Musical Meaning
and
Human Values

Musical Meaning
and
Human Values

Edited by

KEITH CHAPIN AND LAWRENCE KRAMER

FORDHAM UNIVERSITY PRESS

New York 2009

Library of Congress Cataloging-in-Publication Data

Musical meaning and human values / edited by
Keith Chapin and Lawrence Kramer.—1st ed.
    p.   cm.
Includes bibliographical references and index.
ISBN 978-0-8232-3009-9 (cloth : alk. paper)
ISBN 978-0-8232-3010-5 (pbk. : alk. paper)
1. Music—History and criticism.   2. Music—Philosophy
and aesthetics.
I. Chapin, Keith Moore.   II. Kramer, Lawrence, 1946–
ML193.M88   2009
781'.1—dc22
2009003284

Printed in the United States of America
11 10 09   5 4 3 2 1
First edition

CONTENTS

EXAMPLES AND FIGURES

Examples

Figures

Musical Meaning
and
Human Values

Lawrence Kramer

Isolde: Yet our love,
      Is it not called Tristan
      And Isolde?
      This sweet little word: *and* . . .

WAGNER, *Tristan und Isolde*, Act 2

We who think and feel at the same time are those who really continually *fashion* something that had not been there before: the whole eternally growing world of valuations, colors, accents, perspectives, scales, affirmations, and negations.

NIETZSCHE, *The Gay Science*, no. 301

As Wagner's Tristan and Isolde discovered, there is a great deal to be said about the little word *and*. To speak of musical meaning and human values might be to ask how these things, in any of their numerous varieties, reinforce or oppose one another—or, rather, reinforce *and* oppose one another: the ambiguity of music as cosmic or natural harmony and as siren song is as durable as music itself. To speak of musical meaning and human values might be to ask how music expresses values per se or reflects their historical being. Or it might be to ask how values in either of these senses influence music-making as composition or performance, or again how they influence listening. The phrase "musical meaning and human values" leaves both meaning and values underdetermined, and deliberately so. The phrase seems straightforward, but in truth it is an enigma. It is less the designation of a topic than the opening of a question that cannot plausibly be closed. The way to answer, as the essays collected here suggest, is precisely to keep the question open: to keep it opening.

Each of the glosses offered thus far on the title phrase surfaces at one point or another in this collection. But the most important gloss, the one that gives the collection its underlying consistency, is more elusive and more challenging than the others. This gloss regards music as agency no less than as expression. It asks how music *produces* values. It asks, that is, how music shapes, transforms, and even creates values. It asks how music helps install values in the spaces of culture and history through which they circulate.

Perhaps because of its legendary lack of the referential power claimed by images and, especially, by language, music has traditionally been under-estimated as a value-making force. Not many commentators have taken a cue from Nietzsche, who, when he speaks of "the whole eternally growing world of valuations, colors, accents, perspectives, scales, affirmations, and negations," sounds like he is describing the dazzle and dynamism of nine-teenth-century music. He even sounds, in spite of himself, like he is de-scribing Wagner's music, which he regarded as a turning point in the history of values. But among influential modern thinkers, only Adorno gave music the same credit.

Extravagantly admired for its expressive power, beloved in some form by almost everyone, music is all too easy to relegate to the sphere of mere pastime, or what Kant notoriously called pleasure rather than culture. Re-cent musical scholarship, much of it by the authors assembled here, has set out to reverse this systematic illusion, this myth of music's abject de-pendency on cognitive principles that begin by excluding it.[1] The true theme of this collection, therefore—with the differences of topic and ap-proach among the essays duly noted—is the analysis of how making music is also, always, inescapably, making values.

Always, inescapably: but not always or inescapably in the same measure. That music makes values is not a categorical or metaphysical claim but a historical one. The essays collected here testify to this historicity by tracing—sampling—a recurrent moment as it is fashioned in art music from early modern to all-too-modern Europe. Although all the essays visit this moment in one way or another, none of them names it. Walter Benja-min might have called it a *constellation*, and so might Adorno; but a constel-lation is a spatial figure, not, as this moment is, a liminal one. The simplest alternative might be to call it an *epiphany*, but even in literary usage *epiph-any* carries overtones of revelation and sacred mystery that are not neces-sarily appropriate and that in any case lead away from historical time. What to do for lack of a better name? The moment I have in mind is one in which thought assumes the character of an act: a moment of reflection that is also a moment of transformation, a moment in which all the poten-tiality of the *trans-* prefix—to transfigure, transfix, transpose, transcend, transport—comes into play. To capture these qualities, I speak in this in-troduction, albeit a little clumsily, of a moment of *transformative reflection*. Like the title of this volume, the term requires a gloss.

As conceived here, transformative reflection has two principal features. First, it marks the experience of a novel form of subjectivity. It maps the interior space of a developing historical condition. It makes self-recognition available in a new or evolving mode of awareness. The moment is thus reflective. Second, this reflective moment understands its subjective form as correlative not to small or casual changes but to an epochal change. The act of reflection proceeds from a site of distance or disorientation. Whenever it occurs, transformative reflection maps what seems to be the advent of modernity—modernity being a historical condition that keeps on arriving long after it has arrived many times. The moment is thus transformative.

No doubt there are innumerable venues for transformative reflection, but music is perhaps the most immediate of them and thus perhaps the most sensitive as a cultural seismograph.[2] The familiar feeling of its expressive directness comes in part from the bare fact that music can carry an intelligible sense of historical urgency without resort to representation. New sounds go right to the quick. Like the canary in the coal mine, music predicts the atmosphere that lies ahead, but unlike the poor canary it does so not by dying but by singing.

The moment of transformative reflection is most often marked by a sense of loss, danger, or interruption together with a countervailing sense of limited transcendence. In other words, the moment consists of an experience of elevation or sublimation limited by, and perceived together with, the unexhausted remainder of the initial distress. Music, because one and the same music so readily associates itself with different and often divergent states of mind, provides an ideal medium for working out—or failing to work out—this ambivalence.

The process is complicated by the possibility that the formal and emotional trajectories of the music may not be in alignment with each other. Indeed, their alignment or lack thereof is one of the subjective forms that change from one epoch to another. Death and transfiguration, to steal a phrase, may coalesce at the end of both *Tristan und Isolde* and its Hollywood reworking in the film *Humoresque*, discussed in Peter Franklin's essay in this volume, even as the film version veers toward kitsch for reasons of casting, plotting, and rescoring. But at the close of Hans Werner Henze's *Elegy for Young Lovers*, to a libretto by W. H. Auden and Chester Kallman, discussed here in Walter Bernhart's essay, death and transfiguration tear asunder in a moment that, in their stead, conjoins aesthetic greatness with moral abjection.

This historical trajectory suggests that, consistent with the standard narratives of modernization, the limitation on transcendence seems to increase as one era follows another. Each repetition of transformative reflection is also in some sense a diminishment of it. Distances proliferate as the possibilities of irony multiply: the playful or willful self-consciousness of Romantic irony becomes the chastened self-consciousness of historical belatedness, or nostalgic irony, which at some point becomes, has already become, an irony without apparent condition: infinite irony. The limit of limit in one era is surpassed in the next. By the time one surmises, along with T. S. Eliot, that history

> Gives too late
> What's not believed in, or is still believed,
> In memory only, reconsidered passion. Gives too soon
> Into weak hands, what's thought can be dispensed with,[3]

it is long since too late to do anything about it.

Counter to these narratives, however, as the essays collected here make clear, the power of the more compromised transcendental gestures is never wholly lost. Nor is the power of the less compromised gestures ever fully gained. Not all lost: the *Bohème*-like lyricism that effloresces at the end of Puccini's *La fanciulla del West* (*Girl of the Golden West*), an opera that, as Richard Leppert's essay observes, generally eschews the florid style, is powerful nonetheless. It is all the more powerful, perhaps, for its being obsolescent, and—in historical terms—obsolescent so soon, obsolescent even when new. Not all gained: the contemplative slow movements of Beethoven's middle string quartets, as my own essay suggests, constantly risk exposing more loss or pain than they can hope to overcome, and they do so as a very condition of the overcoming.

There is, in short, a continual friction and interchange between transcendence and injury. This dynamic escapes the customary means for understanding forms or forces in opposition. It is a darting and turning that is neither orderly enough to be dialectical nor free enough of its own law of operation to be disseminal, something equally distant from Hegel and Derrida. This state of neither-nor is the threshold of the *and* that links musical meaning and human values. Value inserts itself precisely at the points of decision or indecision that each listener has to make when confronted with a musical moment of transformative reflection. Listening well to such a moment construes it as what Nietzsche described as the fashioning of something that had not been there before, with the added recognitions that this fashioning, or refashioning, is part of a continuous process and that it is enacted *in* the music as it is enacted *by* the listener.

The communicable form of this enactment is a narrative, the story we tell ourselves about the music or the story we tell ourselves that the music is telling. The exact distinction between these possibilities, that is, the exact location of agency, is indeterminate. It is necessarily, even desirably so. To find values in the music we need to feel neither that we ventriloquize the music nor that it ventriloquizes us. For that purpose a complex and ambiguous narrative is required, one responsive to the difficulty—and the difficulty is considerable—of accomplishing this neither/nor. To adopt a phrase from Judith Butler, the question of values arises when we have to give an account of ourselves in relation to the music or, what is almost the same thing, when we hear the music as a demand that we give an account of ourselves.

Butler argues that narrative seeks to stabilize worldly action by turning contingent successions into structured sequences, flows into patterns. Nonetheless, she adds, this effort inevitably fails because narrative is itself a form of action and subject to all the infelicities of action.[4] But is that, so to speak, the whole story? The converse is equally likely. Worldly action is frequently all too predictable, even amid scenes of chaos; action is itself a form of narrative. The narratives we fashion to give an account of ourselves often destabilize the mechanism of action and expand it into the sphere of values. We do not just report on ourselves; we fantasize and embroider and imagine; we tell tall tales. Responsible self-accounting thus depends more on measured excess than it does on any supposed correspondence between stories and events. The moment of transformative reflection is the expression of that excess in the process of taking concrete historical form. At such a moment, music becomes the tangible embodiment of narrative excess by virtue of the excesses basic to musical expression: repetitions and ruptures, changes of intensity, the demands of virtuosity, the channeling of performative energy.

No wonder, then, that the event most likely to prompt transformative reflection is a breakdown in symbolic tradition. I would personally be inclined to give this event a Lacanian gloss and speak of the symbolic order under duress from the Real, but to do so might presume too much of my fellow contributors.[5] Suffice it to say that when we encounter a break in one of the symbolic procedures by which we either stabilize or enlarge our sense of the world, when we come upon a gap in one of the narratives by which we seek to make good our worldly accounts, transformative reflection tends to arise in order both to articulate the gap and to answer the need to mend or at least bridge the gap.

Of course, the moment of transformative reflection is an ideal category each instance of which modifies its concept, and of course, the essays collected here were not conceived under this rubric. Still, the convergences are striking. Susan McClary hears the characteristic friction and interchange in a madrigal's excessive deferral of cadential movement to the final of its mode; Keith Chapin reads the reflective dynamic refracted through moods of enthusiasm and skepticism in E. T. A. Hoffmann's writings as a music critic and as a jurist; I listen to certain slow movements in string quartets by Haydn and Beethoven and hear there the need to avert self-annihilation as a consequence of contemplative absorption; Marshall Brown maps out a continuous play of sonority against form in Mendelssohn's overture to *A Midsummer Night's Dream*; Walter Frisch shows that the interplay of values and meaning inheres in musical performance, here of Brahms's Second Piano Concerto, no less than in the musical score; Richard Leppert tracks the tension between modernizing pungency and regressive lyricism in *La fanciulla del West* in the context of early twentieth-century nostalgia for premodern space and the concurrent reconfiguration of modern time; Peter Franklin traces the transformative reflection of Wagner in the gender trouble and kitsch transcription of the Hollywood melodrama *Humoresque* in the course of pondering the fortunes of late Romantic music in the modernist era; and Walter Bernhart examines the mutual seductions of depravity and genius in Henze and Auden and Kallman's *Elegy for Young Lovers*, as well as in works by Hindemith and Britten, while taking up the difficult question of whether music can represent evil. These summaries do justice to none of the essays, but they do point to a thread that runs through all of them.

A second thread, and an unsurprising one given what I have said so far, is the inescapably historical character of the relationship between meaning and values. This topic demands some reflection of its own. Must we, after all, have history always on our minds? Must meaning, musical or otherwise, always be historical? Must values always be relative to historical conditions? Does the strong concept of values not imply a capacity to persist through the vagaries of historical change? When Nietzsche put the value of values into question, he did so in part because the value of values is precisely what the strong concept assumes and in so doing excludes from the field of inquiry. The existence of true values makes doubt about the value of values literally unthinkable. The frame of mind that would entertain such doubt virtually defines the unthinkable.

A weaker, more historicized concept of values merely evades the problem under the illusion of solving it. Hans-Georg Gadamer suggests as much when he claims that when we historicize too strenuously we bracket the question of truth or validity and thus render questions of value indifferent.[6] Not only is a rigorous historicism bound to be value-neutral, but the moment we begin to write a history of values, the objects of our history cease to be values in the strong sense. They become what Nietzsche called *valuations*, the results of acts of assessment or estimation; they cease to function as standards of conduct that we have, or so we feel, unimpeachable reason to accept.

With music, or art more generally, the change from values to valuations undermines both idealizing claims of meaning and aesthetic enjoyment. It may well seem that, precisely to the degree that works of music enter history, the values they are supposed to embody become diminished. What are we to do, for example, not even mentioning Nazi Germany, about the fact that the "Ode to Joy" from Beethoven's Ninth Symphony was adopted, with a changed text, as the anthem of the racist government of Rhodesia or that the European Union later adopted the tune, without the text, as its own anthem?[7] One usage debases the music and the other merely trivializes it, but is the effect of history not corrosive either way?

The answer to this question is implicit in the asking of it. If we agree about the debasement and the trivialization, we have already made a decision about values. We have assumed the existence in the music of a value-potential with the capacity to resist historical appropriation. The moment that we enjoy the music in one context and wince at it in another, we have both made a claim of value and admitted the claim of that value on us. Our understanding, if we are Nietzschean enough, that what we are doing is making a valuation has no effect on the underlying logic. Valuation becomes value again the moment that it is lived. Music makes values by presenting acts of valuation that rise to the level of values when enjoyed, remembered, imitated, adapted, interpreted—evaluated.

It thus seems virtually impossible, and certainly undesirable, to give up on the idea that music and art harbor genuine value-potential. The wrong conclusion to draw from this premise, however, is the traditional one, the conclusion that tends to dominate reception outside the academic world and still has a solid academic foothold. We should not, that is, suppose that the accessibility of a transhistorical value-potential authorizes us to ignore the force of history. That supposition leads only to familiar bromides about the timelessness of great art and the transcendent quality of genius. And those we can live without—the sooner the better. The better conclusion is that the relationship between the historical and the transhistorical in the sphere of values is positive and mutually productive. What

Michel Foucault claimed on behalf of power can be claimed, mutatis mutandis, about value too.[8] The historical and the transhistorical engender each other and form the necessary condition of each other's coherence. At the same time, each resists the other, potentially providing the negative and critical force necessary to correct both the reductionist tendency of historicism and the inflating tendencies of aesthetic idealism. The same sort of friction and interchange that occurs between disruption and elevation in moments of transformative reflection also may also occur between the historical and the transhistorical in acts of aesthetic reflection. By letting or making that happen, it becomes possible to engage with the history of valuations without bracketing the claims of value.

The essays in this book all seek to do just that. They work in the space between the historical and the transhistorical, the circumstantial and the aesthetic. The authors of these essays understand their own implication in the problems of modernity that they trace through a series of surprising metamorphoses; they act out that implication in their texts; and they show how music, perhaps music above all, with its power to translate meaning into immediate feelings and sensations, implicates its listeners in the same problems, sometimes with solutions proposed, and sometimes not. The hope is that, by so doing, it proves possible to keep faith with both of the spheres that give this book its title and so to clarify the little *and* that unites and divides musical meaning and human values.

The essays in this collection were originally presented at Fordham University in May 2007 at an international conference exploring themes in my work, "Musical Meaning and Human Values: A Symposium with Lawrence Kramer." At the time, the conference participants all remarked on how well the various presentations seemed to hang together spontaneously across wide differences and chronology and culture. Perhaps the topic of values had something to do with this confluence, but more likely the sense of common understanding in these essays stems from the shared conviction of their authors that music not understood in the world is not understood at all. One might, of course, ask *which world? whose world?* since no collection of this kind can include *the* world, as Mahler famously said that the symphony should. But the essays collected here do ask that question, implicitly, at every point.

The one apparent exception, Walter Frisch's chapter on performance, does what exceptions are supposed to do and proves the rule. The essay is also an exception because it appears in lieu of Frisch's conference paper, which was committed elsewhere. Nothing, at any rate, is more "hands on" than performance, which powerfully affects the sensory qualities through which music embodies its values and invites listeners to regard it as an expression of their own values. The little *and* that has supplied a leitmotif to this introduction insinuates itself everywhere, much to our benefit.

I am most grateful to Fordham University for the provision of generous funding and material support for the conference; to Stephanie Pietros and Keith Chapin for doing everything necessary, and much more besides, to organize the event; to Martine Stern for creating and maintaining the conference webpage; to Helen Tartar of Fordham University Press for encouraging this volume; and to Keith Chapin again for acting as host and master of ceremonies.

CHAPTER I

Due Rose, Due Volte

A STUDY OF EARLY MODERN SUBJECTIVITIES

Susan McClary

Modernism comes in many guises. In the early twenty-first century, we are most likely to associate the word with the recent postmodernist turn, with cultural upheavals a hundred years ago, or with the radical questioning of Enlightenment values entailed in the emergence of Romanticism. Pushing the term even further back, many humanities disciplines now refer to the late sixteenth and early seventeenth centuries as the "early modern" period. In musicology, however, the widespread use of period terms such as "Renaissance" and "Baroque" (themselves problematically borrowed from other disciplines and applied somewhat arbitrarily to music) has made it difficult to perceive the "modernity" in earlier repertories. The fact that we have no agreed-upon way of analyzing music from before the eighteenth century causes anything prior to Bach still to appear primitive—anything other than "modern."

The other chapters in this volume quite appropriately focus on later modernist crises, for these are the periods for which Lawrence Kramer has established himself as a leading authority. In his pathbreaking series of books and articles, Kramer has taken the standard classical repertories of the late eighteenth and the nineteenth centuries—long since elevated to the untouchable sphere of "absolute" music—and demonstrated the ways those privileged compositions produce meaning. Allegations to the contrary, he has never sought to undermine the aesthetic worth of classic masterpieces;[1] he simply has wanted to add cultural theory and interpretation to the mix. Rather than the smooth, polished, ineffable entities celebrated by generations of connoisseurs, Kramer offers us documents testifying to ever-changing cultural values, including reactions to the traumas of modernity. Because of his work, the music of Schubert, Schumann, Ives, and many others has acquired renewed meanings—controversial meanings, to be sure, but far more precious for being seen to engage with the messy enterprise of human experience at various moments in history.

Much of my work has addressed the same repertories on which Kramer concentrates his efforts, though I arrived at nineteenth-century studies from the opposite direction. I began my musicological career as a specialist of seventeenth-century music but quickly found that attempts at publishing my analyses and interpretations ran up against the commonly held belief that early music "does not work." Frustrated by this bizarre but apparently nonnegotiable barrier, I decided that I needed to demonstrate the historical and ideological contingency of "absolute" music in order to deal seriously with the cultural values registered by earlier repertories, which in my view ought not to have required such elaborate special pleading. Thirty years after I started, I find it possible at last to address sixteenth-and seventeenth-century musics with the kind of analytical depth and the sorts of questions that Kramer brings to Mozart or Strauss.

My essay concerns two sixteenth-century settings of Francesco Petrarch's Sonnet No. 245, "Due rose fresche." Several sixteenth-century composers set this sonnet to music, most notably Andrea Gabrieli in 1566 and Luca Marenzio in 1585. Musicologists and performers regard both these settings as central to the madrigal repertory. As it turns out, Marenzio alludes throughout his version to Gabrieli's in a gesture of homage and intertextual one-upmanship typical of court-based culture of the time. Marenzio could count on his performers' and listeners' familiarity with the former setting and thereby produce his own reading of both Petrarch's sonnet and Gabrieli's earlier reading of the same sonnet.

The mere nineteen years that separate Gabrieli's setting from Marenzio's proves crucial to their understandings not only of this poem but also of inherited traditions of music composition. Put simply, Marenzio resided on the modernist side of a cultural cataclysm that still resonates even today. Thus, although both composers ostensibly faced only the task of setting a given text, their very divergent assumptions and ideological pri-

orities mark their responses, resulting in two significantly different interpretations of Petrarch's sonnet.

> Due rose fresche et colte in paradiso
> l'altr'ier, nascendo il dì primo di maggio,
> bel dono et d'un amante antiquo et saggio
> tra duo minori egualmente diviso,
>
> con sì dolce parlar et con un riso
> da far innamorare un uom selvaggio,
> di sfavillante et amoroso raggio
> et l'un' et l'altro fe' cangiare il viso.
>
> "Non vede un simil par d'amanti il sole,"
> dicea ridendo et sospirando inseme,
> et stringendo ambedue volgeasi a torno.
>
> Così partia le rose et le parole,
> onde 'l cor lasso ancor s'allegra et teme:
> o felice eloquenzia! o lieto giorno!

> Two roses, fresh and gathered in paradise the
> other day when the first day of May was born,
> a lovely gift by a lover old and wise
> between two younger ones equally divided,
>
> with words and a smile sweet enough
> to cause a wild man to fall in love,
> made a sparkling, amorous ray
> change the faces of both.
>
> "The sun does not see a similar pair of
> lovers," he said, both smiling and sighing,
> and embracing both, he turned around.
>
> Thus he divided the roses and his words;
> and my weary heart still is glad and fearful:
> O felicitous eloquence! O happy day![2]

Written most likely in Avignon shortly before Petrarch learned of the
death of the woman he called Laura (whom he idealized and loved from
afar but never met), "Due rose fresche" imagines a celestial benediction
of the poet and his beloved. A smiling, benign elder presides, offering the
two young lovers the first roses of Maytime along with his blessing. End-

ing as it does with the peroration "O felicitous eloquence! O happy day," the sonnet presents Petrarch at his most optimistic: no misogyny or what Nancy Vickers theorizes as dismembered body parts are in evidence here, only sweetness and light.[3] In fact, musical settings of this sonnet seem to have been performed frequently at weddings in the sixteenth century.[4]

As one might anticipate, word paintings abound in both madrigal settings: their scores present two paired voices alone at "Due rose" and they burst into simulated laughter at "riso" and "ridendo." In short, both pieces indulge in what my discipline deprecates as "madrigalisms." I do not apologize for these figures; there they are in all their glory—though I would remind you that J. S. Bach never encountered an excuse for word painting that he could resist. The problem comes when we assume that the identification of word paintings exhausts the arsenal of critical tools that we can bring to bear on the madrigal repertory. Musicologists have long delighted in pointing out these Mickey Mouse depictions, allowing for a kind of positivistic hermeneutics, and they typically restrict commentary to that level.

Recall, however, that Gabrieli and Marenzio wrote their madrigals a good two centuries after Petrarch had established himself as one of the most insightful theorists of interiority in all Western history.[5] Only if we accept that composers lag woefully behind the cultural agendas of other artists should we content ourselves with pointing at isolated figures and relating them literally to images in the poetry. We do not deal critically with the paintings of, say, Caravaggio by demonstrating that we can identify a represented horse or dog on the canvas, and we should not tolerate this egregiously low standard when we deal with music, either—not even that of early repertories.[6]

Consequently, as I discuss the two settings of "Due rose fresche," I focus my attention on the ways in which the narrator's subjectivity makes itself felt in each setting through moments of affective emphasis, repetitions, changes in the rate of activity, distortions, prolongations, or abrupt shifts. Although the poetic text always informs compositional strategies, such rhetorical choices do not reside at the level of individual words or even clusters of words. Indeed, each composer imposes his own interpretation on Petrarch's sonnet, sometimes causing the text to speak meanings not necessarily evident in the poetry itself. Both, in other words, are already ventriloquizing Petrarch. And in the absence of a pure source, we may as well plunge in ourselves.

Andrea Gabrieli published his setting of "Due rose" in his *Primo libro a cinque* in 1566. As Alfred Einstein explains, Gabrieli was drawn at the time particularly to the fashionable idiom of pastoral poetry, and he infused much of his music with the buoyancy and joy characteristic of that genre. "Even when he turns to literary texts, to Petrarch, for example, as he does five times in his first book and once in his second, Gabrieli does not aspire to a more elevated style. For him Petrarch's sonnet *Due rose fresche* is simply a wedding madrigal which he transforms into a masterpiece of easy grace."[7]

The madrigal operates entirely within G Hypodorian, which offers B♭ and D as well as G as regular points of cadential emphasis. Nothing in the piece challenges these modal limits, nor does Gabrieli rebel against the structure of Petrarch's sonnet: each poetic caesura receives a corresponding cadence. Occasionally Gabrieli repeats a phrase for the sake of rhetorical emphasis or as part of a point of imitation—that is, for purposes of *textural* (rather than *textual*) elaboration. But he accepts Petrarch's verse quite unproblematically with respect to form and also, as we shall see, with respect to content.

As an opening gambit, however, Gabrieli at least toys with the ambiguity most typical of G Hypodorian. The modal octave stretching from D to D has G as its final, but it has a strong tendency to imply an alternative division of the octave at A, with D as the implicit final (Example 1.1). The principal motive in the first three measures traces a powerful descent through the diapente (the interval of a fifth) from D toward G, but it halts each time unfinished at A (soprano, mm. 1–2; tenor 1, mm. 2–3; tenor 2, m. 2). Moreover, by withholding all leading tones, the countermotive refuses to decide between G and D orientations, repeatedly stressing an equivocal F♮ instead.

Many a madrigalist would have used such an opening to plant an internal contradiction that would drive the rest of the composition. But Gabrieli seems to have other priorities. After this passage of delicious, indeterminate hovering, he pivots through the D-minor triad that could have threatened modal integrity to a blossoming B♭ sonority on "paradiso." Not only do we shift from minor to major, but the voices all suddenly lift from their earthbound tessitura to a momentarily sustained glimpse of heavenly heights. Returning us quickly to Petrarch's text, Ga-

EXAMPLE 1.1. G-Hypodorian species and division at D.

Octave divided at G   Octave divided at A

brieli solves the ambiguity of the first line in measure 6 with a cadence confirming G as the final and "maggio" as the end of the first couplet (Example 1.2, mm. 1–6).

Given the radical experiments produced by Gabrieli's contemporaries, this profoundly diatonic beginning—and, indeed, this entire madrigal—

EXAMPLE 1.2. Andrea Gabrieli, "Due rose fresche," mm. 1–13.

EXAMPLE 1.2 *(cont'd.)*

2

might seem conservative or timid. But Gabrieli's agenda here involves the production of rhetorical effects within a secure affective universe. The "easy grace" of which Einstein writes reveals itself in the luxuriant unfurling (like rose petals) of the ambiguous opening point of imitation, the breathless and unexpected simulation of paradise itself, and the deft return to discursive reality for the cadence—quite a bit to accomplish within about seventeen seconds of sound. With expressive mastery such as this, Gabrieli apparently felt no need to go beyond conventional strictures. Instead, he makes the attainment of bliss seem always within our grasp—and within the grasp of the couple at whose wedding such a piece might have provided a musical backdrop.

Gabrieli chooses to begin his setting of Petrarch's second couplet with a melodic motive that recalls the first, though now with a harmonization affiliated with B♭ (Example 1.2, mm. 6ff.) Formerly aligned with "paradiso," this sonority now unfolds as a carefree pastoral landscape in which the imitative voices play an erotically tinged form of tag. The game comes to a temporary halt with a direct descent through the G diapente to a half cadence—still incomplete, as in the opening statements of this motive, but now made functionally clear by the F# that points unequivocally to G (m. 6).

For the remainder of the two-part madrigal, Gabrieli resides within this pastoral universe, occasionally underscoring affectively significant phrases from Petrarch's sonnet (e.g., "con sì dolce parlar," "et sospirando inseme") with slower declamation and intensified harmonies. Most noteworthy, perhaps, is his setting of the words "onde 'l cor lasso," in which he indulges in such a powerful tilting toward E♭, the G-Hypodorian sixth degree, that he nearly sinks into C minor before returning to his normal terrain of joyful exuberance (Example 1.3).

EXAMPLE 1.3. Andrea Gabrieli, "Due rose fresche," mm. 48–end.

EXAMPLE 1.3 *(cont'd.)*

From that point to the end, there is nothing other than the unalloyed joy promised by the lyrics. Gabrieli does recall modal dualism once more by offering in measure 55 a cadence on D for the initial setting of the last line of text, allowing for the entire passage to be repeated for proper closure on G, followed by a plagal prolongation (Example 1.3). This is as certain as happy endings get. Moreover, manifest content aside, this is an image of the Renaissance as we like to think of it, consonant, perhaps, with the pastoral canvases of Sandro Botticelli: balanced, quietly measured, still innocent of the intense, tortured questioning that marks the advent of Mannerism.

Marenzio explicitly takes Gabrieli's setting as the point of departure for his own. In Einstein's words,

> Marenzio . . . might have followed twenty models, but he pays tribute to Gabrieli, who had set the sonnet to music in 15[66]. Marenzio uses Gabrieli's opening as a sort of motto, and the motive relationships are easy to follow from here on; one has the impression that Marenzio aims to prove that the sonnet can be reduced in music to a shorter and more concise formula than Andrea's. At the same time the connection does not bespeak rivalry but rather esteem for the older master who has shown him the way.[8]

In his brief account, Einstein locates the element that most ties these settings together. The melodic motive—the incomplete descent through the diapente—that opens Gabrieli's madrigal and recurs at key moments throughout becomes far more systematic in Marenzio's reworking. For Marenzio recognized in that motivic shape a similarity to a musical device closely associated at the time with the improvised recitation of epics (Example 1.4).

EXAMPLE 1.4. Reciting formulas.

Passamezzo antico

Romanesca

Right from the outset, Marenzio gives the impression that the speaker will proceed line by line with this melodic formula. In its natural habitat, the formula may be harmonized either as if it belonged to G Hypodorian (as with the opening three words, in a standard harmonization called the Passamezzo Antico) or with B♭ (as with the remainder of the poetic line, "et colte in paradiso," a harmonization called the Romanesca). Both linear descents stop before reaching their ultimate goal of G, as the first halts on scale degree 2, the second on scale degree 3; the next line of the sonnet moves twice toward more weighted descents, each time stressing scale degree 4 (C). But everything suggests that these incomplete presentations only serve to delay the inevitable arrival on G (Example 1.5, mm. 1–14).

Note that Marenzio refrains from repeating any text segments from the first two lines. Instead, he seems to be delivering a straightforward reading of the sonnet just as it appears on the page. In contrast to Gabrieli, Marenzio even clarifies the functions of his opening gesture by signing-in leading tones. Gabrieli's delicious ambiguity and slow, imitative unfurling of rose petals is telescoped into a bare schematic presentation. Although Marenzio's setting of "et colte in paradiso" recalls Gabrieli's in its reharmonization in B♭ and the rapid ascent of the lower voices, it denies us the experience of bliss offered by the former version. In other words, his setting does indeed appear to have reduced Gabrieli's exquisite pastoral to mere formula.

Thus, it comes as something of a shock when the phrase "bel dono et d'un amante" becomes a sticking point. Set with the long-awaited diapente descent from D to G, the text fragment is subjected to obsessive iterations; the orderly presentation of the sonnet gives way to rhythmically urgent stammering. Voice after voice attempts the arrival, only to have its

EXAMPLE 1.5. Marenzio, "Due rose fresche," mm. 1–23.

sense of an ending undermined by other voices similarly striving for cadence (Example 1.5, mm. 13–23). According to madrigal traditions going all the way back to Arcadelt's "Il bianco e dolce cigno," such cascading and overlapping grasps at closure are often meant to simulate orgasm.[9] But why would Marenzio select these particular words—a lovely gift by an older lover—for such extravagant affective emphasis?

Moreover, after all the anticipation churned up by the repeated descents to G, the modal final, the cadence that appears suddenly with the words "et saggio" tonicizes D instead. In measure 20, the soprano's A, the second degree, which ought by rights to move down by step to affirm G, is harmonized instead with C# in the tenor and A in the bass, forcing the soprano to continue down the D octave to its unexpected conclusion (see again Example 1.1). I suspect that Petrarch too would have been a bit disconcerted by this passage, given that it wreaks havoc on the structure of his sonnet: we should not have a major cadence point at the end of the third line of the quatrain. Marenzio continues to run roughshod over

Example 1.5 *(cont'd.)*

Petrarch's formal design by presenting the quatrain's last line, "tra duo minori," as a new beginning, parallel with the opening "due rose."

Of course, it might be in part the possibility of producing that parallel that motivates Marenzio to distort the sonnet, for if he wishes to mark clearly the new beginning on "tra duo minori," he has to do something to seal up the first strain. Still, he does not truly need that insistent push for closure that ends up in the wrong place. Neither the *prima parte* nor, indeed, the finale to the entire madrigal features a cadential point nearly so emphatic—or anxious.

That cadence on D in measure 23 continues to resonate well into the next section (Example 1.6). If the very beginning of the madrigal casually (and unusually) sported F# leading tones to point unequivocally to G as the final, the return to the reciting formula in measure 24 finds itself harmonized ambiguously, ready to tilt at a moment's notice to either D or G. Only the E♭ and F# in measures 27–28 confirm a G orientation—but just in time for another displacement, this time to C on the word "diviso." As

EXAMPLE 1.6. Marenzio, "Due rose fresche," mm. 24–38.

a modal theorist, I understand this move syntactically as another emphatic descent to scale degree 4, thus shoring up a renewed attempt at moving down to G. Yet something cataclysmic happens at that moment, causing the ongoing momentum to stop cold in its tracks. In the wake of this abrupt break, the upper voices pull themselves up hand over fist until they reestablish G. The expected cadence on G, when it does finally occur in measure 38, is undermined, however, by the overlapping entry of the lower voices.

Nevertheless, the melodic contours return to the narrative formula of the beginning. The words "et l'un' et l'altro" even recall the two other formal anchors of "due rose" and "tra duo minori." But no sooner is order restored than it gets upended. Our older lover casts a magic spell that transfigures Petrarch and Laura, lifting them and us temporarily and affectively out of the mode and causing the composition to hover in a realm distinct from reality. In fact, this remote realm is A, the same pitch on which the incomplete diapente descents usually paused and also the pitch that produced the sudden, disruptive cadence on D in measure 23. But as it becomes its own temporary key center, it cancels out the markers of G-Hypodorian identity: B♮ replaces the mediant B♭, and G# replaces the final. Marenzio does not leave us stranded there in midair, however. Making use of A as a pivot, he repeats the words concerned with metamorphosis, now grounded in D—a more closely related region, the key associated with the older lover—for the conclusion of the *prima parte* (Example 1.7).

Over the course of this first part, Marenzio's narrator has found his reciting formula deeply shaken three times: once with the bizarre expansion of "bel dono" and the introduction of the older lover, then with the abrupt drop to C at "diviso," and finally with the out-of-body experience as the faces of the younger two lovers find themselves transformed. Of course, Petrarch's sonnet explicitly signals a rite of consecration, a wedding ceremony in which two separate individuals become one flesh. At the beginning of the sonnet's second half, the shaman tells his charges that the sun sees no lovers to equal them, and as the *seconda parte* continues, he turns around them, showering them with light. Perhaps he is the Sun itself, the Phoebus Apollo who also bestows his blessings at the union of Orpheus and Eurydice—which is why Peri's and Monteverdi's operas incorporated or alluded to lines from this sonnet in their marriage vows.[10]

But I suggest that Marenzio has also set Petrarch's sonnet in a way that makes it something like the organ toccatas composed for the elevation of the host and wine in the Counter-Reformation Catholic Mass. Elevation toccatas strive to immerse congregants in a world of mystery in which

EXAMPLE 1.7. Marenzio, "Due rose fresche," mm. 51–61.

everyday materials undergo transubstantiation. In intoning the words "behold the body of Christ," the priest performs the miracle that lies at the core of Christian communion (the Latin "hoc est corpus" became the "hocus pocus" later uttered by street magicians to accompany their sleights of hand). In either case—wedding or communion—an officiating priest offers a precious gift, divides it, and administers it as a sacrament, thereby transfiguring all who participate.

Moreover, Marenzio has read Petrarch's sonnet in such a way as to delay transcendent effects until this moment. Recall how casually he brushed past the opening line's reference to "paradiso"; a singer familiar with Gabrieli's version might well feel cheated by Marenzio's offhand setting of that word. But here he presents not only an intense affective experience but one made possible only by stepping outside the realm of modal normality.

The quotation from the older lover that opens the *seconda parte* presents a direct scalar descent through the complete D octave—more emphatic this time than in the passage that marked the introduction of this character in measures 20–23. After this self-contained statement, the madrigal revisits many of the events of the *prima parte*, as if trying to recover whatever it was that happened at the moment of transformation. A syncopated halt on melodic C in measure 73 parallels the passage setting "diviso" in measure 31; both these breaks are followed by hand-over-fist attempts at ascending by step; another attempt at direct descent to G in measure 85 finds itself diverted at the last instant to D instead—once again marking the intervention of the older lover.

But in place of the experience of *rapture*, Marenzio gives us *rupture* in the *seconda parte*, for the passage beginning in measure 87 falls abjectly by thirds through an implied C minor. If in this piece D is the sun and A that moment of brilliant insight, C resides in outer darkness, nearly as far to the flat side as A is to the sharp. To be sure, Petrarch does refer to his weary heart—a heart now far removed from the innocence of youth and Maytime, a heart cognizant not only of his failure to unify his life with Laura's but probably also of her death—and he goes on to couple fear with gladness before ending with his rejoicing in this happy memory. Even Gabrieli had to contend with this somewhat pessimistic line in his otherwise joyous madrigal, and his decision to mark this affective ambivalence with a nod toward C minor obviously serves as Marenzio's model. But Marenzio allows the piece to bottom out on "lasso," and neither the dancing on "s'allegra" or even the final perorations manage to save him from the realization that he cannot go home again. Even though this section ends with a cadence on G—the first such cadence in the piece—it serves only to mark the word "teme" in a very gingerly fashion (Example 1.8, mm. 86–92).

And here we might recall that the older lover's action at that moment of blinding insight was actually *division* rather than union, which may account for the fact that Marenzio sets the word "diviso" in measure 31 as a mysterious cataclysm. The predominance of the number two—never one—also underscores this aspect of the sonnet and its setting. In essence, it takes the remainder of the madrigal for us to understand that the officiating shaman has never bequeathed anything other than the irreparable separation that continually haunts Petrarch's poetry. We might finally understand in retrospect the overemphatic presentation of the words "bel dono": it is as if the narrator were trying even at that early point in the madrigal to convince himself that the gift was indeed lovely. Only the

EXAMPLE 1.8. Marenzio, "Due rose fresche," mm. 86–end.

EXAMPLE 1.8 (*cont'd.*)

shaman gets to present an intact octave, and his agency brings about most of the madrigal's cadences—on D rather than the established final, G. Compared with this model, the narrator's always-truncated diapente descents seem miserably inadequate.

The Romanesca narration formula dominates the final page, with "o felice eloquenzia!" twice ending on incomplete half cadences. The phrase "O lieto giorno" glances quickly back at all those cadences on D and then repeats for a final cadence on G—the only one in this Hypodorian piece that apparently set out to do nothing other than to confirm its final. But although the tenor voice does manage something of a diapente descent from D to G at the end, the highest voice (which has been our guide throughout the madrigal) concludes equivocally, longing in vain for a return of that wondrous day and its miraculous feeling. Like so many pieces in late Beethoven or Schubert in which a moment of escape into a blissful or dreamlike flat submediant proves unrecoverable, Marenzio's "Due rose fresche" both delivers the experience of transcendence and also demonstrates the incompatibility of that experience with the real world. The would-be ecstasy of "o felicitous eloquence, o happy day" sounds provisional at best, leaving only a residue of bittersweet melancholy (Example 1.8, mm. 93–end).

I should warn you that several of the points I have made in this chapter may not be audible on many recordings, most of which strive primarily to make everything "musical" or pretty. As one of my professors once told me concerning Renaissance music, "It didn't matter to them where they started or ended or where they cadenced. They just worked through their texts and stopped." But I think you can imagine a rendition in which singers project rhythmically urgent stammering, cataclysmic shifts, moments of mystical transfiguration, and so on. Indeed, my work is driven in large part by my concern that performers understand and bring to life those dimensions of music that may not be exactly pretty but that speak to more complex, often contradictory aspects of human life. I want drastic experiences just as much as the next person when I listen, though this requires me to turn my (if you will) gnostic gaze at the score.[11] Surely that kind of mediation between the inert dots on the page and performers qualifies as one of the musicologist's duties.

Earlier I bracketed off explicit word paintings so as to focus on larger rhetorical events. Now, in closing, I bracket off altogether the verbal text that motivated Marenzio's particular strategies in order to address some broader issues. In composing this Mannerist madrigal, Marenzio allowed himself to step away from the certainties of standard modal practice, which provided the secure ground on which Gabrieli could operate and which contemporaries such as Artusi regarded as repositories of metaphysical truth.[12] When Marenzio moves to A near the end of the *prima parte*, he cancels out the crucial identifying pitches of the final G (which becomes G#) and the signed-in mediant B♭ (which becomes a heavily weighted B♮). The experience of that vision cannot be forgotten, but neither can it be reproduced at will. Moreover, the failed attempt at reentering that mystic realm not only apparently conjures forth its opposite in the abject collapse into C minor but also renders the return to diatonic Hypodorian too mundane to serve as a satisfactory telos.

The conditions for necessary closure, in other words, no longer arise from within the economy of the piece itself; they come to seem arbitrary or simply stuck on—as do the lunges for tonic conclusions in so much nineteenth-century music after the certainties of eighteenth-century tonality had been called into question. In both historical periods, excesses in subjective expression violate the constraints of socially established conventions of rationality, leaving us unable to believe either in the ecstasy or in the material world, now embittered by that remembered taste of bliss. Both moments of modernist self-consciousness leave musicians and listeners in the ambiguous state described by Petrarch in "Due rose fresche" as a mixture of gladness and fear, of exhilaration and apprehension. We may celebrate the demonstration that mere humans invent culture and can deconstruct it at will, but that very demonstration—that taste of the Fruit of the Tree of Knowledge—separates us from the Eden afforded by unproblematic belief in a higher authority.

My reference here to the beginning of Genesis suggests that this Modernist Condition runs throughout the development of Western civilization. Psychoanalysts often theorize the trauma of such moves as the inevitable result of differentiation from the Mother. But such stories also proliferate at times of cultural or social upheaval. María Rosa Menocal explains at length the ways in which Petrarch himself formulated this structure of subjectivity as a complex response to his banishment from Florence.[13]

Yet I am not arguing here in favor of archetypes, which tend to sacrifice historical specificity in favor of possible universals. For every transgressive crisis there stands a prior period of consolidation. Consequently, we need explanations not only for moments of rebellious experimentation but also for those—such as the High Renaissance and the Enlightenment—that allow for the cultivation and celebration of formal conventions.[14]

    In other words, the beautiful symmetries and syntactical certainties of
Gabrieli's "Due rose fresche" demand—no less than Marenzio's acting
out—a sense of historically grounded self-consciousness. Already audible
in Gabrieli is the drive toward rhetorical emphasis, the oratorical stance
that encourages him as an individual artist to bend his chosen text to his
expressive will, even though he works to balance those impulses with the
exigencies of socially sanctioned procedures.[15] But the collective move
toward the consolidation of those procedures themselves serve—however
inadequately—to shore up a sense of rational order in the face of cata-
strophic events such as the Sack of Rome and the Reformation.

    Gabrieli does not write from the innocence of Eden but instead from
the compensatory sphere that art can offer to a beleaguered world all too
aware of its fallen condition. To be sure, he pushes Petrarch's internally
conflicted sonnet in the direction of wholeness, attempting to smooth over
or minimize with his lush rhetoric the dimension of division palpable in
the poetic text. As we have seen, Marenzio reads the sonnet differently.
Indeed, he takes those instances of rhetorical plenitude in Gabrieli's setting and uses them as crowbars to upend and deconstruct the smooth surfaces of his predecessor. If we do not have Vickersian body parts as the
result, we certainly have fragments of a shattered entity. But, again, Gabrieli was already attempting to postulate through his own maneuvers a uto-
pian vision in the face of a damaged world. For this longing for a simpler,
not-yet-corrupted time is always the terrain of the pastoral genre.[16]

    Earlier I cited Alfred Einstein's claim that settings of "Due rose
fresche" were often performed at weddings, and it may seem unlikely that
Marenzio's setting as I have here described it would have been deemed
appropriate for such occasions. Recall, however, that the period we call
the Baroque was ushered in by Peri's *Euridice*, a pastoral based on the myth
of Orpheus and composed for a grand Medici wedding in 1600. In keeping
with the nuptials, Peri and his librettist, Rinuccini, did alter the ending of
the usually tragic story, allowing Orpheus to bring his bride back to life to
live happily ever after. Like Gabrieli, the collaborators chose to emphasize
the affirmative side of their model.

    Seven years later, Monteverdi and Striggio returned not only to the
same mythological source but quite deliberately to Peri and Rinuccini's
pioneering effort. And like Marenzio, they put pressure on the moments
of Peri's greatest achievement—his laments—and produced a much darker
reading; they even planned to end their *dramma per musica* with Baccante
tearing the singer to shreds (body parts yet again!) to punish him for his
oath to shun women. The court censors objected, even though the per-

formance took place during Carnival rather than a wedding. Consequently, the version that survives concludes with a deus ex machina, in which Apollo—exasperated by Orpheus's grief-stricken plaints—simply airlifts the hero into the skies to shut him up. Closure occurs, as it does in Marenzio's "Due rose fresche," but in both cases, the doubts raised over the course of the proceedings continue to resonate.

Such pairs, in which one version constructs a simulation of *paradiso* and the other deconstructs it along the faultlines of its rhetorical emphasis, occur throughout cultural history. In the words of Argentine novelist Ernesto Sabato, in his classic *Sobre Héroes y Tumbas* (*On Heroes and Tombs*),

> Pessimists are recruited among former optimists, since in order to have a black picture of the world it is necessary to have previously believed in that world and its possibilities. And it is an even more curious and paradoxical fact that pessimists, once they have been disillusioned, are not constantly and systematically filled with despair, but rather seem prepared, in a manner of speaking, to renew their hope at each and every instant, although by virtue of a sort of metaphysical modesty they conceal this fact beneath their black envelope of men suffering from a universal bitterness—as though pessimism, in order to keep itself strong and ever-vigorous, needed from time to time the impetus provided by a new cruel disillusionment.[17]

And perhaps it is this alternation itself rather than the rebellion against images of plenitude alone that constitutes the Modern Condition.[18]

In going beyond the identification of mere madrigalisms, I have risked moving into the realm of the "low and soft" hermeneutics that Lawrence Kramer and I so often stand accused of practicing.[19] I might even plead guilty of imposing once again my own latter-day semiotics on a temporally distant and defenseless culture, though the heated controversies concerning mode, dissonance control, and tuning—labeled at the time as debates of the ancients versus the moderns—reveal that the stakes were widely perceived much as I have presented them.[20]

But in any case, if what I am doing is ventriloquizing, I vastly prefer it to accepting the notion that musicians in the Renaissance were simpleminded and incapable of anything we might want to acknowledge as the articulation of subjectivity. We can learn a great deal about how our predecessors experienced the self and interiority, but only if we take the music itself seriously as historical evidence.

CHAPTER 2

Sublime Experience and Ironic Action

E. T. A. HOFFMANN AND THE USE OF MUSIC FOR LIFE

Keith Chapin

Try as he would, E. T. A. Hoffmann never lived exactly the life he wished. In a well-known "Highly Random Thought" from *Kreisleriana*, one finds a motif that Hoffmann often varied in his literature and letters: "What artist has ever troubled himself with the political events of the day? He has always lived in his art alone, and only in it did he stride through life." Hoffmann, it would seem, looked away from politics and worldly action. If he ever did dabble with the rabble, it was only because the Napoleonic Wars forced him to do so. Thus the less-than-random thought continues: "A fatefully hard time has grasped humanity with an iron fist, and the pain has forced out sounds that were once foreign to it."[1]

This image, anyway, is the one that Hoffmann inspired. Both literary critics and musicologists have at times taken at face value his rigorous distinction between life devoted to art and life devoted to current events.[2] This acceptance is no fault of theirs, for it was Hoffmann himself who first professed this goal, practiced it in part, and provided inspiration for later artists to follow suit. Only Stephen Rumph has seriously challenged the commonplace view, arguing that Hoffmann devoted himself to the aesthetic state in the hope that the political state would follow suit.[3] In this interpretation, Hoffmann continued a line of thought begun by Plato and later repeated time and time again: musical order serves as a symbol for political order.

Although there is much to this point of view, it is important not to pass over the concrete ways that Hoffmann approached the political events of his time, and especially those that occurred late in his career. Hoffmann could indeed separate two types of activity, one directed toward art, the other directed toward worldly action and politics. With the help of motifs drawn from the theoretical tradition of the sublime, he construed the life of an artist, paradigmatically the life of a musician, as one set off from society. Yet with the help of a motif drawn from the theoretical tradition of irony—the tension between statement and counterstatement, or, as Friedrich Schlegel put it, between "self-creation and self-destruction"— he presented the life of art and the life of worldly action as complementary. The retirement and retreat of the life of art, grounded in the sublime moment of transport, became a type of self-creation: intuition, enthusiasm, and yearning helped one to form an identity. Worldly action, on the other hand, became a type of self-destruction: reflection, criticism, and skepticism helped one to reflect critically on the actions of society and to disrupt complacent self-understandings.

Although Hoffmann walked both apolitical and political paths throughout his life to some degree, his engagement with the world attained a specifically political dimension after 1814 in Berlin, once he returned to his career as a judge after eight tenuous years as a musician. In the last years before his death in 1822, Hoffmann jousted with the ministers of King Friedrich Wilhelm III, combating their arbitrary extensions of monarchical authority into the rule of law. In this case, art offered Hoffmann a position from which he could engage the life of worldly events. With a gentle nod to Nietzsche, one could say that ethical action was born from the spirit of music. By tracing a path through Hoffmann's opinions as a jurist into his life as an artist, this essay seeks to show just how that happened.

Liberal Judge and Romantic Musician

Hoffmann's legal opinions have withstood the test of time less well than his music criticism, not to mention his tales, though legal scholars in the past twenty years have found in them a Hoffmann who would surprise those who know only the musician and the writer.[4] As a musician and a writer, Hoffmann was fascinated by the ways that human actions revealed themselves as controlled by superindividual processes. As a judge, by contrast, Hoffmann demanded the autonomy of the individual, both in matters of criminal law and in those of politics. He used Prussian law to resist arbitrary infringements on individual rights, whether from above (Prussian ministers) or below (revolutionary student societies). A brief review of his duels with the Prussian state will serve both as a reminder of how Hoffmann differed from other politically minded Romantics, despite his great admiration for them, and as an introduction to the essential division that marked his approach to the world.

Hoffmann was educated in law in Königsberg, today Kaliningrad. He worked his way up the Prussian bureaucracy in Berlin and then in various East Prussian, now Polish, cities from 1795 until 1806, when French armies took Warsaw and Hoffmann found himself out of a job. He was not wholly unhappy with the turn of events, for he used it as an excuse to devote himself entirely to music, long his dream. From 1808 until 1814, he held various musical posts in Bamberg, Dresden, and Leipzig. Finally, tired of financial hardship and the uncertain life of a musician, in the summer of 1814 Hoffmann decided to reapply for a bureaucratic post, though he did not relish the prospect.[5] When he reentered the bureaucracy in October 1814, he hoped for light work as an "expediary secretary" in the Ministry of the Interior, essentially as a copyist, so as to pay bills and leave time for artistic activities.[6] His discernment, his diligence, and the needs of the Ministry of Justice trumped his wishes, however, and he was promoted up the ranks until in 1821 he reached the highest court in the Prussian system of justice, the High Appellate Senate of the Judicial Chamber (*Oberappellationssenat des Kammergerichts*). In 1819, he was further assigned to a special panel instructed to investigate ostensible demagogic and revolutionary activities against the state, the Immediate Investigatory Commission (*Immediat-Untersuchungs-Kommission*). During his years on the court, Hoffmann singled himself out as a judge for his fascination with the psychological nuance, for his ability to see his way through complex cases, and finally, and most important for this study, for his defense of individual rights and the rule of law and his opposition to arbitrary assumptions of power.

Though not the only instance, Hofmann's work on the Investigatory Commission best illustrates his strict respect for the rule of law. King Friedrich Wilhelm III and his ministers established the commission as a specific response to the murder of the playwright August von Kotzebue by the nationalist Karl Ludwig Sand on 23 March 1819, as well as to Karl

Loening's copycat attempt at the murder of Carl von Ibell on 1 July of the same year. The task of the commission was to prosecute "high-treasonable societies and other subversive activities," that is, those real and imagined revolutionaries who wished to challenge the monarchical status quo.[7] Although the commission was part of a general reactionary realignment of policy after the Congress of Vienna, it was directed above all toward an ostensible terrorist movement among student societies, the *Burschenschaften*, and several student leaders were brought before the tribunal, including Friedrich Ludwig Jahn, Georg Ludwig Rödiger, and August Follen.

Although many of the defendants had espoused German nationalism and hoped for some sort of popular representation, few had broken any laws. But it mattered little to the police or the royal ministers whether the defendants had actually committed crimes or represented credible threats, and the police took a free hand in illegally imprisoning defendants, fabricating evidence, and coercing confessions. More interested in results than in proof or protocol, they clearly hoped that the Investigatory Commission would take an aggressive stance against perceived enemies of the state.

The king and his ministers were severely deceived. Although the judges on the commission took action in egregious cases, they nonetheless repeatedly incited royal and ministerial ire, for they persistently asked for evidence and annoyingly found many of the investigated "demagogues" not guilty. It is easy to hear the frustration in the response of police director Karl Albert von Kamptz to the liberation of Georg Ludwig Rödiger, one of the speakers at the Wartburg festival in 1817 and a leader of the Jena *Burschenschaft*. "Instead of opening the investigation," wrote von Kamptz, "the commission responded to the ringleader's brief statement, which contravened protocol, by declaring him not guilty and liberating him."[8] Though not alone, Hoffmann was among the most proactive of the members of the commission in insisting on proper evidence, and many of the commission's letters and reports carry his signature.[9]

The king eventually tried to resolve what he perceived as the insubordination of the commission by creating a further ministerial commission outside the Justice Ministry. Its purpose was to review and to approve or veto the judgments of the Investigatory Commission, and it thus constituted a severe attack on judicial independence. When the ministers vetoed a decision of the commission, Hoffmann, speaking for himself and his colleagues, directed an appeal to the king. He asked that their decision be carried out or that they be relieved of their duties.[10] The king fulfilled neither request.

Although Hoffmann had often voiced vigorous nationalist hopes, especially during the Napoleonic Wars, he defended the demagogues, as they were called, out of respect for legal principle, not out of sympathy with their cause. He looked with horror on the patently twisted or even fabricated arguments of the police and their blatant disregard of individual rights. As he wrote to his friend Hippel on 24 June 1820, "knowing me you can imagine my *mood* as I saw an entire web of unholy arbitrariness, cheeky disregard of all laws, and personal animosity develop before my eyes." Although he felt that legal action against revolutionary "deeds" (*Taten*) was justified, he would have no truck with legal action against "sentiments" (*Gesinnungen*).[11] (He did draw a line, however, when he dealt with individuals who sought to take the law into their own hands, as in the case of such radical *Burschenschaftler* as August Adolph Follen. The case is discussed at the end of this chapter.)

Hartmut Mangold has suggested that as the conflict within the Prussian government heated up, Hoffmann did go beyond his initial neutral defense of legal procedure and invested himself personally in his opposition to the prosecutions.[12] Yet he did not sympathize with the goals of the defendants. He had little respect for the student societies, whose self-anointed messianism he mocked in his novel *Die Lebens-Ansichten des Katers Murr* (*The Life and Opinions of the Tomcat Murr*).[13] Their nationalism seems to have struck him as narrow-minded, as did much of the bigotry that pervaded Germany after the Restoration.

Hoffmann's nuanced distance from Romantic ideals can be read in many of his late stories. In the self-exculpatory "Meister Johannes Wacht" (1822), he combined a tribute to German Protestant burghers (properly outfitted with honesty, work ethic, and craft) with a critique of their intolerance toward lawyers. In the beginning of the tale, burghers and lawyers function, respectively, as figures of deep, authentic culture and of shallow, fabricated civilization. Meister Wacht shows true burgher colors in his disdain for a stepson who chooses the legal path. Yet he thereby also exemplifies a danger of the burgher mentality, the "disdainful, even sinful valor of a hardened spirit," as the narrator states after Wacht has mended his ways.[14] Hoffmann did not rescind his own faith in German culture, but he did temper his praise with a pragmatic awareness of the dangers of insularity and narrow-mindedness.

Hoffmann extended his satirical forays against ministerial and prosecutorial caprice and willful interpretation in his tales of 1821, including "Die Marquise de la Pivardiere" and "Die Doppelgänger." The late novella *Meister Floh* is especially worthy of note, for in it Hoffmann satirized Po-

lice Director von Kamptz, one of the primary instigators of the dema-
gogue persecutions. Unwisely, Hoffmann found inspiration for the satire
in classified documents. Although he borrowed innocuous material, he
thereby laid himself open to vengeful prosecution by Kamptz.

The Investigatory Commission had reviewed in one case the alleged
revolutionary, homicidal intentions of the student Gustav Asverus, who
had once described himself in a diary as "bloody lazy" (literally, "murder-
ously lazy" [*mordfaul*]). Taking the expression out of context, Kamptz had
used it to incriminate Asverus. Murder was obviously on Asverus's mind,
Kamptz suggested. In *Meister Floh*, Hoffmann invented the character of
Privy Counselor Knarripanti to ridicule Kamptz's strained arguments. To
curry favor at a small, unnamed court, Knarripanti hopes to suggest that
Peregrinus Tyß, a shy and retiring merchant's son in the free city of Frankfurt, has seduced the daughter of Knarripanti's lord, although Knarripanti
knows full well that the princess had long ago eloped with a traveling
actor. Knarripanti finds the term "bloody lazy" in Tyß's diary and points
to it as evidence of his bad character. Imagine the man who can find himself too lazy to murder on a given day!

Another passage in the Knarripanti episode points to the basic problem
of the real-world prosecutions, the lack of evidence. When the Frankfurt
connoisseurs of law who comment on Knarripanti's arguments note that
there is no *corpus delicti*—no material evidence that a crime had been committed—Knarripanti insists on prosecution nonetheless. He cares little
about the *delictum*, he says, so long as there is a *corpus*, and Herr Peregrinus
Tyß is the *corpus*.[15] Even though Hoffmann suppressed the Knarripanti
episodes in the published version of *Meister Floh*, word flew. Kamptz suc-
ceeded in having Hoffmann impeached for betrayal of state secrets, that
is, the harvest of the *mordfaul* argument from internal documents. Hoffmann died before the affair reached a resolution.

These examples should suffice to illustrate some of Hoffmann's basic
tenets as a judge. He allowed citizens liberty of thought and freedom of
action so long as they did not envision actual crimes. By the same token,
he restricted the jurisdiction of the state. Its leaders were not to fashion a
society to their taste. *Raison d'état* should not overturn the rule of law. As
Mangold has pointed out, Hoffmann was a liberal in his legal thought,
even a Kantian in his firm belief in the necessity of positive law and the
assumption of individual autonomy in all matters before the court.[16] He
insisted that individuals should be judged as if they had freedom of the
will. Furthermore, the law of the land should be enshrined in concrete
form and should not be altered to suit a monarch's fancy. In order to

protect the rights of individuals, Hoffmann divided the public and private spheres quite strictly. As long as individuals behaved according to the law, they could develop their own individual lives in the directions they wished.

Hoffmann owed his liberalism on the bench to his early training in law and to a well-established tradition within the Prussian judiciary. Even though he pointedly avoided Kant's lectures in Königsberg, he had studied law under Daniel Christoph Reidenitz, a follower of Kant. Although Reidenitz held that states should be led from above rather than through democratic processes, he did not propose that individuals lost all their rights in consequence. Instead he taught the separation of powers, the equality of citizens before the law, and freedom of speech.[17] Indeed, although Prussia was no constitutional monarchy, it did have a well-established body of law that enshrined such rights, as well as a professionalized judiciary jealous of its independence.[18]

Heinrich Heine commented in his *Briefe aus Berlin* (1822) that Hoffmann was neither Romantic nor Liberal.[19] It would be more accurate to say that he was both. As a musician and writer, Hoffmann tended to be a Romantic: unknown forces ruled human desires, activities, and history. As a judge, he was a Liberal: individuals had free will. On the one hand, imbrication of human agency with larger forces; on the other, autonomy. These two political tendencies can be seen to privilege opposing perspectives on the nature of human agency. On the one hand, any human decision or act can be seen as determined by a potentially infinite chain of causes and effects; on the other hand, the same acts or decisions can be seen as willed by the individual. Hoffmann parted intellectual company, though he did not break his personal ties, with many of his friends and idols among the Romantics at the point where they embraced religious mysticism, political conservatism, and apologies for monarchy as an expression of the organic state. Yet he never gave up on the metaphysics that inspired such regressive positions. Instead, he found another way to relate the metaphysics to politics.

Self-Creation and Self-Destruction:
Irony, Mood, and the Construal of Identity

To show the relationship between Hoffmann's metaphysics and his politics, it is necessary to examine two topics of great interest to the Romantics: irony and mood. Hoffmann used the binaries of irony not only to elaborate on the existential division between perception and reality that he believed afflicted all human endeavors but also to distinguish between two different categories of mood that determined human reactions to this division. As I discuss later, music and law served as activities that both emblematized the two sides of irony and sprang from the two categories of mood.

The Romantic writers that Hoffmann read carefully, especially Friedrich Schlegel, Ludwig Tieck, and Jean Paul, found existential significance for their various theories of irony in a rhetorical technique known since classical antiquity: a speaker says one thing and means another.[20] Romantic critics broke down the conflict between the said and the signified and analyzed its component parts, focusing in particular on the mental attitudes that can underpin the making of a statement. For example, the statement "nice day" might be taken as a straightforward remark, say, on the beauty of a summer day, or as a critical remark, to comment on assaults of rain and hail. Friedrich Schlegel, who stimulated much of the critical thought on the issue of irony, took the contrast between the straightforward use of linguistic conventions (a statement signifies according to linguistic convention) and the critical destabilization of linguistic conventions (a statement goes in a different direction than its conventional meaning) and worked it into the other dichotomies popular among writers of the time: instinct and reflection, emotion and reason, enthusiasm and criticism, and naïve and sentimental. Common to all these dichotomies was a belief that individuals acted and reacted in the world dualistically. There were two different modes of being, two fundamental attitudes toward the world.

Furthermore, critics developed common systems of value judgment to relate these two modes or attitudes to each other. Romantic critics appreciated the immediacy and surety implicit in "naïve" instinctive and emotional attitudes toward the world, yet they were hardly about to give up on the subjective freedom and richness of experience achieved through the "sentimental" reflective and rational attitudes. Irony offered Schlegel and other Romantics a way to relate these two types of attitude to each other. They transformed the distinction between the straightforward and the critical aspects of irony in several ways. First, they transformed it into a conflict between the true nature of the world and human perception of the world.[21] In their pantheistic speculations about the true order of things, Romantics of all stripes proposed that superindividual forces imbricate all human utterance and action. For Schlegel and Hoffmann, these forces were metaphysical in nature, to be intuited through instinct or poetic enthusiasm.[22] Hoffmann himself was less interested in language than in the interpenetration of biology and psychology, especially as manifested in sexual desire and dreams. But no matter whether the superindividual forces were physical-psychological or linguistic, they put the reach of rationality and the claims of agency in doubt and on notice. On the other side of the coin, the world as perceived by human beings was the world of rational reflection and willed action, the world where human beings seemed to control their actions.

Hoffmann commented on this gap between perception (ostensible free agency) and reality (actual determined action) at the beginning of "Meister Johannes Wacht":

> As it weighs and orders the fate of its children, nature follows her own dark, unfathomable path. That which people conveniently designate as the true tendency of being in ideas and reflections won from a narrow life, is to nature only the cheeky play of beguiled children who think themselves wise. But the shortsighted man often finds an incurable irony in the contradiction between the convictions of his spirit and that dark reign of the unfathomable power, a power that had once held and cared for him on her maternal breast but then abandoned him. This irony fills him with horror and terror, for it threatens to destroy his own self.[23]

Irony played into this conflict between "unfathomable power" and short-sighted "convictions" in two ways. First, human beings related to these two aspects of the world through intuition and rational reflection, respectively, and thus their mode of existence itself embodied the conflict at the center of irony. Even as they believed they acted rationally, exercising their free will to achieve their quotidian ends, they might still intuit the unfathomable powers that controlled human destinies. Second, the metaphysical forces that suffused the world pulled perpetual fast ones on short-sighted human beings, and the mismatch between the finite actions of men and the infinite workings of the world produced a close cousin to dramatic irony.

It should be noted that even as Hoffman used this first Romantic transformation of the principle of irony to define his worldview, he was a master of the more traditional rhetorical irony and often let rhetorical and Romantic irony intertwine. When he or one of his characters felt the ironic disjunction between the world as it was in truth and the world as it was perceived by human beings, he offered wry commentary on the delusions and foibles of society. Hoffmann thus found a role for the critical function of classical irony at the point where the existential divisions of life described by Romantic irony became too grave to ignore. Classical irony then served to reveal to people trapped in a narrow walk of life the blindness of their ways. In *Die Lebens-Ansichten des Katers Murr*, the Frau Counselor Benzon censors the irony of Kreisler (the nonfeline protagonist): " 'With this fantastic agitation, with this 'heart-rending irony,' retorted Benzon, 'you will never cause anything but unrest, completely dissonant confusion of all conventional affairs and things as they now stand.' "[24]

Hoffmann himself commented on this critical function of classical irony. In the programmatic essay on Callot that Hoffmann set as preface to the *Fantasiestücke*, he noted that "irony of the sort that, by putting the human into conflict with the animal, mocks man in his pitiable doings and efforts lives only in a deep spirit, and so Callot's grotesque shapes created from animal and man reveal to the serious, deeply penetrating viewer all the mysterious allusions that lie under the veil of scurrility."[25] The implication is that humanity does not live up to the humanistic ideals of the caricaturist and ironist.

Hoffmann also drew on a second Romantic transformation of the theory of irony, even if he did not explicitly theorize it. Friedrich Schlegel took the conflict between the said and signified (or instinct and reflection) and worked it into an existential conflict between "self-creation and self-destruction" (*Selbstschöpfung und Selbstvernichtung*). Schlegel set out the framework of this conflict in the first sentences of the "Athenäums-Fragment No. 51":

> Naive is what is or seems to be natural, individual, or classical to the point of irony, or to the point of continuously fluctuating between self-creation and self-destruction. If it's simply instinctive, then it's childlike, childish, or silly; if it's merely intentional, then it gives rise to affectation. The beautiful, poetical, ideal naive must combine intention and instinct. The essence of intention in this sense is freedom, though intention isn't consciousness by a long shot. There is a certain kind of self-infatuated contemplation of one's own naturalness or silliness that is itself unspeakably silly. Intention doesn't exactly require any deep calculation or plan. Even Homeric naiveté isn't simply instinctive; there is at least as much intention in it as there is in the grace of lovely children or innocent girls. And even if Homer himself had no intentions, his poetry and the real author of that poetry, Nature, certainly did.[26]

Always allusive, elusive, and multifarious in his intended meanings, Schlegel cleverly manipulated the principle of irony to address many issues.[27]

One of Schlegel's central interests was literary. He took the conflictual aspect of irony (the contrast between statement and counterstatement) to

ground a type of literature that flirted with the classicist ideals of verisimilitude and formal unity yet that undermined both the dramatic and formal
foundations of classicist illusion. To achieve the semblance of reality (a
story in which one forgot the artificiality of the writer's narrative and art),
a prototypical "naïve" writer relied on inspired "genius," that is, a form
of intuitive creative power based in the emotional wellsprings of the self.
Genius allowed an artist to weld his materials and his message together
into a striking whole. The successful artwork hid its artificiality and provided an illusion so powerful that it seemed real, the semblance of nature.
By contrast, although Schlegel's ironic writer still worked within the basic
classicist parameters of formal unity and narrative verisimilitude, he used
critical rationality to puncture the illusion of the classicist whole and, most
important, to transcend the formal and narrative limits (and resulting autonomy) that accompanied classical goals. The purpose was to create a
work of art with less balance and less verisimilitude than the classicist work
of art but, thanks to its provocative meditations on its own formal and
narrative means, a work that achieved greater subtlety and richness. Although even Homer had his place in the scheme, Cervantes, Shakespeare,
Sterne, and Goethe served as Schlegel's models. All four authors constantly allowed their narrators and characters to reflect critically on the
generic and poetological traditions of the stories that they told. The instinctive and critical modes that underpinned enthusiastic statement and
skeptical counterstatement intertwined.

This program of literary reform could easily map onto the many programs of human betterment that circulated at the time. Ultimately, Schlegel conceived irony as essential to an ideal of social and civic formation of
ancient heritage and modern relevance. "When it is said to a philosopher,
'Sacrifice to the Graces,' this means the same thing as 'Possess yourself of
irony and form yourself to urbanity.' "[28] In other words, individuals should
bypass limited constitutions of identity, governed by the "naïve" acceptance of the modes of behavior customary to a society (the statement), and
they should strive to expand their imaginative and spiritual life into new
dimensions through "sentimental" reflection (the counterstatement).
Greece provided an idealized model for the "naïve" form of behavior. The
Romantics viewed Greek antiquity as an age when the individual had lived
at one with the world, but they also believed that the Greek model had
seen its day and could no longer suit the conditions of modernity. Romantic souls had to leave the finite world behind, allow reflection to expand
infinitely, and ultimately search for a second nature, a second naïveté that
might offer a new yet richer holistic identity.

As much as Hoffmann admired Schlegel, he only followed him in part. Although the future of literature did not concern Hoffmann overly, he did find use for Schlegel's thoughts on the existential and critical potential of irony. With the conflict between self-creation and self-destruction, he could address different types of mood and attitude as well as their functional significance for the constitution or performance of identity. He thereby tapped into another widespread interest of Romantics: mood.

Mood, or *Stimmung* (literally, "attunement"), can be defined as the meeting point of a person's emotional life (which juts into consciousness as instincts and intuitions) and the person's intellectual life (which strives toward rational behavior and a critical distance from the surrounding world). It is also the point at which it is difficult to distinguish between the action of the world on an individual (paradigmatically represented for Romantics by human emotions and desires) and the action of an individual on the world (paradigmatically represented by the will and rational and moral freedom). Writers such as Goethe, Schiller, Humboldt, and Fichte used the concept of mood to explore the points at which the Enlightenment distinction between the human power over nature and the human enthrallment to nature breaks down, whether in the process of artistic creation or in the process of natural experience.[29] Hoffmann's interest in mood can be easily read in the diaries he kept from 1811 to 1814. Many an entry does little more than note his mood that day.

More to the point, in his criticism, in his fiction, and in his life, Hoffmann was fascinated by the divisions and distinctions between two basic categories of emphatic mood, or *Stimmung*. On the one side stood moods of melancholy, yearning, and exaltation, that is, moods that encouraged intuition and instinctive activities. On the other side stood moods of bitterness and estrangement, so conducive to self-reflection, criticism, skepticism, satire, and irony. These two categories of mood represented the outer edges on the spectrum of emphatic human experiences, and they engendered quite different types of activity and attitude. Yet they had something in common. Hoffmann portrayed such emphatic moods as always in essence existential, related to the maintenance of the self or, as Hoffmann put it, the *Ich*. In both types of mood, a person sensed that there was more to the world than met the eye: one sensed the ground of existence, those forces that determined the destiny of individuals, nations, and history. Emphatic moods also opposed a rather diffuse and eclectic assembly of everyday moods and sentiments. Emphatic moods, for Hoffmann, did not occur in lives complacently lived or directed toward economic gain and social prestige. Hoffmann's phenomenology of the spirit, as it might be called, was normative. Rightly or wrongly, he was willing to disregard many moods simply because he believed their materialistic motivations to be false.

Hoffmann frequently staged violent shifts from one category of emphatic mood to the other. In the *Lebens-Ansichten des Katers Murr*, to take a literary example, the Capellmeister Johannes Kreisler at one moment muses enthusiastically and longingly, absenting himself from his surroundings. In the next moment, he lays into a gauche and philistine princess with savage vigor: "As soon as the princess began to speak, the stranger [Kreisler] turned suddenly and looked her in the eyes, but his entire countenance seemed to have become a new one.—Gone was the expression of melancholy yearning, gone every trace of a spirit aroused in its innermost depths. A crazily distorted smile intensified the expression of bitter irony to a prankish and scurrilous point."[30] In *Der goldene Topf* (*The Golden Pot*), Hoffmann shows the Archivarius Lindhorst pass in the opposite direction, from skepticism to enthusiasm. Lindhorst expects the protagonist, Anselmus, to fail at the task of copying a mysterious manuscript covered with strange characters: "With a strange smile he strode to the table. Anselmus stood up silently. All the while the Archivarius looked at him with a mocking smirk, but hardly had he glanced at the copy that the smile was drowned in the expression of deep, solemn seriousness, to which all the muscles of his face contributed."[31] Similar dramatizations of the rapid passage of mood can be found throughout Hoffmann's fiction, from early to late.

By bifurcating instinctive and critical modes of human consciousness, Hoffmann found in the principle of irony a powerful potential. With it, he could address the ways that human beings give a rhythm to their lives and construe their identities, now retreating from the world at large, now turning toward it. Schematically put, moods of enthusiasm, yearning, or exaltation (associated with instinct and intuition) permitted and pushed one to turn away from society, to devote oneself to a small group of friends, to a loved one, to religion, to wine, or to music. To take up Schlegel's dichotomy, one "created" one's self, either at the personal level or through a form of intuitive communion with another. Forgetting cares, plans, and projects, a person falls back to the point at which individuality becomes coterminous with the superindividual forces. On the other hand, moods of bitterness or estrangement led a person to take up rational activities such as criticism and skepticism and to turn attention toward society. One addressed the behavior of others critically, whether through wry remarks, fantastic stories, or finely tuned legal arguments. Here one "de-stroyed" the unity of self as one attended to worldly events.

Both the centripetal movements of self-creation and the centrifugal ones of self-destruction arose from an intense sense of the duality of exis-tence, from the gap between the inner world of the spirit and the outer world of human events. In fact, both processes involved species of retreat and engagement with the world, though in quite different ways. In mo-ments of melancholy, exaltation, or yearning, one derived strength from the intuited sense of a connection to the forces that propel the world. One felt situated and emphatically present in one's space, a feeling for which German philosophical taste and tradition later coined the term *Geborgen-heit* (roughly, a situatedness with overtones of safety). If such experiences were a token of the estrangement of humanity from metaphysical founda-tions, a token that everyday life failed to meet its potential, they were also a way to reconnect, to strengthen resolve in the continuation of life. A person turned away from the chaotic everyday world and attended rather to the constitutive forces that might provide some stable identity.

Such stability of identity was of course something of an illusion, but it was a useful illusion. Indeed, so important was its function that the idea cannot easily be set aside, as the reformulations of the principle attest. In a marvelous article titled "The Mysteries of Animation," Lawrence Kramer has noted that the moment of transcendence so essential to nine-teenth-century aesthetics is an example of a process by which an individual comes to terms with the symbolic order of language, or the "big Other," as Jacques Lacan called it. As Kramer notes, Lacan developed aspects of an idealist tradition. Music acts as an "ideal or authoritative subject." In order for human individuals to infuse their particularity with a sense of universality, they either accept the symbolic order wholesale or they come to some sort of negotiated settlement with it. This is a process not re-stricted to music, but it occurs whenever individuals experience something that seems to point beyond their limited experience. The particularity of music, Kramer argues, lies in its capacity to make the process pleasurable rather than painful. Music allows human beings to experience the myster-ies of animation, to allow their participation in imbricating orders to rise above the mechanical, and ultimately to achieve the semblance of imme-diacy.[32]

This moment of self-creation had profound repercussions on human action in the world, for the strength and confidence derived from the sense of immediacy, no matter how illusory, allowed one to act with the full confidence of a grounded self. The process might be schematized thus:

only when one realizes the extent of one's enthrallment to imbricating forces can one gain the ability to rise above them, to exercise true free will and self-determination. Hoffmann gave many examples of such freedom, among them, examples that feature the liberation that composers of genius possessed. In "Ritter Gluck" (1809), a man describes his banishment from the ground of existence (the realm of tones) to the harsh reality of Berlin, but, thanks to his contact with the metaphysical realm of tones, he makes wonderful music. (Hoffmann blurred the boundary of fantasy and reality and left the identity of the man ambiguous. The musician is perhaps Gluck himself or a deranged man who thinks himself Gluck or some combination of the two. His preeminent musicality, however, is not in doubt.) Hoffmann ascribed the same freedom to composers in his criticism. Beethoven, like Haydn and Mozart, "separates his self from the inner realm of tones and acts over it as an absolute ruler."[33]

Critical moods such as bitterness involved an alternate negotiation of the two sides of human identity. Once again, such moods arose from the emphatic experience of a gap between the dualities of human nature and experience, between determined destiny and self-determination, and between the world as it truly is and the world as it seems to be. But where instinct-oriented moods of yearning, melancholy, and exaltation provoked a person to turn inward, to shore up the self, bitter moods incited ironic comments on the world around the self. This constitutes a form of self-destruction, not only because Hoffmann and his heroes turned outward to focus on the deficiencies of the world, often as manifested in the activities of others, but also because the bitter and sardonic mood gave no incitement to overcome the dualities of life, or at least not directly. The bitter mood arose from and provoked recognition of human foibles and delusions, whether one's own or those of others, and led one to comment on them. Of course, insofar as irony had a revelatory function, it did help people see the error of their ways and thus cleared the path toward reform. But the energy and impetus to overcome the divisions of life had to come from elsewhere.

In Hoffman's music criticism and fantastic tales, he offered many images of such self-creation and self-destruction. Indeed, he owed much of his popularity in his own day—and his relevance today—to his awareness that the self was not always on firm ground. It is rare to find a story or critique by Hoffmann in which the self is not threatened. But in order to distinguish creative and destructive impulses, Hoffmann also needs to be read carefully, for the threatened self reacts in a variety of ways to its situations. One can differentiate between situations in which a person

works toward some individual or group identity and situations in which a
person deals with society at large. In the first case, the force of some affect-
ing experience produces a mood that empties the self of its everyday sentiments and concerns. The self is brought back to basics, so to speak. In the
second case, the awareness of the gap between human perceptions of the
world and the imbricating forces that determine human action encourage
the threatened self to offer critical commentary on human practices and
foibles. In one situation, then, the instinctive capacities of a person are
awakened; in the other, the reflective and critical ones are.

Moods of Retreat, Sublime Shock, and the Construal of Identity

Among the activities associated with instinct-oriented moods, Hoffmann
gave an especially high place to music. As he saw it, music elicited moods
that marked the point at which human identities fuse with some larger
whole. "Music opens to man an unknown realm," he famously wrote at
the beginning of his review of Beethoven's Fifth Symphony. "It is true
music from the other world (*musica dell'altro mondo*)," he wrote of Palestrina
in "Alte und neue Kirchenmusik" ("Old and New Church Music").[34] To
a large extent, Hoffmann simply took motifs of music aesthetics and the
philosophy of history common at the time and linked them to the compositional specificities of styles and works. Like Rousseau, Herder, and many
others, he dignified moods of enthusiastic ecstasy and yearning as physio-
logical and psychological reminders of origins. The reasoning was simple.
If the progress of history had estranged and alienated humanity from its
original compact with nature, and if primordial oneness with the order of
things had given way to Doppelgänger twoness or an imperfect mismatch
between the world as it was perceived and the world as it was, music offered humanity an opportunity to rekindle the link and rediscover the ori-
ginary state, if only momentarily. Thus, as has often been noted,
Hoffmann's metaphysics of art music stood close to religion. Nonetheless,
although the moods had a revelatory function, they also served other,
more humanistic ends. They allowed individuals to construe their own
identities.

   To deal with the centrality of music in the construal of identity, Hoffmann relied on an essential motif in contemporaneous theories of the sublime. In the moment of transport, ordinary life ceases. This cessation of
ordinary life was the centerpiece and keystone of the tripartite structure
of many theories of the sublime, nicely and concisely analyzed by Thomas

Weiskel: first, ordinary experience; second, sublime shock and radical severance from ordinary experience; third, a transfigured state.[35] Hoffmann worked the moment of shock into his music criticism and his fiction often, though he varied the temporality of the moment liberally to accord with the diverse types of transport that music can produce. The sudden striking moment so important to classical theories of sublimity could be mapped onto truly sudden events (brutal chords), onto extended passages (especially loud and massive textures), and, perhaps most important for his own particular renegotiation of classicism, to whole movements or works.[36]

Hoffmann manipulated contemporaneous theories of sublimity in exemplary fashion in his review of the Fifth Symphony (1810). Carl Dahlhaus has argued that Hoffmann took Kant's theory of the sublime as his basic model but substituted religious pathos for Kant's moral pathos.[37] It would perhaps be more accurate to say that Hoffmann balanced moral and religious pathos, for the sublime moment did not just reveal a metaphysical order. It also cleared the way for a rich sense of individual identity. Hoffmann took the tripartite structure of the sublime and gave significance to the emphatic moods felt during and after the act of devoted listening.

Hoffmann had no need to mention the first stage, ordinary experience. The banality of the complacent life was ever Hoffmann's unstated foe and must be read into his critical remarks. The second stage of the sublime experience, radical severance from ordinary life, he treated in various ways, for he was as anxious to capture differences in musical character as he was to respect the special nature of the musical experience as a distinct type. Haydn's symphonies, he wrote, "[lead] us into infinite, green groves, into a joyful, colorful throng of happy people. . . . Mozart leads us into the depths of the realm of ghosts."[38] Whatever the character of the musical moment, whether pastoral, uncanny, or violent, the moment served to sever a person from everyday modes of experience.[39]

Hoffmann then proceeded to describe the move from the second to the third stage of the musical sublime. As the music proceeds, it destroys the contents of experience, in particular the emotions, and replaces the sated consciousness characteristic of the first stage with a radically stripped down, transfigured state. The Fifth Symphony, for example, is filled with "giant shadows," part metaphorical descriptions of Beethoven's unruly themes and gestures, part poetic circumlocutions of the effects of his music. They

> swell up and down, close us ever more tightly in, and destroy everything in us, with the exception of the pain of infinite yearning. In this state, every

desire that had arisen with the jubilant tones falls and is extinguished. We live forth in this pain [of infinite yearning] that consumes love, hope, and joy, though it does not destroy them, and that wants to explode our breasts with a many-voiced sonic simultaneity of all passions. We are ecstatic ghost-seers.[40]

For all its poetry, this description of the auditory experience contains both philosophical acumen and musical good sense, though to move beyond the dazzle of metaphor it is helpful to review some of its terms.

Early in the review, Hoffmann dismissed feelings that could be named by concepts (*durch Begriffe bestimmbare Gefühle*) as incommensurable with the realm opened up by instrumental music.[41] Although his intention was in part to drive a wedge between "pure" instrumental music and ostensibly impure vocal music, he was also working with a contemporaneously discussed and thoroughly valid distinction between mood and emotion.[42] Moods are affective states and lack intentional direction. Emotions build on moods but are directed toward specific people, things, or ideas. Anxiety is a mood; fear is an emotion. Of course, Hoffmann did not strictly distinguish his terms, but he did separate the unspecific emotions presented in instrumental music and the specific emotions proper to vocal music (and to everyday life, in which intentions are an essential part of human dealings) in a fashion that points toward the modern distinction between mood and emotion.

The unspecific category of mood was essential to the particular character of the second and third stages of the sublime experience. In Hoffman's description of the experience of Beethoven's symphony, he suggested that music manipulates human desire (*Lust*) so as to strip a person of the detritus of the everyday, that is, such definite emotions as love, hope, and joy. These emotions, linked to a person's everyday experience by motivations and intentions, are different both from the exalted moods elicited during the experience of music, that is, the second stage, and from the mood of infinite yearning left over after the music is over, the third stage. If, for Edmund Burke, human beings felt delight after the moment of sublime shock, for Hoffmann, as for many of his German contemporaries, they felt infinite yearning. This peculiarly Romantic mood provided the foundation for a more intense experience of life.

The power of music to cleave one type of experience from another— the transfigured from the everyday—underpins not just Hoffmann's Beethoven criticism but also his approach to all music that he felt was worth speaking about. Even music that might have been termed "beautiful" in the dichotomies of the eighteenth century, insofar as it elicited special states, could lend itself to the tripartite structure of the sublime.[43] Thus, the special quality of the affective state that Hoffmann linked to Beethoven extends to the special qualities of the more "human" music of Haydn and Mozart. "Haydn crystallizes the human in human life in a Romantic fashion," wrote Hoffmann. "Mozart takes claim on the superhuman, the marvelous, which lives in the inner spirit."[44] Although the moods elicited by Haydn and Mozart lacked the violent and radically emphatic character that Hoffmann valued in Beethoven, and thus were more commensurable with everyday life, they were no less moods, without intentionality and without direction. They too were idealized, without specific links to the concrete experience of a person.

If Hoffmann focused in his criticism on the effects of music on individual listeners, in his fiction he again took up the principle of severance and again addressed the constitution of identity at the level of the individual. But he moved on to deal with the constitution of small group identity, both heterosocial and homosocial. As individuals engaged in intimate music making, they found harmony with other kindred spirits. It might seem that in this respect Hoffmann fell back on eighteenth-century theories of beauty. Edmund Burke, for instance, famously argued in his *Philosophical Enquiry into the Sublime and the Beautiful* (1757) that beauty awakened the soft sentiments related to social interaction, whereas sublimity awakened the violent sentiments associated with individual action.[45] But even as Hoffmann addressed social interaction, sublimity structured his thought about the effects of music. In the first of the *Kreisleriana*, "Johannes Kreislers, des Kapellmeisters musikalische Leiden" ("Musical Sufferings of the Kapellmeister Johannes Kreisler"), Kreisler admits that a woman's singing is what keeps him from fleeing society. Her singing "carries him into heaven," and an hour at the piano with her "pours the balsam of heaven in the wounds inflicted by the all the mangled tones of an entire day" of worldly life. She too takes musical refuge from the hyperactivity around her, playing the piano in duo sonatas by Mozart and Beethoven and singing scenes from Gluck or Mozart. It is because music carries both parties to hidden regions that they experience their special bond. Only because they share a common individuating experience are they able to form their common identity.[46] This strategy also allowed Hoffmann to attribute a metaphysical significance to love and desire. Fancy clothes and social position might draw ordinary beings together, to paraphrase Hoffmann's logic, but the sensual sparks that united Kreisler and his pupil Amalie were proper to the underlying order of things.

In other words, for Hoffmann, music individuated and isolated individuals in their private moods, as eighteenth-century theorists of the sublime had suggested; but insofar as individuals could share these moods and moments, they could still form some group identity. Hoffmann thereby allowed the individuating function of the sublime to merge with the community-forming function of the beautiful. In the eighteenth century, beauty had owed its social function to its ability to awaken social sentiment, in particular the sensitivity to the natural moral or sensual links that bound human individuals together in society. As Barbara Naumann has noted, however, the early Romantics, beginning with Wilhelm Heinrich Wackenroder, began to doubt that such a natural community between human beings could ever exist. For Hoffmann, the individuating power of the sublime offered a way to reinstate the social function once assigned to beauty, if only at the level of the small group.[47]

In sum, Hoffmann played out the second, core moment of sublime shock in two ways to describe the construal or performance of identity. First, in the musical experience both individual moments and entire works provide the shock that will pull individuals from their daily affairs. Second, in moments of making music with others the sublime experience disrupts the ordinary course of affairs and allows those involved in the music to commune together. It offers a moment away from the divisions and complexities of the world, as well as a token of a possible reconciliation of such divisions and complexities. In both the individual and the communal moment of severance from the everyday world, a person stands off from directed emotions. He or she finds refuge in moods prejudicial to intuition and often associated with interiority: exaltation, melancholy, yearning. And in all of these cases, the emphatic experience allows or forces a person to turn away from everyday life.[48]

Before moving on to Hoffmann's engagement with worldly events as a judge, it is good to review some of the deficiencies of his approach to music, for only then does one take it with the seriousness it deserves. As noted, music for Hoffmann elicited moods linked to intuition and instinct. It was a force that brought human beings back to themselves, so to speak. Yet although the best music for Hoffmann did include instinct's opposite, that is, rational reflection and the free choice of the composer, it was still a one-sided affair, directed toward mood and intimations of imbricating forces.

Hoffmann purchased this power of music at the price of other valuable functions of the art. He was blind to many potentials of music, even the music he loved best. First, because he associated music so strongly with enthusiasm and instinct, he mistrusted any music that wore its critical spirit on its sleeve. Playful jokes, or *tändelnde Lazzi*, as he put it, were not his cup of tea.[49] Second, he overemphasized the centrality of synthesis and coherence in the musical sphere, even to the point where he ignored formal disjunctions and changes in affect.[50] Third, he restricted music's significance to affect, character, and the expression of the absolute.[51] He rejected programmatic music and willfully ignored the signifying potential of style. Finally, insofar as he acknowledged that music had other social functions, he roundly scorned them. Had he known the work of Lawrence Kramer, he would have learned much.

But the fact that Hoffmann wore blinders as an aesthetician of music should not blind one to the larger framework of his aesthetics. The power of music to crystallize new states in the subject, however defined, has long been legendary. For all that Hoffmann insisted on the priority of such states, they existed in constant and productive tension with their nominal opposites, moments of critical reflection and engagement. One need only look at the many glorious *tändelnde Lazzi* among his stories to see that the enthusiastic practice of music was not his only course of action.

Moods of Engagement, Legal Action, and Social Criticism

Hoffmann never explicitly presented his legal activities as a form of irony, that is, as a way to destabilize complacent and misguided self-understandings. Nonetheless, the parallels between his attitudes and actions as an ironist on the one hand and as a judge on the other are striking. Most important, in both roles he took a critical and engaged stance toward the world around him. In both he relied on moods conducive to reflection and criticism, not those—so important to music, religion, and the communion with friends—directed toward the intuitive surrendering of a past self. Furthermore, in both roles he set himself to the criticism and "destruction" of limited self-images and self-understandings, both his own and those of others, including the Romantic nationalists. As we have seen, he also insisted that the law treat people as if they had free will. Law thus demanded of human individuals the same free will and critical distance from emotions that the fantasist required in order to produce the strange juxtapositions of humor.

Although Hoffmann did not always care for the particular form of social engagement that the legal profession offered him, at the end of his life he practiced it with care, maintaining the cool mood that enabled him to act critically. He most certainly did not approach it with the zeal of an ideologue who enthusiastically identified a political agenda with the law. To his colleagues, his efficiency and rationality on the bench could seem to oppose the fantastic flights of his fiction. As his superior Friedrich von Trützschler wrote in an internal review in 1818, "His work as a writer, to which he at times devotes his hours of relaxation and leisure, in no way hinders his industry, and the luxuriant fantasy and tendency to the comic that reigns in it contrasts in a remarkable way with the cool calm and seriousness with which he approaches his work as a *judge*."[52] It would be a mistake, however, to take Trützschler entirely at his word and divorce Hoffmann's mood as a judge from his mood as a fantasist. Trützschler would not have mentioned Hoffmann's work as writer had he not wished to calm apprehensions about them in the Ministry. The mistake would be dire. History has shown too well that devotion to duty and to the letter of the law can blind just as dangerously as euphoric engagement for a cause. Calm alone does not make the ironist.

Hoffmann combined the cool collectedness described by Trützschler with a critical outlook born of indignation. In Hoffmann's letter to Hippel of 1820, quoted earlier, he himself spoke not of his cool and calm but of the emphatic mood provoked by the ministerial nest of wasps: "Knowing me you can imagine my *mood* as I saw an entire web of unholy arbitrariness, cheeky disregard of all laws, and personal animosity develop before my eyes."[53] (The emphasis on "mood" is Hoffmann's.) Although he does not elaborate on his dismay, it is redolent of the bitterness and estrangement that so often inspired ironic commentary in his fictional characters. Hoffmann may not have put irony and comedy into play in his official letters and judgments, but the strict and sober forms of Prussian legalese served his purpose just as well. Under his pen, the chancellery style of government bureaucracy contrasted grotesquely with the ludicrous leaps of logic taken by lawyers and defendants and the brash overstepping of roles by overzealous government ministers.

In alliance with this critical spirit, Hoffmann's engagement with society through his activities as a judge, and above all his insistence that Prussian law be upheld, allowed him to negate or "destroy" self-understandings. As noted earlier, these self-understandings could be either his own or those of others. The personal self-destruction can be read in the softened tone and nuanced positions that he developed in his late fiction and that suggest that Hoffmann understood his own position better. Through his activities on the Immediate Investigatory Commission, he had to engage with nationalists who made use of the very principles he had expounded earlier in his own writings. The experience seems to have made him distance himself from the nationalist enthusiasms he had expressed at the height of the Napoleonic Wars. For example, in "Meister Johannes Wacht" he moved away from the idealization of German culture and a phobic antipathy toward French civilization. A representative of civilization, Wacht's French Huguenot neighbor, Monsieur Pickard Leberfink, is more circumspect and fair in his sentiments than is Wacht, the German burgher and symbol of culture. At some point, it would seem, Hoffmann learned that the achievements of "civilization" should not be lightly tossed aside. Even if he did not rid himself of his prejudice in favor of "culture" over "civilization," he did nuance his views considerably. As he engaged with the nationalists as a judge, he distanced himself from a system of values and a vision of the world that he had held earlier in his career and that had been important to his earlier self-understanding and identity. Criticism, in the form of "self-destruction," allowed him to achieve a new self-understanding.

Such criticism also aimed at the self-understandings of a society, and indeed of the very modes by which a society construes itself as a community. It depended on an implicit distinction between two ways in which modern societies regulate themselves: in part through ethical and behavioral codes (often driven by moral sentiments) and in part through a political authority or state that formulates explicit directives and laws. Natural law was the foundation of the one, positive law the foundation of the other. Hoffmann distinguished sharply between the two. He invested great faith in civil society as an ideal way to form a nation but then used positive law as a way to restrain the delusions that can arise from the deeply felt ethical codes of individuals.

In Hoffmann's idealized fictional portraits of civil interaction, he advocated instinct-driven values of love, sympathy, honor, patriotism, and faith—in short, a bourgeois moral code. His stories glorify a system of values (and prejudices) that, in Hoffmann's telling, produce a chaotic, if ultimately peaceful, society. In the end, Hoffmann hoped that the values of civil society would unite humanity. At the end of "Der Dichter und der Komponist" ("The Poet and the Composer"), Ferdinand, the poet turned warrior, proclaims, "The golden gates are opened and in a *single* flash science and art alight the holy striving that unites humanity to a *single* church. Thus, friend, cast your gaze upward—courage—trust—faith!"[54] The three values of courage, trust, and faith serve as a call to spiritual action and as a parallel to the military action undertaken by Ferdinand. Ludwig, the composer and reluctant patriot, does not object, though he does not seem to overcome entirely his skepticism about the explicit political actions undertaken by his friend.[55] Hoffmann was, however, well aware of the dangers of such communal identities inspired by instinct-driven values and codes.

To counterbalance in his legal opinions the enthusiasms and yearnings that he encouraged in his fiction, Hoffmann used the law as a negative, critical control. In the realm of governance—that is, the political sphere narrowly construed—he demanded the rule of rational logic in the legal profession and in government policy. Here, Prussian law acted as an arbiter of sorts, a check on the enthusiasms and delusions of all from the lowliest peasant up to the king's ministers. If civil society adhered to an ethical code grounded in instinct and intuition, state power had to obey a different standard.

Hoffmann's opposition to the intrusive and excessive prosecution of "demagogues" by royal ministers provides one example of how he used the law to control the enthusiasms of society. The fear of revolutionaries had made the rulers and their ministers so eager to suppress dissent that they grouped innocent members of student groups with committed revolutionaries. Individual rights were not overly a matter of concern, and as they discovered guilt by association, the representatives of the state fell into a form of fanatical behavior.

The case of August Adolph Follen offers another useful example of the way that Hoffmann used the law as a regulative and critical tool. In the judgment that he wrote on behalf of the six members of the Investigatory Commission, dated 8 November 1819, he developed an argument that took direct issue with the politicization of intuition. Follen was among the leaders of one of the most radical of the student societies, indeed the society from which Karl Ludwig Sand (Kotzebue's assassin) had sprung, the Jena Blacks (*Schwarzen*). In Hoffmann's judgment, he drew on letters and essays by Follen, but at a crucial point he responded critically to an essay by another member of the society. Writing of a desire to "destroy" a finite existent life in order to achieve the triumph of the infinite, the essay's author developed a logic that owed much to the dialectic of self-creation and self-destruction described by Schlegel:

> As I cannot see why the spirit requires the form of the finite to live, that is, why there is anything beyond God and the beatitude of spirits, so then the content and goal of nature and of human life are for me empty and completely without substance. For this reason I cannot act merely for the improvement of the human condition, but rather will devote my entire power

to the destruction of nature and human life. I will do this by attempting to develop within me and to realize the idea of spiritual beatitude, of the true spiritual life, and of freedom (that is, negatively expressed, the destruction of all finite and of all change). Thus after this task the transcendence of this life is nothing more than the triumph over form, which should of course lead progressively to beatitude, for namely everything finite itself in its essence must lead progressively to beatitude, so that that which is, is nothing but God.[56]

According to this logic, the first round of self-creation would produce a finite life. The self-destruction that followed would be governed by a type of mystical reason and reflection proper to God. The mystical terms of the argument are close to those developed by other Romantics, including Friedrich Schlegel, in the years after the Restoration.[57]

Rejecting this logic, Hoffmann warned presciently against the dangers of subjectivism in political action. When individuals believe that their private conviction entitles them to take the law into their own hands, he argued, social anarchy threatens:

When the inner conviction of right and wrong, without consideration for law and civil order, is the sole norm of all action; when this conviction is the forum before which a man believes himself justified to call and to judge the acts of his brothers; when he believes that any means is allowed him to reach a goal, so long as that goal seems right and good according to that conviction; and when he holds any person who diverges from what he believes within himself as worthy of death and he himself warranted to carry out this judgment of his inner views, then all ties of human society are destroyed. The riotous activity of a fanatic craziness that wishes to see in itself an omnipotent and all-judging god must manifest itself then in crimes of all types.[58]

The two sides of irony (self-creation and self-destruction) underpin the arguments of both Follen's colleague and Hoffmann, though in quite different ways. The unknown author had hoped to overthrow the "finite" life represented by the current political system and material conditions and to "destroy" this finite life with an infinite freedom directed toward God. The passage cited by Hoffmann in his judgment leaves unclear whether this destruction is the metaphorical one of a person turned toward God or the real one of a political activist aiming at revolution, but the two types of destruction could easily coincide and did indeed coincide within the radical student societies. Hoffmann, by contrast, rightly viewed the infinite freedom professed by the author as a type of fanaticism. If inner conviction went so far as to overstep positive law, it became one more form of the same human self-delusion that he dealt with in his tales. Hoffmann's critical activity, in this case, consisted in an attempt to block the self-aggrandizement of the religiously motivated political activist.

This study has moved far beyond the discussion of music per se into a discussion of Hoffmann's politics, both as he practiced them in his confrontations with Prussian royal authority and its opponents and as he abstracted them in his stories. But the movement beyond music is precisely the point. Although Hoffmann never mentioned music in his legal opinions, its power as a token of imbricating forces and as a symbol of the sphere of intuition and enthusiasm functioned as an implicit buttress of his distinction between the natural law of civil society and the positive, contractual law of state authority. If the force of the musical experience was powerful and sublime, causing him to intuit another world or the pantheistic imbrication of human action in world-historical tendencies, the sublime force also allowed him to insist rigorously on the strict limits of state action. As a figure of everything that transcended human reason, a figure of the inexplicable and the intuited, music allowed him to insist all the more stringently that reason should rule when fallible human beings exerted power over others. Hoffmann, in other words, certainly appealed to the symbolic political value of harmony, but he did not associate it with state action.

This essay has shown one way that autonomy aesthetics could have a political function, and there is no doubt that Hoffmann, separating musical from other life activities, pursued a version of autonomy aesthetics, just as there is no doubt that his autonomy aesthetics, oriented toward transformative experiences and a process of identity formation, little resembled those of later proponents of the platform. It should be remembered, of course, that the politicization of art (propaganda) and the politicization of the aesthetic (messianic prophecy) were avenues on which Hoffmann ventured at times and that many of his contemporaries claimed triumphantly as their own. But for Hoffmann, more skeptical of state power than were many of his contemporaries, music was political in an extended sense only because it was not political in a narrow one. He thereby discovered a potential long dormant in the art of music. As Lawrence Kramer has written, music has with its authoritative voice the power to call individual subjects to attention, to provide a means by which they can take on or come to terms with the subjectivities offered by the music.[59] In other words, individuals negotiate a settlement with the gestural world offered by pieces of music, conforming to it in varying degrees and in varying ways. Thus, as music transforms its public, it envoices the imbricating forces (or symbolic orders) that determine human lives. It helps or forces human beings to an identity. But these imbricating forces need not be coterminous with state power. On the contrary, for Hoffmann, music competed with a state anxious to reserve this disciplining power for itself.

With Hoffmann one sees a striking transformation of the political function of harmony. He took the ancient ideal of harmony, so often used metaphorically to glorify state authority, and associated it with real music and the sphere of intuition, including natural law. But because he distinguished natural from positive law and demanded that the state restrict itself to positive law, he reinterpreted the political value of harmony at its root. No longer a sign of state authority, harmony became a sign of where the state should fear to tread.

CHAPTER 3

The Devoted Ear

MUSIC AS CONTEMPLATION

Lawrence Kramer

Central Europe, the late eighteenth century: the slow movements of cyclical instrumental works embarked on a metamorphosis. Instead of expressing sustained states of feeling drawn mainly from the varieties of serenity and pathos, some slow movements began to explore the possibilities of internalized drama. Others enacted a process of contemplation. One group sought to grasp interiority as something complex and heterogeneous; the other labored to elevate the spirit through acts of attention.

These two aims sometimes overlapped. Each was consistent with the era's increasing interest in the psyche as a structure, a realm, and a puzzlement. But this interest covered the dramatic strain more fully than it did the contemplative, which was more concerned with spirit than with feeling. The protocol of elevation in the contemplative slow movement corresponded with a certain practice of devotion—"a certain practice" because its devotedness had no object. It assumed the form of religious illumination but without specific religious content. It was a meditative exercise in the spirit of Kantian aesthetics: devotedness without devotion.[1]

Where did the concern with such illumination come from, and how did it find its way into music? What is the genealogy of the contemplative slow movement? I do not mean this question as a stylistic one that might lead, say, to the traditions of hymnody or operatic prayer or the setting of the Benedictus. It is a question, rather, of cultural formation, the development of a certain type of expressiveness that even today retains much of its power.

One likely agent in this development was the inclusion of contemplative thought among the basic routines of cultivated life. Another was the overlapping practice of seeking opportunities for reflection in both the traces of history—sites, monuments, relics, ruins—and scenes of beauty in nature. The spiritual element in these practices coincided with the drift of religion from something the truth of which was assumed to something the truth of which might be questioned or denied, something that those who maintained it might have needed to defend. This drift, and not a simple turn from belief to unbelief, was the primary form of post-Enlightenment secularism. Its outcome was not yet the art-religion of the later nineteenth century but the creation of aesthetic practices meant to tune the spirit and give sensory pleasure at the same time.

The contemplative practice of the age was literal in its seeking: the thinker or artist walked out into the world and paused for contemplation when something arrested the walker's progress. To wander became a source of wonder. Both Rousseau's *Reveries of a Solitary Walker* and Byron's *Childe Harold's Pilgrimage*, key texts of the post-Enlightenment moment, and widely read, helped model this fusion of the *via contemplativa* with the *via practica* in which the seeds of modern tourism also germinated (think of Fingal's cave, which Keats invoked in verse and Mendelssohn in music). Thus Byron, recalling the ruins of the Roman capital of Switzerland:

> By a lone wall a lonelier column rears
> A gray and grief-worn aspect of old days;
> 'Tis the last remnant of the wreck of years,
> And looks as with the wild-bewildered gaze
> Of one to stone converted by amaze,
> Yet still with consciousness; and there it stands.[2]

Byron's image of consciousness both stilled and heightened by a transformative gaze points to the frequent aim of the contemplative practice that his text exemplifies. The contemplative slow movement represents a concurrent, mutually reinforcing trend that replaces the gaze with an intensive practice of listening and thus allows the mind both to wander without a map and to arrest its own progress without a monument. What follows are some thoughts on how this happens, and to what end.

Haydn's String Quartet in G Minor, op. 74, no. 3, dates from 1793. It is nicknamed "The Rider" for the memorable galloping theme that opens the finale. A decade later, the finale of Beethoven's Piano Sonata in D Minor, op. 31, no. 2 (1802), nicknamed the "Tempest," would give the sound of a passing horseman a distant nocturnal quality, the aura of romance, not of adventure. But Haydn evokes a clipped, roughshod energy, a rocking and surging still audible in the mid-nineteenth century in Robert Browning's poem "How They Brought the Good News from Ghent to Aix" (1845): "I sprang to the stirrup, and Joris, and he; / I galloped, Dirck galloped, we galloped all three."[3]

Such horsemanship aside, Haydn's quartet is dominated by its long and deeply expressive second movement, marked "Largo assai" (very slow), an exceptional tempo for Haydn. To this movement the work's shorter, mercurially witty other movements serve as pendants. Music like this Largo was a rarity in the 1790s. It combined the static powers of traditional pathetic expression with the dynamic, reflective, developmental powers of sonata-based forms. So the quartet presents itself as misproportioned. The slow movement overshadows the rest. And it seems to do so purposely.

Why? It is not enough to say that the work as a whole contrasts gravity and energy, seriousness and wit. That would be a normal proceeding, and the contrast here is anything but normal. The gravity is very serious, the seriousness very grave. The rupture, to give it a better name, is neither mended nor rationalized nor confined to one place. Haydn takes pains both to link the Largo to the whole and to detach it from the whole. The movement's key, E major, is remote from first movement's G minor, so that the passage from one to the other comes as a change of expressive worlds. You need not recognize the keys to hear this; what you hear is not the change of key but the change of world. On the other hand, the Largo's three-part harmonic scheme, E major–E minor–E major, forms a mirror image of the scheme of the subsequent Minuet, G major–G minor–G major. One world is the other in a pond. The Minuet even adds its own touch of disproportion, with a middle section notably longer and more expressive than the outer sections.

So powerful is the Largo that five different piano arrangements were published during the 1790s, two of them within two weeks of each other, and the piece was adapted for use in a memorial cantata shortly after Haydn's death.[4] The movement formed a prototype for the independent slow movement as a site of special depth, truth, or spirituality, corresponding to the social idea that these qualities are to be found in the unique interior of the individual independent of both sacred and mundane norms. This independence would consolidate with Beethoven. The instance that caught everyone's ear came early, in the opening Adagio of the "Moonlight" Sonata.[5] But the works in which Beethoven thought the concept through and brought it to the pitch of extremity are the three string quartets of his op. 59, the "Rasumovsky" Quartets. The slow movements of these works form a kind of trilogy leading from grief to ecstatic contemplation to absorption in the mystery of things. Before we turn to this music, though, let's dwell a little longer on Haydn.

Haydn's Quartet in D Major, op. 76, no. 5, suggests a fit of impatience with the kinds of emotional drama afforded by the typical layout of classical symphonies and quartets. The year is 1797, late enough for a *not that again!* at the prospect of another instance of the four-movement generic sequence: fast movement–slow movement–dance–finale, corresponding roughly to the dramatic sequence: conflict–reflection–release–celebration.

The opening movement of this quartet is a set of variations that mimics but also mocks, amiably enough, a standard first movement in sonata form. The quartet movement stretches the obligatory minor-mode variation into a development section and arrives at the typical first-movement tempo only with what would be the recapitulation and coda—if there were a recapitulation and coda. The second movement, Largo cantabile e mesto (slow, songlike and sad), shifts from the first movement's affectionate detachment to unrelieved absorption. Like its precursor in the "Rider" Quartet, this is a long, very slow, quasi-devotional song of contemplation. Its key, F# major, lies several removes from the common tonal orbit of its day. Its expressive design follows a course of profound involution as the opening texture of melody and hymnlike accompaniment recurrently evolves into intricate counterpoint. The music adheres to the norm of beauty generally followed by the classical slow movement, but in its depth of seriousness and sadness it is, again like the "Rider" Largo, unusual to the point of being out of place in a classical string quartet.

The ensuing Minuet goes to the opposite extreme; it is so sturdy and earthy that it seems (and is meant to seem) false. The sinister minor-key trio seems to mock its Breughelesque surroundings, as if to ask just who the minuet thinks it is kidding. The finale is an orgy of Hungarian tunes and rhythms: an irresistible piece, but one hard to place sensibly in its disrupted context. Overall, op. 76, no. 5, counts as one of the first truly modern works of music: works that challenge at least as much as they please, works that risk—for better or worse—the considerable pleasure that may be offered by their parts by refusing to let those parts add up to a self-evident whole. And ironically, the agent of this disruption is the quartet's most beautiful movement, the Largo.

In the three Rasumovsky Quartets of 1806, Beethoven greatly expanded the scale of the string quartet, as he had done for the symphony with the *Eroica* a few years earlier. Each of these pieces has an extended slow movement of exceptional intensity. I have considered some of this music before,[6] but I return to it here as a way of exemplifying the contemplative principle I now want to find in votive or devoted slow movements: the work of contemplation is never finished; the fullness with which divine mystery is revealed always demands a further revelation. These slow movements, unlike their antecedents in Haydn, all seem to respond to something in the movement preceding them rather than to step unforeseeably into an alternate expressive universe. This comparison may sound like a compliment to Beethoven, but it is neither that nor the opposite. On this subject, a brief side comment is necessary.

Beethoven's career coincided with an unprecedented rise in the status of music in Western culture. Still equivocal for Kant in the 1790s, music soon came to be regarded as one of the peaks of human accomplishment, the equal of painting, sculpture, and poetry in revealing the truth and depth of feeling, even the substance of mind and spirit. Together with the other arts, music had become more than merely functional or ornamental, and it had not yet fallen into the modern orbit of entertainment. (Entertainment in the modern sense did not yet exist, though the nineteenth century was about to invent it with the notable help of virtuoso pianists and singers, who were among the first performers to become stars with fans trailing in their courses.) Beethoven was caught up in this cultural change, which his music helped shape both at the time and in retrospect and for which he became a supremely charismatic spokesman.

In the first decade of the nineteenth century, Beethoven engaged the new status of music by posing the question that this status made both obvious and inescapable: Just how big could music become? This was both a technical question (how could the standard forms of the day be amplified?) and an imaginative one (how deep, how high, how far could music go?). The answers on both sides were diverse. The technical side is not my concern here. On the imaginative side, the answer most pertinent to the history of exalted slow music involves the belief in a deep inner self associated with the hidden and sometimes disturbing truths of human being. The discovery of this inwardness, which is to say the development of a language and a mode of thinking that made experiencing the world in terms of such inwardness possible, was another basic event in progress across Europe in Beethoven's lifetime. Beethoven's perceived ability to tap into inner feeling is a familiar theme in discussions of his music from that day to this, but not until recently has this theme become the object of historically informed reflection.[7] A long time had to pass before the idea could be set at an ideal interpretive distance, neither too close nor too far away.

The culture of inwardness is still our own, all the more so because it is beginning to erode. The accelerating contemporary tendencies toward multiplicity, decenteredness, dispersal, and virtuality—call them postmodern or posthuman or what you will—no more simply abolish inwardness than the Enlightenment simply abolished religious belief. The effect of these latter-day forces is once again not a simple yes or no but a question of status. As a basic measure of human authenticity, inwardness may now seem quaint, the remnant of a defunct modernity, but it survives, even thrives, as the object of an increasingly nostalgic longing. The spiritual has become the spectral. Part of the reason why classical music seems to have fallen of late on hard times is the continuing loss of confidence in the music's claims to give access to true subjectivity and to truths about it. If we want to say, as I do, that classical music still matters, we need to ask about the possibility and the value of recovering the kernel of truth in the musical claims that grew out of the cultural and political revolutions of the late eighteenth century. And we need to do so without merely recycling habits of thought that may still put up a good front but are conceptually bankrupt.

On the evidence of their music, Haydn would probably be more comfortable in a postmodernist time machine than Beethoven would, but, again, the point of the contrast is not to anoint one or the other composer as the higher genius but to suggest how we as twenty-first-century subjects can continue to hear ourselves addressed by their music. There is a pitfall in describing Beethoven in particular with reference to inwardness. The lingering prestige of the idea tends to make the descriptions seem worshipful to the point of fatuousness. It is hard to fight this tendency, but I will try.

The agenda of the First Rasumovsky Quartet seems to be amplification. This piece really is asking how big music can get, as the lyrical breadth of its first theme, backed by a calm and tireless pulsation, announces in all but words. The first two movements expressly seek the limits of scope and force available to their genres, the sonata allegro and the scherzo, especially the latter, which here becomes gargantuan in scale and manic in

impulse. To behave accordingly, the slow movement has to find an affective topic that requires—not permits but requires—extravagance of feeling.
What it decides to do is plumb the depths of grief. The movement, like
the Funeral March of the *Eroica*, is a lamentation, a modern dithyramb.
After one of the sketches for the first theme, Beethoven wrote, "a weeping
willow or acacia over the grave of my brother." But the brother is anyone
and everyone, any participant in the Enlightened ideal of the brotherhood
of man.

The choice of lament is risky, and not just aesthetically. This slow
movement plumbs so deeply, so insistently, that it borders on simulating
classic melancholia, grief turned limitless because it is turned inward. But
that is just the point: to suggest the power of human emotion to make or
to find itself limitless, to open inwardly onto an abyss. The point becomes
explicit when the movement, like every movement of this quartet a full-
dress sonata form, keeps to the minor mode for its second theme. The
second theme would normally turn to the relative major and relieve the
sadness. Here that change is deferred until the beginning of the development, which thus becomes a place apart within the enveloping shadow of
the weeping willow. Only at the inner core of lament is solace found.
Afterward, the darkness gathers relentlessly across the recapitulation despite a brief glimmer of respite. A stop, but not an end, comes after the
first theme, returning one last time, is roughly curtailed before it can finish, as if its emotional burden—now resonating through the most richly
scored texture in the movement, indeed in the whole quartet—could not
be borne for one more second.

A transitional passage leads from here to the brilliant finale. Beethoven
evidently felt that he could not simply jump into festivity as if nothing had
happened. He often felt this way; such transitions are famously a feature
of his mature music, including the Third Rasumovsky, in which the finale
emerges from a mysterious coda to an otherwise genial minuet.

Some listeners to the First Rasumovsky feel that its finale comes back
from the brink, others that it can only pretend to. Either way, that is its
appointed task, which it helps to establish as a basic task of modern emotional life. Haydn shows more confidence in simple difference, which
might be glossed as a confidence in forgetting, a willingness to take the
present moment as sufficient unto itself. As Nietzsche remarked a century
later, the art of forgetting is necessary to mental survival;[8] the trouble with
Beethoven is that he never forgets anything. For Haydn, emotional depth
is a fact, not a mandate; he lives in a culture of feeling where emotions
more often coexist than interact. This is an attitude that Beethoven, for

better or worse, can no longer adopt—and for better or worse, it helped set the agenda for later music and later modes of emotional experience. Beethoven's procedure is consistent with a discovery that his and subsequent generations felt impelled to make: that feeling, understood as the truth of human inwardness, imposes burdens and tasks on those who feel. Or, as W. B. Yeats memorably expressed it, "In dreams begins responsibility."[9]

The slow movement of the Third Rasumovsky Quartet is mysterious, evocative, and in various ways overtly irrational. It begins like a sonata movement and ends by warping the sonata design almost beyond recognition. But it does so without drama. It sustains a mood of mysterious brooding throughout, except for a somewhat old-fashioned passage of delicate filigree that proves to be of surprising importance. The music is haunted by the sonority of its opening, a deep cello pizzicato line supporting a hypnotic, throaty triplet theme. Heard in this context the filigree passage is deeply nostalgic, like a sepia postcard. It is also faintly troubling in its blithe disregard of its own uneasy context, as if the dark but lustrous brooding of the first subject could evoke only an equally but differently impossible mood for relief.

The business of the movement is to sustain and deepen its mysterious opening, especially by traveling constantly into new harmonic worlds. Or so it seems at first. The real business, only gradually revealed, gradually discovered, is to absorb the filigree passage into the prevailing mystery and thus to reveal a mystery even greater. This process turns out to coincide with the acme of formal disruption—the principle of Haydn's op. 76, no. 5, turned further inward. The climactic arrival at the remotest harmony possible ($E\flat$ major, a tritone removed from the tonic A minor) is also the moment of maximum fascination and serenity: the restatement of the filigree theme stripped of its nostalgia to reveal something genuinely delicate and luminous.

The "form" of the movement consists of absorbing everything into its dark contemplative state, at the peak of which everything changes: the darkness turns inside out to reveal a tranquil light, high tessitura replaces low, and the filigree theme transforms the brooding by which it has been transformed. Although the filigree's old-fashioned phrasing remains intact, its somewhat faded prettiness has become the expression of a transcendental delicacy. That delicacy unexpectedly blossoms into a liquid shimmer as the melody settles firmly in its strange new tonal sphere. And it is from this point of furthest remove that the music returns directly but enigmatically to its origin as the first violin and cello move progressively apart, one rising, the other falling, one in long bowed notes, the other in pizzicato triplets, one mirrored by the inner voices, the other on its own, until all come to hover on a static threshold. The remainder of the movement is transfigured by these events, clarified by them, even though it never refers to them; once consummated, the filigree vanishes, never to be heard again. Whereas the filigree originally ignored the brooding, the brooding ultimately absorbs the transfigured filigree as its deepest secret.

In doing all this, the slow movement forms a vast expansion of the slow introduction that begins the quartet. This introduction consists of a mysterious, nearly atonal series of chords drawn along by a steadily rising line in the first violin and a steadily falling line in the cello, the same elements that carry the slow movement from climax to threshold, from sudden illumination to returning darkness. Once again, the question posed by the remainder of the quartet is how to come back from this beyond. And once again, the actual answer—form run wild, a fugue-finale that unreels at breakneck pace—is less important than the question it addresses, a question that is no longer simply musical or aesthetic but social and emotional. With Haydn, it is possible to accept such a finale on its own terms. With Beethoven, the finale no longer has its own terms. The difference is not one of value or relative genius—it is perfectly reasonable to prefer either alternative—but of changes in the culture of feeling. Beethoven's procedure helps to articulate those changes, which, in turn, find in his procedure a potent means of dissemination.

The slow movement of the Second Rasumovsky Quartet is calmly contemplative, more like its antecedents in Haydn than its partners are. Like Haydn's, this very slow music of Beethoven's is disposed to form rich, organlike sonorities as a sign of spiritual depth, to convert the sociable four-voice quartet texture into the communal voice of a chorale. Like Haydn's, Beethoven's movement combines expressive solo writing with free counterpoint to suggest the workings of intense concentration of mind. And like Haydn's, this movement poses the question of how to return from a voyage into the beyond and unknown that is also a voyage inward—but poses them with the differences already noted between Beethoven's and Haydn's senses of what the question demands. The differences are particularly telling here because the Second Rasumovsky, like the "Rider," is in a minor key. And whereas Haydn pointedly avoids making high drama of the minor in his fast movements, preferring incisiveness to turbulence, Beethoven gives minor-key turbulence free rein—at least at first.

A good way to hear this E-minor quartet is as a large-scale effort to keep the turbulent outbursts that begin the first movement from sponsoring a climate of chaos, belligerence, or irrationality. This is something that the first movement itself tries to do by turning from E minor to E major for the second half of its recapitulation and by calling for a repeat of the already lengthy development-recapitulation sequence. But an extended, dramatic E-minor coda follows to announce that the wild rumpus will not be placated so easily.

The ensuing slow movement possesses an extraordinary serenity, but a serenity that is asked to absorb disturbances both from the accompaniment and from the effects of development—for the movement is in full sonata form. In that respect this Molto Adagio refers back to the Adagio molto e mesto of the First Rasumovsky Quartet and prepares for the dissolution of sonata form in the Andante of the third. The movement also mediates between its two counterparts. On one hand, the melody of the Molto Adagio often travels in a soaring and dipping arc that anticipates the triplet line of the third quartet's Andante, but as contemplation, not as brooding. On the other hand, the movement allows itself to be haunted by the grief of the first quartet's Adagio in the form of a hiccoughing staccato accompaniment that twice prevents the contemplative melody from forgetting its earthly sources and sorrows.

The contemplative side of this passage takes the form of slowly evolving three-part counterpoint heard against repetitions of the staccato figure (Example 3.1). As the passage proceeds, the contrapuntal voices begin one

EXAMPLE 3.1. Beethoven, Adagio of String Quartet in E minor, op. 59, no. 2, dotted rhythm and counterpoint.

by one to mirror the rhythm of the figure while remaining legato against the figure's persistent staccato. Restrained when first heard, the imitative pattern proliferates and intensifies when the passage is recapitulated; no voice but the accompaniment's remains unchanged. It is as if the contrapuntal voices were seeking to find a sacred paraphrase for a profane truth. The gesture suggests an effort to reconcile the weight of the world with the need to cast it off. But although the counterpoint, this second time, is more supple and searching than before, the accompaniment is darker and heavier. Contemplation edges toward sublimation; the cost of increased devotion in the counterpoint is an increase in the ominousness of its worldly shadow.

No wonder, then, that the gesture of reconciliation proves to be premature. For this movement continuously heightens its intensity of feeling and concentration until it passes the point where such heightening seems tolerable. Its hiccoughing reminders of care have been a portent. Very near the end, the hiccoughs become a rift in the music. In the twinkling of an eye, a crisis erupts. For a long moment, a fierce, sonorous, polyphonic outcry seems to consume the whole movement (Example 3.2). When the moment ends, the serenity returns. But it has been shaken; it is no longer what it was.

Haydn avoided climaxes like this one, especially in the Largo of op. 76 no. 5. His model of contemplation requires a spirit more at peace with itself, though not a spirit blind to discordant prospects or fearful of the need to confront them. The difference between his model and Beetho-

EXAMPLE 3.2. Beethoven, Adagio of String Quartet in E minor, op. 59, no. 2, climactic chorale.

ven's sounds out clearly in the two composers' musical images for ongoing
contemplative serenity. Both images emerge with the second theme of a
full sonata form, Haydn's as the theme itself, Beethoven's as the combination of melodic counterpoint and hiccoughing accompaniment noted earlier. Both images serve to suspend without wholly denying the tendency
of sonata form to foment drama. But Beethoven's version is vulnerable in
a way that from Haydn's perspective is improbable, even unthinkable.

Both versions make expressive use of dotted rhythms. Haydn's theme
is highly concentrated, only six notes long. It consists of a pickup from
which to embark, a strong beat on which to land, and, in between, two
legato dotted figures, a falling leap answered at a distance by a falling step
(Example 3.3). The result is a kind of serpentine shape perhaps reminiscent of the S-curve often associated with visual beauty in the eighteenth
century. The result is both an involuted figure and a figure of involution.
To this figure the music continually recurs, linking the theme's extended
appearances with chains of dotted rhythms and thus imparting a kind of
S-curve to the large-scale deployment of the theme as well as to its shape.
At both levels, the melodic motion continually closes the loops it continually draws, continually pulls away from the music's steady quarter-note
pulse and continually yields to it. The texture is as secure as it is serene.
The theme centers the attention like a sacred word or image pored over
from every possible perspective. Contemplation is less something it evokes
than something it induces.

As well it might: the contemplative force of the movement depends on
it. Haydn's second theme seems to arise as a condensation, or, better, a

EXAMPLE 3.3. Haydn, dotted theme from Largo cantabile e mesto of String Quartet in
D, op. 76, no. 5 (mm. 9–11).

paring down to its imperturbable essence, of his first. The two themes intertwine both melodically and contrapuntally. The first theme moves with a solemn, even tread, but it takes on a certain interior momentum by breaking stride at midpoint to incorporate falling dotted figures, the substance of the impending second theme, before three successive paces (Example 3.4). The second theme responds to this change like a spirit to an invocation; as soon as the first theme is done, the second appears in the tonic, as if come from afar before its time. When the second theme subsequently returns on the dominant, as a second theme should, its bass line—quarter notes devolving onto a falling dotted figure—is the head of the first theme.

Despite this affinity, though, the two themes are anything but inseparable, and they have very different destinies. The first theme carries the burden of whatever darkness or distress Haydn's Adagio admits of. It alone, and more particularly its head phrase, submits to the uncertainties of motivic and harmonic development. The second theme stands almost entirely aloof in its serenity, or better yet, it comes to do so, and with no apparent effort. The theme yields to a touch of pensiveness at the end of the exposition, but its recapitulation is wholly radiant and extends through the conclusion of the movement. The second theme returns to restore a calm that the theme itself proves to have been inviolable. Its serpentine shape, its inward turning, encloses not only the theme and its vicissitudes but also the entire Adagio within the perfect self-mirroring space of contemplative devotion.

EXAMPLE 3.4. Haydn, first theme from Largo cantabile e mesto of String Quartet in D, op. 76, no. 5.

This is an outcome that Beethoven can only wish for. His dotted figure, that gasping accompaniment, is a disturbance. For Haydn's melodic concentration, Beethoven substitutes a persistent jabbing against melody. Not only is his figure played staccato, but it is also broken by rests. Heard in the exposition on first violin like a nervous drumming of fingernails, the figure becomes more relentless in the recapitulation, where the cello plays it in the bass. In both versions, the texture is one in which the possibility of rupture or dead silence hovers at every moment. Perhaps the most surprising thing about the rupture that eventually does break out is that it does not happen sooner.

Haydn is willing to speculate on the same possibility but not to realize it. The Largo of op. 76, no. 5, allows its development section to wander through a weird and distant region. After hovering around the subdominant of the home key, F# major, the music cadences unexpectedly into G major and drifts through a series of uncertain harmonies sustained by the throbbing of thickly clustered chords (mm. 50–58) before settling on the dominant (mm. 59–62; the throbbing continues through m. 60). This detour might be heard as a necessary descent, as if the movement had to catch a glimpse of the suffering that its contemplative spirit transcends. The way down, as contemplative tradition holds, is the way up. But the passage does not falter and it does not sear.

Beethoven's climax does both. In form, it is a chorale built of dissonance piled on dissonance, intensity piled on intensity. It halts—disrupts, undoes, suspends, transcends—the melodic flow of the movement and seems to slow time itself, even to stop it dead. This climax is almost as excessive with respect to the Adagio as the Adagio is with respect to the normal classical slow movement: isolated, supercharged, blistering. It changes everything, not only within the movement but well beyond it.

The subsequent scherzo is a model of artistically controlled excitement, suggesting that this quartet can handle well enough the emotional extreme it has just been through. But the trio, heard twice like the development-recapitulation sequence of the first movement, is aggressively exuberant— indeed a little crazy. It is as if the memory of a well-nigh unbearable transcendental vision had come back into the form of sheer looniness, the quality that Beethoven's contemporary, the philosopher-critic Friedrich Schlegel, called "really transcendental buffoonery."[10]

The craziness bursts forth fully in the finale, probably the most transcendentally buffoonish movement that Beethoven ever wrote. When it begins with a theme on two left feet, a lurching dotted figure in what seems to be the wrong key, we know we are in for a wild ride—and sure

enough the harmony lurches as well as the tune. This key-switching is a
travesty of the first movement's mode-switching. It makes neither formal
nor dramatic sense, nor is it supposed to. Instead it represents a Lacanian
"sinthome," an action full of "idiotic pleasure," in Slavoj Žižek's phrase,
a pleasure embraced precisely because it is mindless, meaningless, heed-
less.[11]

It is a good idea to hear this music as if it were literally out of control,
a whirligig of energetic babble that seems compulsive, as if any break in
the craziness would spell disaster. And if that is right, the reason may
once again be the presence of the slow movement, which introduces into
Western music the idea of a beauty that drives the beholder mad, that
estranges the psyche from all worldly life and reaches a depth so inner, so
true, that it is almost an abyss. With this contemplative exercise, backed
by Haydn's precedents and his own, Beethoven installs the model of the
sublime Adagio that would haunt concert music for a century and more
and would later become a key component of film music—not to mention
a key component of the way we think about ourselves. People who have
never heard this music, or heard of it, have nonetheless been shaped by it.

In the context of this wider process neither Haydn nor Beethoven matters
much as an individual. Nor does it matter much that Haydn seems to have
been conventionally if not ardently religious, and Beethoven—an oratorio
and two masses notwithstanding—a committed secularist in all but name.
At best these facts may have helped predispose the two composers toward
the contemplative topic. What is really at stake here is not the personal
details of their involvement but the force of a cultural tendency that demanded to be put into discourse.

Contrary to the gruff, commonsensical view of Richard Taruskin that
only people can do things,[12] the things people do often take on lives of
their own. Works and words acquire charisma; they assume something like
the pull of fatality or necessity; they produce a field of attraction toward
which the things people do as individuals tend to gravitate. This process
cannot be dismissed as mere reification; its existence has to complicate our
sense of human agency in general. As Judith Butler observes of names, the
force of an utterance is an effect of its historicity, "[the history] installed
and arrested in and by the name . . . the sedimentation of its usages as they
have become part of the very name."[13] Shelley made much the same point
in the language of 1819: "Every man's mind is . . . modified by all the
objects of nature and art; by every word and every suggestion which he
ever admitted to act upon his consciousness."[14] The devoted slow move-

ments of Haydn and Beethoven neither form nor follow a mandate in any simple sense. Instead they intervene, to powerful effect, in a conversation about private devotion that takes place in the public sphere. They demonstrate how the questions of inwardness and the sacred might be posed in musical terms and how those questions might be answered by finding the right ways to slow the music—to slow music—down.

But why is that the answer? Why—to ask the obvious question that has so far lay hidden behind a scrim of seeming self-evidence, and not just in this chapter—should the music be slow? Why is it slowing music down that produces the genre of the devoted Adagio, a term I want to invest with the multiple meanings of "devotion" and "votive," referring on the one hand to spiritual absorption and on the other hand to sacrifice, the annihilation of self in the contemplative act. Why, for nearly three centuries, has a slow tempo seemed the natural one for this and cognate purposes?

The answer itself must come slowly, as a series of partial reasons to be pondered. First, time slowed by just the right amount fosters a sense of timelessness. Devoted movements are not just slow but very slow, stretching out the interval between downbeats so as to dilate the sense of time, to replace passage with *durée*.[15] Second, the phenomenological effect of a very slow tempo is to allow each note and chord to be heard for itself, a possibility that progressively declines as the tempo increases. Slowness creates the sensory form of contemplative involvement. And finally, in cultural terms, in symbolic tradition, slowing or halting is the bodily form that contemplation takes, especially when one is confronted with a monument or memorial, a point of resistance to time as the progress of oblivion. As I noted earlier, this idea has close associations with the wandering or wayfaring that at the turn of the nineteenth century was both a familiar literary figure and a spur to modern tourism. The underlying trope, associated with the Latin phrase "*siste, viator*" (pause, traveler), goes back to the funerary poetry of ancient Greece and persists to the present in the aesthetics of cultural memory. In Haydn's and Beethoven's time, occasions of slowed or arrested motion overlapped with the appeal of ruins and monuments as simultaneously points of aesthetic breakthrough and of contemplative gravity.[16]

There is a tradition that takes such points as gateways to the divine or the eternal, each one "the point of intersection of the timeless / With time."[17] The quotation comes from T. S. Eliot's *Four Quartets*, the title of which supposedly alludes to the late quartets of Beethoven. But the devoted Adagio does not really belong to this tradition, Eliot notwithstanding. The history of the votive slow movement is in part a history of secularization, the apprehension of divine mystery in a religious form empty of religious content. This secularizing process enables the performance of devotion without sacrifice. It forms a means of appropriating the power of religious experience without making any commitments to religious truth—although in so doing it may also be claiming to establish the form of religious truth in an Enlightened world.

This impulse may even be felt in explicitly religious works: in Haydn's virtual omission of the fall of man from *The Creation* or in Beethoven's transformation of the Benedictus into a higher-order violin concerto in the *Missa Solemnis*. At the same time, however, the devoted slow movement incorporates an opposite tendency. It represents an attempt to recover the very sense of religious mystery that the Enlightenment supposedly extinguished, but to recover it by Enlightenment means. The music in this context may be heard as avoiding the expression of religious truth in order to find the truth that religious experience embodies but that it cannot express without hardening truth into dogma. On the one hand, the music secularizes a religious tradition. On the other hand, the same music renders a secular experience religious.

This duality of secularization and sacralization brings us back to Byron's image of the Roman column, which captures this precarious balance of forces in exemplary terms. The column is reminiscent of a funerary marker, and it halts the traveler precisely as do the inscribed stones of the *siste, viator* tradition. As a cenotaph for Roman civilization, the column is an index of the relationship between time and eternity. Yet it is also a purely material form: a massy, almost featureless thing bare of any actual inscription. The column is a historical fossil, and in its historicity, insofar as it is the relic of an age and a memorial of the spirit of that age—both *saeculum* in Latin—nothing could be more secular.

This duality is itself doubled in the column's uncanny union of animation and the inanimate. Byron describes this union as the embodiment of an astonished gaze ("the wild-bewildered gaze / Of one to stone converted by amaze, / Yet still with consciousness"): the transformation of a sublime perception into its own object. In this respect, the column is also the embodiment of contemplation itself, a condensation of subjectivity into a singular and impossible form. The column is sentience in stone. In Hegelian terms, it is pure substance become pure subject. In its absolute singularity, something inscribed in its very shape (the one, or I, standing lonelier than the lone wall), the column embodies both what the mind seeks in contemplation and the mind that seeks it.

In the Largo and Adagio that I have taken as best examples of the devoted slow movement, Haydn and Beethoven produce—seem inexorably drawn to produce—acoustic parallels to Byron's column. Haydn's serpentine second theme, immune from disturbance and folded over on itself, is a kind of spiritual monad. Beethoven's dissonant chorale, in the ferocity of its concentration and the insistence of its sonority, brings contemplation to the same point of petrifying inspiration that Byron imagined at a safer distance. These musical images are affective opposites; but both of them are unlike anything else in the music to which they belong, and both complete the work of contemplation in which the sacred becomes the secular and vice versa.

This balance of forces could not remain stable for long; perhaps it could never be stable at all. Hegel thought that that devotion itself, *Andacht*, was no more than a mystical warm bath, "a musicalized thinking."[18] Beethoven and Haydn sought to give such thinking a real, if nonspecific, conceptual integrity precisely by musicalizing it, investing it with the compositional rigors of counterpoint, detour, and disruption. But their moment was brief. The tradition of the contemplative slow movement probably comes to symbolic closure in 1882 with the languorous spirituality of the prelude to Wagner's *Parsifal*. Or else with what the prelude foretells: the logical-illogical conclusion by which the opera performs the grail-like miracle of slowly transfiguring the key of D major into its tritonal antithesis, the A♭ major with which the prelude begins and the opera ends.[19] The tritone transformation carefully framed by the Andante of the Third Rasumovsky Quartet here becomes the frame itself. The contemplation that this music asks for is sheer astonishment.

Nor is that all. The *Parsifal* prelude reverses the idea of devotion without sacrifice; without sacrifice as a premise, this music is scarcely conceivable. It is the music for a ritual of excruciating yet ecstatic self-surrender, a surrender meant to consecrate the very stage on which the music is performed. Just how, or whether, this consecration can take hold in the absence of divine sanction, or just how, rather, the stage ritual is supposed to sanction the divine in a world that lacks assurance of it, remains the open question that continues to sustain *Parsifal*, much as the open wound of Amfortas sustains the brotherhood of the grail. There can be no Parsifal for *Parsifal*.

After the *Parsifal* prelude, it is hard to find devoted Adagios unmarked by a sense of anachronism, even if the later nineteenth century tended to luxuriate in the anachronism itself. If Wagner had "closed" the genre by going to its limit, he had by that very closure prompted its proliferation, but only in the distance. The devoted slow movement of Saint-Saens's Third Symphony (1886) fades away into an alternation of off-key chords that the composer labeled "mystical." The famous Largo of Dvorak's Ninth Symphony (the *New World*, 1893) begins and ends with a mystical chorale of its own but fills the space between with melodic nostalgia and longing. Each in its own way, the slow finales of Tchaikovsky's Sixth Symphony (the *Pathétique*, 1893) and Ives's Fourth (1910–16) whittle themselves down to nothing, the Tchaikovsky inverting contemplation to lamentation, the Ives pursuing a spiritual exercise in self-abnegation. Elsewhere, the second movement of Richard Strauss's symphonic poem *Also Sprach Zarathustra* (1896) turns devotedness to deliberate kitsch, a process repeated more stridently in the sub-Parsifalian rantings of Jochanaan in Strauss's opera *Salome* (1905). Perhaps only the series of Bruckner's symphonies, a long epilogue to *Parsifal*, continues the devoted genre without submitting it to reflective distance or to the darkening temporal distance, the melancholy datedness, that I called nostalgic irony in the introduction to this volume.

Walter Frisch identifies this type of historically directed irony specifically with German modernism,[20] and it will not have escaped notice that my primary examples of the contemplative slow movement are Germanic. The source of this bias is probably the installation of Beethoven and Wagner as points of symbolic origin and closure in the culture of classical music. This development, which was by no means limited to German-speaking Europe, had contradictory consequences with which musical scholarship is still trying to cope. On the one hand, it replicated the trope of German music as national or "racial" in origin but universal in form, the paradigm of music as such; on the other hand, it situated this universal model at an impossible historical remove, in an exclusive sphere barred by the figures of genius who established it.

Yet another layer of irony arises in the *lack* of irony with which the devoted Adagio, along with other nineteenth-century expressive modes, emigrated to Hollywood in order to live on—a process noted by Peter Franklin in his chapter in this volume, and one that considerably disturbs what he calls, with another sort of irony still, the Narrative of Modernism. Frisch's chapter on the Andante of Brahms's Second Piano Concerto reveals a more rarefied form of the same irony in twentieth-century performance practice, which sometimes produced devoted Adagios by playing nineteenth-century Andantes in the acoustic equivalent of slow motion.

It should thus come as no surprise that nostalgic irony casts a diaphanous veil over Mahler's two principal examples of the devoted slow movement, the Adagio finales of his Third and Ninth symphonies. These movements are valedictions; they are always already in the distance.[21] In the history of Mahler reception, the current high status of these Adagios arrived only belatedly, with the Mahler revival of the 1970s, almost as if modern reception, like modern performance, had stepped in to provide what modern composition had long since given up on. In the Ninth (1910), the key of the Adagio, D♭ major, sets it at a remove not only from the symphony's D-major first movement but also from the D-major Adagio of the Third (1895–96). But the earlier Adagio is already at a remove from itself. Its main theme is a revenant, a spectral remainder of its counterpart in the contemplative slow movement, Lento assai, cantante e tranquillo (very slow, singing and tranquil), of Beethoven's final string quartet (no. 16 in F, op. 135). The Adagio of the Ninth carries this haunting to something like the zero degree by basing its own main theme on an elemental musical figure, the turn, a foundation that could hardly be frailer or more dated. What enables the figure to hold the music up as long as it does, before all crumbles away at the end, is the simple fact of being slowed down.

These Adagios by Mahler are hardly too little, but they are too late. The twentieth century witnesses a split in the contemplative mode, half of which trends toward phantasmagoria, half toward the ceremonial. The one half produces the uncanny, semipsychoanalytic nocturnes in Mahler's own Seventh Symphony and numerous pieces by Bartok; the other half yields the almost anthropological depiction of liturgical ritual in certain works by Stravinsky and Poulenc and many by Messiaen, whose devotedness is once again devout. But that, as they say, is another story.

CHAPTER 4

Music and Fantasy

MARSHALL BROWN

Lawrence Kramer's brave new book, *Why Classical Music Still Matters*, climaxes with an account of the saving grace of Beethoven's *Pastoral* Symphony. The music, he says, imagines "an unbroken continuity of tradition." Is this really imagining? Well, not exactly. "Imagining it, that is, in music." What kind of imagining is that? "It is never just a simple image of a lost paradise. . . . Rather . . ."[1] Kramer's moment of hesitation stems from the association of imagination with images, hence with visual experience. Imagining "in music" is never "simple." To be sure, pictorialism was an old tendency in music, but with the exception of onomatopoetic sound imitation it was never natural but always mediated conceptually—down for us was up for the Greeks—and as Susan McClary shows in this volume, it was not the last word even in the traditions with which it has been most closely associated. Romantic aesthetics, however, upped the ante. Starting in the late eighteenth century, imagination acquired a heightened prestige, transcending the merely pictorial. Musicians might have envied the imagination, but they were hard-pressed to capitalize on it. That pressure and the resistance to it are the subject of my reflections.

Genre

What does music say to imagination? The *New Grove Dictionary of Music and Musicians* has no entry for *image* or *imagination*. "Images" as a musical title seems to originate simultaneously with Bartók and Debussy, followed by Ibert. "Bilder" starts with Schumann's *Bilder aus dem Osten* for piano four hands, with few successor titles beyond Musorgsky's imitation of paintings. (Musorgsky actually uses the diminutive "Kartinki," suggesting prints derived from the paintings and hence a derivative or inferior status for music.) Music typically has other ways to think than in images. Meditation is a possible alternative to imagination, but the *New Grove* has no entry for *meditation* either, and so far as I can tell from checking my library catalogue, composers have been less into meditation than packagers of recordings have been; Massenet seems to have started the belated fad, such as it was, but the sporadic examples from Tchaikovsky, Widor, and Ravel hardly ground a countertradition to visuality. As musical genres, neither image nor meditation offers much.

Instead, composers fought back with the term *fantasy*. *Fantasy* derives from the Greek word for *imagination*, but the Greek verb *phainomai* is not so decidedly visual as the Latin noun *imago*, and a *phainomenon* could be any kind of appearance or manifestation. Hence, Hanslick, following the aesthetician Friedrich Theodor Vischer, defines *Phantasie* as "the organ for the perception of the beautiful," characterizes its mode of perception as "looking with understanding" (*Schauen mit Verstand*), then detaches perception from visuality by shifting terminology from *Schauen* to the Kantian *Anschauung*. "Moreover, the word 'intuition' [*Anschauung*], long since transferred from visual representations to all sensory manifestations, corresponds admirably to the act of attentive hearing."[2] By highlighting the divide between the two closely related aspects of the mind, imagination and fantasy, I intend to suggest a direction for listening to Romantic music that differs from commonly accepted analytic forms.

As the Romantic imagination transcends the older pictorialism, so fantasy in Romantic usage (and as I propose to employ it) supersedes earlier meanings. "Fantasia" appears early and commonly in musical titles for either a free-form or a purely instrumental composition. These older usages survived into the eighteenth century, when, as the *New Grove* reports, the term generally declined, although examples from the Bach family, Mozart, Czerny, Spohr, Schubert, and others suggest its persistence. Schumann revived the term in his *Phantasiestücke*, which were inspired by E. T. A. Hoffmann's collection of stories, the *Phantasiestücke in Callots*

Manier, themselves inspired by a graphic artist, Callot. The rivalry with visuality is thus built into the modern usage of the genre term *Phantasie*.

Hoffmann's collection incorporates his writings about music, and Jean Paul's preface to it emphasizes its musical dimension. The preface speaks of the author's "camera obscura" or "dark room"; the brief opening sketch dedicated to Callot concerns the fantastic quality of his fantasy, and it is followed by "Ritter Gluck," with its ghostly appearance of the composer in an opera box. Visualization in Hoffmann's *Phantasiestücke* is thus Romantic, not enlightened; dark, not light; more visionary than visual. Fantasy here is inseparable from reverie; *Phantasiestück* joins another title shared by Hoffmann and Schumann, *Nachtstück*.

Between Mozart (or C. P. E. Bach) and Schumann came Beethoven, who wrote a free-form fantasy for piano solo and another as a piano prelude to the "Choral Fantasia." More important to the genre history, though, are Beethoven's two piano sonatas, op. 27, both subtitled "quasi una fantasia." Although the sonatas share some characteristics and sonorities, the first one is more closely associated with the earlier tradition, marked by a free-form first movement and by the linkage of all four movements through "attacca" designations; the second sonata was perceived early on to be in the reverie mode and was given the label that Kramer has written so brilliantly about, "Moonlight."[3] The moral of this genre history is clear. *Fantasy* changed meanings with the Romantic movement and became the musical alternative to *imagination* as a dark, brooding or dreamy, meditative kind of thought. Romantic fantasy overlaps with Enlightenment fantasia in the Beethoven sonatas, but overall, the later meaning displaced the earlier meaning rather than continuing it.

Aesthetics: Kant

The divide between imagination and fantasy emerges in Kant, who variously credits imagination with both perception and representation. As perception, imagination reproduces and schematizes immediate sensations to make them accessible to understanding; as representation, it is productive and deals in imagined situations as well as imaged realities. A striking comment in Kant's *Anthropology* defines its wiles: "We often like to play with the imagination; but the imagination (as fantasy) just as often plays with us, sometimes very inconveniently."[4] Whereas the reproductive imagination regulates mental processes, the productive imagination, otherwise known as fantasy, threatens to disorder them again. "The imagination, insofar as it produces spontaneous imaginings, is called fantasy. Anyone who is accustomed to regard these as (inner or outer) experiences is a fantasist [*Phantast*]" (§25, B68). The true and false or good and bad versions of imagination are hard to tell apart; for the bad, productive kind, Kant has the adjective *unwillkürlich*, which I translate as "spontaneous," but *Spontaneität* is also crucial to the operations of the good, reproductive kind of imagination. Still, it seems evident that there are two kinds, and that the kind called *Phantasie* is not to be trusted. Nor, in Kant's eyes, is music to be valued. Königsberg schools and churches offered modest musical opportunities at best, and Kant's exposure fell well below even the local norm until his middle years, when he was a regular guest for pro-am entertainments at Count Keyserling's, overseen by a moderately talented daughter. Hence, when the *Critique of Judgment* famously calls music "enjoyment rather than culture" (*Critique of Judgment*, §53, A218), it is not so much invidious as responsive to Kant's real situation: he describes music exactly as he found it.[5]

But Kant's resistance to music and to fantasy also implies temptation.[6] As a philosopher of the late Enlightenment, Kant wants universal judgments of taste based on knowledge and subject to concepts. But as a philosopher of incipient Romanticism, he wants them to be free. Consequently, the relationship between imagination and clarity remains highly problematic.[7] The crucial ninth section of the *Critique of Judgment* persistently speaks of "play," "harmony," and "accord" (*Stimmung*). To be sure, these are not self-evidently musical terms. But it is hard to assign them to any other terrain; surely Guyer's translation of "proportionierte Stimmung" (*Critique of Judgment*, §9, A31) as "mutual agreement" loses the flavor of the phrase.[8] Kantian "free beauty" belongs to families of brightly colored birds that Kant most likely had never seen and "presupposes no concept of what the object should be" (§16, A48); it "represents nothing" (A49), and its climactic instantiation, in this paragraph of the *Critique*, is musical "phantasies (without a theme)" (A49; a rare variant in the third-edition text has "Phantasieren," phantasizing, which is even more dynamic and less conceptual). Guyer surveys alternative readings of the free play of imagination as precognitive, multicognitive, and (his proposal) metacognitive, but these various pigeonholes constrain a freedom whose thrust is, willy-nilly, more nearly anticognitive. Although Kant, like his contemporaries, recognizes that music is based on mathematical relationships that schematize the sonic spectrum, he also says that mathematics has "not the slightest share" in musical charm and affect (§53, A220).[9] Nightingales sing freely, not subject to rules, and their song gives more pleasure than any human music. Nightingales must be "unwill-kürlich" ("spontaneous"; "General Note to the First Part of the Analytic," A73; the same word used for *Phantasie* in the *Anthropology*); if their song is consciously imitated, Kant twice writes, the resultant artificiality is pro-foundly disenchanting (§22, 42, A73, 172–73). And so, Kant's praise of the spontaneity of birdsong leads immediately to the contrast of imagination and fantasy that concludes the "Analytic of the Beautiful." An unremarked pun hints at the divide between the imagination that orders perceptions and the free play of that other imagination properly known as fantasy. For the German word for the nightingale's song is *Nachtigallenschlag*. In musi-cal renditions by Beethoven, Schubert, Schumann, and Brahms, even the nightingale's song sounds like beats, often distantly echoing. But the true *Schlag* of the nightingale is not the mathematically regular imitation found in songbird songs. It is productive, not reproductive; "it seems to contain more freedom and therefore more for the taste than even a human song" (§22, A72), and its freedom, surely, leaves it more like a *Herzschlag*, or heartbeat, than like a drumbeat. The true beauty of music belongs, after all, to fantasy rather than imagination.

Traditional "musical logic" seeks the inspired coherence of the work in a dialectical process proceeding from initial statement via developmental analysis toward a resolving synthesis. I associate it with the lucid clarity of the imagination, Coleridge's *In-eins-Bildung*, or esemplastic power. Even the richly plural treatment of classical form in Charles Rosen's *Sonata Forms* evinces a bias toward unification: for Rosen, even tonal drift or de-nial of closure merely provides alternative kinds of "integration," which is his term for structural unification. Only in some works of Schumann is Rosen's book prepared to acknowledge an "attack on . . . the integrity of classical form" that is genuinely "inexplicable by classical aesthetics."[10] The last chapter of Rosen's later book, *The Romantic Generation*, then por-trays Schumann as the hero breaking through the barriers of classical sense. Schumann here is the musician's musician, the true man of fantasy. He is likewise the hero of John Daverio's *Nineteenth-Century Music and the German Romantic Ideology*, which pivots on the op. 17 Fantasie, understood as "a musical critique of the very idea of unity."[11] I suggest, however, that Schumann did not so much break with musical tradition as consummate it or that indeed he may not be so special as these accounts claim.

Suppose we take unity not as the substance of music but rather as the foil for expression. While a Bach fugue, after all, displays the composer's constructive power, it revels in the ever-changing inventions of horizontal and vertical spacing and overlapping pulses. Haydn's jokes are not disruptions of form but explosions of its potential. Mozart is being himself when he introduces a new theme at the beginning of a development section, as is Beethoven when he drops into a radically unexpected key. Musical thinking is not made by predictability, grammar, or logic but by fantasy, and the extremity of Schumann's more daring works does not indicate that he was rejecting his predecessors but that enough territory had been occupied that it was harder for him to achieve results like theirs. Already the first movement of Beethoven's String Quartet, op. 59, no. 2, barely touches on the tonic chord; the cello finally sustains the root of a tonic only at the recapitulation of the second theme in the first group, but the movement drives to the dominant from the opening pair of chords, and dissonant overlays make the rendition in the recapitulation less stable than the version in the exposition, where the bass pedal is a B (Examples 4.1a and 4.1b). Joseph Kerman thinks that performing the written repeats would clarify the logic: "If both repetitions in the E-minor movement were played, the compressed flow of ideas might sit in the ear less cryptically than it is apt to do in most current performances. The symmetry would have to be coped with."[12] The bias in favor of the mathematical imagination is evident in Kerman's invocation of symmetry. But I do not

EXAMPLE 4.1A. Beethoven, String Quartet in E minor, Op.59, no. 2, first movement, mm. 11–14 (first theme in exposition).

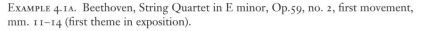

EXAMPLE 4.1B. Beethoven, String Quartet in E minor, Op. 59, no. 2, first movement, mm. 151–54 (first theme in recapitulation).

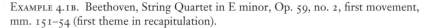

think this quartet shares the bias: the first ending at the second repeat undertakes a genuinely weird slippage down a minor second that is anything but clarifying (Example 4.2). More to the point, we might not want to replace mystery with symmetry. Fantasy is what music is all about. Beethoven loved the fierce energy of minor-second clashes; there are some slashers in this movement, and they are no easier on the ear the second time around. Endings are difficult because in them music comes to rest, and that is not its natural forte.

Painting, arguably, does its job when it frames the continuities of the visible world to give them shape. But the job of music, on this account, is to shake up the mathematical regularities inherent in pitch. Of course, it cannot shake regularities up if they are not first recognized: it depends on the pitches to introduce harmonic and melodic surprises, as it depends on the formal models to destabilize them with ironies, to unsettle them with anxieties, or even to propel them toward calm. But it remains thought in motion, resisting teleologies as long as it can. Perhaps the most representative function of sonata-form repetitions is not to allow the ear to rest but to alienate the sense of logical progress.[13] As an eighteenth-century commonplace has it, painting depicts but music moves.

Poetics: Verlaine

Still, fantasy is not license. The fancy etches its visions with precision; it is a distinct mode of thought, not to be associated with vagueness or antithought. To a post-Romantic sensibility, fantasy comes tarred with the feather of impressionism, the exemplary art of fancy, especially in the dreamy soft-focus of the musically named Whistler's Nocturnes. In literary impressionism, too, much seems to imply a linkage of fantasy with the dreamiest of reveries. In the poem "Harmonie du soir," Baudelaire writes

EXAMPLE 4.2. Beethoven, String Quartet in E minor, Op. 59, no. 2, first movement, mm. 208a–d.

of a "valse mélancolique et langoureux vertige" (melancholy waltz and dizzy languor), leading the musical reader to think perhaps of Musetta on Prozac. And in "La Musique et les lettres," Mallarmé writes of the "vibratory near disappearance" of natural facts, as if thinking of church bells in the fog. But freedom remains the goal, not the means. Even in impressionism the musical imagination that I am calling fantasy has sharp contours. The impressionists were craftsmen, first and foremost, and their mastery precedes their reverie. Naturally, careful students of impressionism have no reserves about the nature of its best practices. To take just one classic example, Jean-Pierre Richard concludes his massive study of Mallarmé with pages on the poet's *presque*, but Mallarmé's ambiguities and approximations prove for Richard to be conduits toward a "total structuration" in which chance will be absorbed into a prismatic geometry.[14] Among scholars crossing the music-poetry divide, I could mention the brilliantly meticulous essays of David Code as well as Elizabeth McCombie's attempt to specify what she calls "the poetics of discontinuity" in Mallarmé and Debussy in terms of a repertoire of particular Boulezian gestures—*éclat* and *explosion fixe*, *déchirures* and *intrusions*.[15] Fancy and its impressions do not make their mark if shorn of rigor.

But a focus on Mallarmé could stack the cards in favor of wit over fancy. Verlaine is a better test of the parameters of musical fantasy. For the signature line of Verlaine's "Art poétique," "De la musique avant toute chose," appears to proclaim that impressionistic poetry should bypass words in favor of sounds, subordinating meaning to sensation. The characteristic tracery is evident in lines such as these, from Verlaine's poem "Kaléidoscope": "Un instant à la fois très vague et très aigu . . . / O ce soleil parmi la brume qui se lève" (A moment at once most vague and most sharp . . . / Oh this sun amidst the mist, rising). Most sharp, perhaps, but the vagueness washes over it, leaving uncertain whether it is the sun that is rising or the mist. But "music before everything" certainly means musicality within language—not music denying rhythm and grammar—for Verlaine immediately continues with his prosodic recipe: "Et pour cela préfère l'Impair" (and for that prefer uneven lines). Nor does the call in "Art poétique" for nuance and dream come dreamily. The traditions of poetry are to be wrenched into shape: "Prends l'éloquence et tords-lui son cou" (take eloquence and wring its neck). The demand on the poet is for more technique, not less. Speaking of his bugaboo, weak rhyme, Verlaine writes, "Quel enfant sourd ou quel nègre fou / Nous a forgé ce bijou d'un sou / Qui sonne creux et faux sous la lime?" (what deaf babe or what mad black / forged this groat's-worth jewel / that sounds hollow and false under the file?). Verlaine's diction both soars and sinks—it sinks, for instance, in the Anglicism "toute chose" and the piquantly antipoetic "cela"—but never casually. He wants to use the file, not to discard it. His verse is, and has, pro-file. Indeed, the signature rhythm, the *vers impair*, is anything but free verse. Of the poem's thirty-six lines, all but one have a word break after the fourth syllable, and all but three of those have a caesura there. The rhythm is regular, the gesture decisive: a weighty first half-line, sometimes with four monosyllables of equal importance, offsetting a swifter second half-line with only two beats in five or (with a feminine ending) six syllables. The hold-and-release pattern is essential: the method, like the doctrine, entails not freedom per se but a determined liberation and discharge.

In sum, the vagueness that characterizes musicality and fantasy is an achieved effect. Hence, Verlaine calls for attentive supervision of the rhyme, for joining the indistinct to the precise. Vague yet sharp, musicality needs to be bracing, like a strong herb: "Que ton vers soit la bonne aventure / Éparse au vent crispé du matin / Qui va fleurant la menthe et le thym" (Make your verse an escapade / loosed to the wince of the morning wind, / smelling of mint and thyme). Verlaine's music can be languidly Swinburnesque, to be sure, as in the well-known "Chanson d'automne": "Les sanglots longs / Des violons / De l'automne / Blessent mon coeur / D'une langueur / Monotone" (The long sobs of autumn violins wound my heart with monotonous languor). "Flitting among the shadowy dead," decadence, in its full efflorescence, appears to be shorn of cadence, approaching "unheard sound," "opening vistas of music hitherto unseen."[16] But the sharp wind can just as easily pick up, as in the self-pastiche "A la manière de Paul Verlaine": "Des romances sans paroles ont, / D'un accord discord ensemble et frais, / Agacé ce coeur fadasse exprès; / O le son, le frisson qu'elles ont" (Romances without words [the title of an earlier collection of his poems], / With a harmony discordant at once and fresh, / Have vexed this mawkish heart on purpose; / Oh, the sound, the thrill of them). "Accord frais"–"frisson"– the quasi-echo, quasi-pun is poetic self-indulgence raised to the pitch of genius. Verlaine is hardly a difficult poet, and I do not know how much of the sharp wit in his languid effusions really needs to be pointed out. Suffice it to say that his impressionism does not succumb to the sensations of a moment but fixes them for an eternity. And thus, finally, "De la musique avant toute chose" does not mean "music first" but "music foremost," not "before something else" but "above all."

The counterpole to Verlaine may be seen in the musical realism of Liszt in his symphonic poems.[17] To the extent that Liszt's genre label suggests a narrative model, it is misleading. Formally, Liszt's symphonic poems and successor works by the likes of Frank, Saint-Saëns, and Dvorák are episodic, their true models being not poems but certain musical predecessors, notably Schubert's "Wanderer Fantasy" and some of Beethoven's more picturesque and episodic works such as "Les Adieux" and the late string quartets. There are indeed affinities with the other arts, but chiefly where the other arts approach the dreamy logic of music, as does Byron's poetry, which is often as episodic as Liszt's. The twelfth symphonic poem, *Die Ideale*, evokes atmospheric fragments rearranged from a philosophical ballad by Schiller, but the words elucidate the direction of the music more than the music illuminates the words,[18] and the poem finally proves less illuminating than the added section titles "Aufschwung," "Enttäuschung," "Beschäftigung," and the concluding "Apotheose," which has no parallel in the poem. *Hunnenschlacht* (Battle of the Huns), the eleventh symphonic poem, is based on a painting rather than a poem, privileging color over story (the term in the score is "*Kolorit*") and rendering a battle without audible sides, until a chorale emerges to allegorize the Christian victory. Brief motifs permeate these works and provide a simple unity: an identity constituted by repetition rather than organic development. Conversely, the pseudonarratives serve to separate parts and thus to create an illusion of symphonic variety that falls short of a logic of connections.

But the symphonic poems are vitiated by their representational aims. A picture envy undermines the potential for musical fantasy. Swelling or subsiding energy, often scripted by Liszt's calls for tiny accelerations or retards, replaces actual development. The best known of the works, *Les Préludes*—again referring to a poem (in this case by Lamartine) that Liszt rearranged to suit his convenience—takes its initial motto from the "Muß es sein?" motif in the last movement of Beethoven's op. 135 string quartet but renders it static by turning Beethoven's questing, minor-key sequel into a harmlessly pentatonic diatonicism.[19] Liszt was capable of fantasy in other works, and indeed in direct transcriptions of the music of other composers, but the symphonic poems, on the whole, figure in my argument as negative examples of a music that substitutes energy for pulse and tableau-like portraiture for the kind of fantasy that is music's answer to the shaping spirit of imagination. Their conduct is oratorical, pompously affirmative in tone, even though it is never in the nature of music to specify contents. But short of imputing irony to the sententious repetitions, it is impossible to align Liszt's compositions with Verlaine's impressionist fantasy. "Take eloquence and wring its neck," is Verlaine's line; the affirmative character of the symphonic poems has a stentorian grandeur innocent of Verlaine's wry bent. Of course, Verlaine often fell into a Lisztlike religiosity that reduced musicality to a cheering chorale.[20] And conversely, as Kramer has eloquently shown, Liszt at his most interesting, in the *Faust Symphony*, approaches imaginative realization full of the dark hesitancies of fantasy.[21] But the characteristic gestures of the symphonic poems surge forward too enthusiastically into the steady light of the ideal. Aiming at imagination, they betray fantasy.

Music: Mendelssohn and Beethoven

Liszt has more in common with Mendelssohn than either composer was ready to acknowledge. They share fireworks, sententiousness, religiously tinged kitsch, bright fleetness with an inclination to the demonic that is, to be sure, more common in Liszt than in Mendelssohn. These surface similarities suffice to set off the more deep-seated contrasts. For when Mendelssohn's genius emerges, it takes the form of a fantasy that defies logic. I instance the Overture to *A Midsummer Night's Dream*, perhaps too easy an example for my case but still a good illustration of what I mean by fantasy. It is full of surprises of a kind too rare in Liszt.

The overture is, of course, in perfect sonata-allegro form. After a brief introduction, the exposition consists of a tonic area composed of a series of themes beginning with the minor-key fairy music and continuing with march rhythms that come to be combined with a major-key variant of the fairy music, followed by a transition to the dominant that is securely approached by way of eight measures of its dominant seventh; the second key area features a lyrical, relatively chromatic love theme followed by the donkey music and a closing, fanfare-like motif. Predictable development and recapitulation follow, with the expected harmonic transformations, and phrases throughout are almost monotonously in repeated four-measure units, yielding a textbook example of Riemannian *Achttaktigkeit*. The music closes by returning to the introduction, replacing a Beethovenesque teleology with an equally recognizable, cyclical alternative. An image of "musical logic" remains audibly in place.

But there is little corresponding process. What I have called themes are really more like character motifs. As in many opera overtures, the real aim is to set a mood or to define a range of moods; the overture is the foundation, not the building. *Thematische Arbeit* would undermine the nature of the enterprise. The motifs are tossed around, sometimes combined, never significantly transformed. But whereas, for instance, the similarly busy overture to *Così fan tutte* operates with a facsimile of sonata form, bandying about a motif even if it is not altered, Mendelssohn's overture systematically confronts formal expectations. It begins with a curiously notated introduction, slow and unmetered to the ear but subsumed to the eye under the Allegro di molto designation (Example 4.3). Strings take over from the winds, twice briefly interrupted by winds. The *fortissimo tutti* march abruptly replaces the *pianissimo* fairy music, which proves in retrospect not to have been in the principal tonality of the piece but in the tonic minor. Displacement rather than development marks the entire work, in evocation of the superimposed worlds in the play. The retransition to the recapitulation takes a form that became almost standard practice with Mendelssohn, that of a relaxation toward stasis, sometimes followed by a quick crescendo, sometimes, as here, by a dissolve into the opening. Rosen quotes it in *Sonata Forms* and says it "is not a climax but the lowest point of tension"; in *The Romantic Generation*, he calls it "an effect of extreme exhaustion after an access of passion."[22] Given that the quiet *espressivo* in measures 376–93 follows sixty-four measures of *pianissimo* or *piano*, these narrativizations strike me as imaginary. Tension, climax, and exhaustion are Beethoven characteristics that could not be more pointedly countered here. The movement simply falls asleep and dissolves back not into the first subject but into the introduction (which explains why the introduction is notated as part of the allegro); the final chord of the introduction motif is sustained for longer than in the opening, and the violins now overlap with the winds, but the shift to the minor is just as sudden as at the start (Example 4.4, mm. 390–404). Fanciful transubstantiations replace imaginative transformational process throughout. There is an antiorgani-

EXAMPLE 4.3. Mendelssohn, Overture to *A Midsummer Night's Dream*, mm. 1–8.

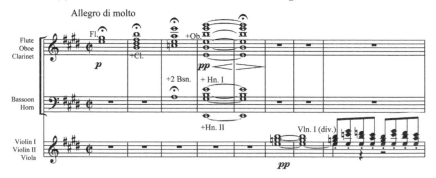

EXAMPLE 4.4. Mendelssohn, Overture to *A Midsummer Night's Dream*, mm. 390–436.

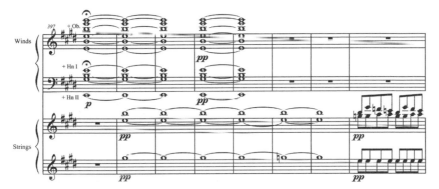

Example 4.4 *(cont'd.)*

3

EXAMPLE 4.4 *(cont'd.)*

cism that critiques the notion of identity as *Bildung*. The themes (or motifs) here are personae, not persons, and Mendelssohn's fancy brings the overture into a dream world of fixed extremes that displaces the daylight world of midlevel volumes and ongoing labor. That is how extreme speed can come to coexist with the motionless chords that begin and end the overture and also how major and minor can alternate without disorientation.[23] Fast or slow, the overture goes nowhere but rather exists in the delight of its moods. (So, for instance, the descending half-note scale motif that first appears in measures 78–83, with four overlapping entries and every note marked with an accent—this is theatrics, not melody [Example 4.5].) The fancy lies in the dissolve of structure; music's appeal is in the joints more than in the flow.

One moment stands out from all this—or at least, performed as I envision it, should stand out. The recapitulation adds to the fairy music a set

EXAMPLE 4.5. Mendelssohn, Overture to *A Midsummer Night's Dream*, mm. 76–84 (winds).

of punctuations. Pizzicatos had joined the continuation of the fairy music in the exposition; here the fairy music begins with a viola pizzicato note, echoed by an oboe pip two measures later, then, always at two-measure intervals, clarinet and flute half notes, held low notes in bassoon and then horn. The ophicleide in the deep bass comes next, yields to a drumbeat in the timpani, only then to return with an eight-measure low G (Example 4.4, mm. 428–36). The ophicleide solo is my favorite moment in the piece. Otherwise the instrument appears chiefly in *forte* and *fortissimo* massed sonorities (sometimes with the brass marked *mezzo forte* to keep them from dominating). The pedal tone here is unearthly, harmonically unproblematic but hermeneutically almost uninterpretable. Sonority typically belongs to character rather than structure, and the swampy buzz of the keyed serpent links the imagined, romanticized heavens back to the earthly flesh. But I call it uninterpretable because the dark fantasy flesh is only a challenge to the rational, imaginative order of recapitulation; the ophicleide does not make a statement or enter into a dialogue. Instead, it punctures the fabric, reconstituting the terrain under the aegis of reverie rather than reason. It marks the perfect sonata form as merely the most delightful of Mendelssohn's illusions. Paintings are defined by their frames, music by the moments when it breaks out of its frame. Kramer has punningly adopted the term "scoring" for music's disruptive, attention-grabbing force.[24] That is the kind of listening encouraged by reorienting from imagination to fantasy.

I suggest, then, a donkey's-ear approach to the *Midsummer Night's Dream* Overture. As in the play, the most distinctive element in the music is the donkey's bray. Formally, this is the second theme in the second group. The entire second group is virtually ignored in the development section, and then its main body is repeated measure for measure in the recapitulation. In that sense, the donkey has a merely mechanical presence; it is not even first in its own section, and it is impervious to any developmental logic. It remains in the ear partly because it cannot be dealt with. But let its huge leap downward define an alternative hearing of the whole piece. Over the ophicleide buzz, for instance, wind notes pitted against the fairy music sink downward and spread out in length. But especially listen to the introduction and its later repetitions upside down. The first flute takes the lead, rising through a first-inversion tonic chord. But the distinctive aspect is the increasing spread as instruments are successively added and the fundamentals move rapidly into the bass (Example 4.6). It is awkward enough at the start of the overture, and it sounds perilous no matter how perfectly it is played. In the coda, the oboes are omitted; the chord spacing grows more open, and a timpani roll with a swell is added, slightly unnervingly on the dominant (Example 4.7). The music has stretched out temporally; it also stretches out spatially, but it does not exactly relax. Fantasy keeps it on edge.

The task for an interpreter or listener is to determine which way the edge of fantasy cuts. What categories are disrupted, what expectations dynamited? The notable absence in the overture is eroticism. The love theme proper has a quietly contemplative, hymnlike texture, and the only swell that might code an outbreak of passion leads abruptly to the donkey's bray. Upon its recapitulation, the pounding half notes with their comical

EXAMPLE 4.6. Mendelssohn, Overture to *A Midsummer Night's Dream*, mm. 1–4, bass notes only.

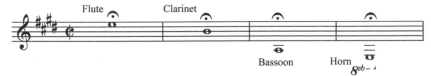

EXAMPLE 4.7. Mendelssohn, Overture to *A Midsummer Night's Dream*, mm. 682–86.

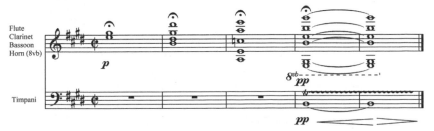

fortissimo enter earlier, overlapping with the build-up. We know now what is coming, and it is only a delusion. There can be no genuine erotic union in this work built out of so many displacements. Many other elements of Shakespeare's play are omitted here as well: the rage, the tyranny of authority, the luxuriant exoticism. But if threats to selfhood are glossed over by Mendelssohn's fantasy, the compensation is a celebration of individuality. Notable, for instance, is the brilliant use of the winds in constantly varying combinations and textures, letting the instruments play with and around one another, in delightful, occasionally piquant sonorities. (Measure 434, for instance, elaborates a fantasy of C major above the ophicleide's G pedal, but with the flutes on low C and G and a bass C pizzicato creating a rare sonority while leaving the harmonic status shadowy—root position if the pizzicato counts, second inversion if the pedal dominates—and the Neapolitan function momentarily in suspense.) The play of lights is never oppositional; indeed, by the time the overture concludes with a resumption of the initial wind chords, the integration of major with minor has become naturalized as part of the work's vernacular (already as early as a passing I–IV–iv–I progression in a triumphant, unclouded *fortissimo* at measure 77). Regular symmetry and clear boundaries make character stand out with unmistakable definiteness, yet all kinds of fluid combinations and sudden illuminations become possible. Thus, the whole principle of form is transmuted, as desire yields to dreamy submission to the passing moment, as character (in the form of sonority) loses its positivity and becomes combinatorial, and as logic revels joyously in the perfection of its accomplishments. Mendelssohn mastered the art of the narrow escape; he can find the way out of any sonic trap. A light and sociable tone is constructed out of remarkably diverse elements, high and low, as with the opening chords, where the flute arpeggio projects social order, while the traveling bass line grounds it in diversity of identity. The hymnlike moments and plagal cadences may suggest a reverential or confessional attitude toward social harmony, but in the generally humorous context they can hardly be felt to imply a rigorous discipline. Mendelssohnian fancy is as alien to Adornian critique as to Ernst Bloch's messianic utopianism, though if Bloch had not been so fixated on intensities of expression, he ought to have been able to open himself to Mendelssohn's way of making light of formalism.[25] The word that echoes throughout Puck's closing speech in the play is "mend," and Mendelssohn behaves as if his very name had made him Puck's heir.

But perhaps an evocation of the fancy in early Mendelssohn is making too easy a case. Everyone knows that the *Midsummer Night's Dream* Overture is fun, even if it is not always so readily accepted that good cheer can be a quality of deep cultural significance.[26] Consequently, I turn to a final example that probably has never been called a dream vision: Beethoven's Fifth Symphony. Yet I hear it too as a work of uncanny fantasy rather than of imaginative logic. The symphony is short and compelling, and some of the more interesting readings have pointed out numerous features that make it taut and tense rather than persuasively triumphant.[27] It fights its way toward its fabled logical integration.

Fantasy raises the question of the boundaries of the work, and the Fifth Symphony presents that question with particular acuteness.[28] Apart from the two pastorally tinged symphonies in F major, Beethoven's symphonies all have some kind of introduction: the First, Second, Fourth, and Seventh have formal slow introductions, the Ninth has its mysterious gestation out of silence, and even the heroic Third has two preparatory chords. In all of these, it is easy to say where the introduction ends. There are frame and content, setting and substance, invitation and dance. The Fifth Symphony is different. As its first movement is the shortest of the nine symphonies' first movements, so it is the most compact and inwrought in its utterance. And so it begins swift, yet with immediate fermatas, first on what might be the tonic but eventually proves to be the mediant, then an even longer one on a note evidently belonging to the dominant area. But only thereafter is the key definitely established as C minor rather than E♭ major. This introduction passes too quickly yet hesitates too much to establish a firm tonality. For a bit longer, the symphony might be thought to enact a more extended introduction, if at an eccentrically fast tempo, leading up to the well-prepared dominant in measure 21, a crashing orchestral chord (unlike the unison texture at the beginning, strings and clarinet alone), though with everything dropping out from beneath, leaving only the isolated first-violin G to be held through. Point of arrival or only point of passage? In English, we have the same word for both, *landing*, depending on whether it is a boat landing or a staircase landing, and indeed the genius of the symphony, from the present perspective, lies in its willful confusion of the two. Then an urgent hush, rising to yet another climax, this one, however, already being the transition to the relative-major key area and to the second subject, with unison horns landing solidly on the dominant of the tonic major. Finally, gone out hunting, we have firm ground after the frenzied bustle of preparation, whether the first subject is decoded as preparations for war or as Machiavellian maneuverings in the palace.

In a noted essay on anxiety in the work, Joseph Kerman draws attention to the opening fermatas and to the frequent stuttering effects throughout, though to my mind he still does not articulate how thoroughly it problematizes the entry of music into ideas.[29] For the dominant chord steps aside for a louder crash, strings and woodwinds together, though the trumpets and tympani drop out. And if the entire first subject is regarded as an introduction, what does that do to the balance of the movement? Indeed, it never quite finds its grip. Asymmetries ruffle the feathers of the second subject (Example 4.8). It comes in four-bar units, with the fourth measure always the point of arrival; the pattern is set by the horn call (mm. 59–62) and then supported by the regularly appearing motto in the bassi (with points of arrival in mm. 66, 70, 74). As notated by Beethoven, the melody is phrased 3 + 1 when it sounds in full, then 2 + 2 in measures 75–82, when it is reduced to its stepwise motif, but still with the motto and the feminine ending every fourth measure. Then, however, the violins reverse the large beat; their part (in mm. 83–93) is phrased 3 + 2 + 2 + 4, and the stepwise downward pair that had been the arrival notes abruptly become the launch notes, starting rather than concluding the larger patterns. In a further destabilization, the crescendo lasts ten measures (mm. 84–93), with the violins playing the same figure four times then varying it for an asymmetrical fifth to arrive at the next *fortissimo* crash. It would have been easy to cut two measures to balance the passage, but balance is precisely not the effect the exposition aims at. Nor—to advance into the development—does Beethoven strike a balance in the long passage in half notes alternating between strings and winds (mm. 196–227), where the ear grows confused as to which voice leads and which follows.

The Fifth Symphony is full of obvious structural surprises, expressive clashes, and raw humor. It does finally end triumphantly, though the last-

EXAMPLE 4.8. Beethoven, Symphony no. 5, Op. 67, first movement, mm. 71–94.

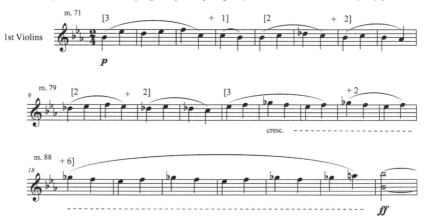

movement coda is notoriously reluctant actually to have done with it. But along the way it is constantly pulling up short, tipping tipsily, halting the progress for an odd little oboe cadenza, a *misterioso* quickening (*più moto* in the slow movement) followed by a meditative relapse, many more fermatas and abruptly unended snatches of theme (in the scherzo), and the return of the scherzo in the finale. My reference to some details in the first movement is intended only to underscore how much more attuned the symphony is to questioning than to responding and settling doubts. In its compact intensity, it is a triumph of form, for sure; the blending of introduction and implementation brilliantly fulfills the postulates of Kantian or Schillerian organicism. Yet it fulfills them only to show the impossibility of form ever disentangling itself from the spooky, mysterious energies in which it is implicated and with which it is activated. If it seems ever on the verge of a grand statement, or even to be making a grand statement whose content is uncertain, that is because it never finds the proper way to open its mouth. It has Lisztian magniloquence in abundance, but the sententiousness is never beyond doubt. Liszt's own idealism flowers into transcendence, marking boundaries at every turn; Beethoven's idealism pulls punches nonstop. The symphony is as much a dramma giocoso as *Don Giovanni* is. It mixes Dionysian and Apollonian elements, shadow and light, storm and repose. To be sure, the mixtures that constitute successful form are not a smooth blend, the Kansas of the imagination. A greater or lesser degree of lumpiness gives each work its distinctive expressivity. And the lumpiness can be both horizontal—an alternation of roles or, to adapt Hölderlin's word, of tones—or it can be vertical, with a polished surface covering a dis-ease beneath.

Fantasy—imagination in its musical form—is a questioning presence.[30] Musical answers come, if at all, in codas, tail ends. Meanwhile, the expositions are problems, the developments analyses of the problems, and the recapitulations memorial reprocessings. And sonata style guarantees that the problematics of contrast will infect phrases and melodies even under the aegis of different large-scale organizational schemes. Musical erotics (as Kramer has tirelessly argued) destabilize gender identities, but the musical fantasy equally questions the claims of power, sociable ease, ethnic localization (forgetting the great example of Dvořák, think even of the tensions between color and form—Norway and Germany—in Grieg), historicism (since, given the impossibility that music might reproduce the continuous fabric of a time line, the past must appear as an alien bloc), and any other concept it is able to propose. The underlying reason is the lack of a statement form to shore up against the restlessness of a pulse. The imagination proper operates on the counters of language; the fantasy operates outside them. Where fantasy does not audibly trouble the musical surface, the absence of trouble itself becomes problematic, forcing the questions: What means the repetitiousness of Beethoven's pastoral? What swirls within Debussy's sea and clouds? What is Steve Reich driving at? And musical mysticism (Messiaen, some of Glass, parts of Ives) can seem so powerful precisely because of its fantastic triumphs over fantasy, as the realism of Messiaen's bird calls—above all in the piano music—appears to wrest an impossible victory by reproducing and stabilizing seemingly unanalyzable noises.

Again, though, the Fifth Symphony might be the paradigm. Heinrich Schenker's monograph on the symphony opens with a careful argument that the opening motif is the complex of eight notes, two interlaced thirds, rather than the simple motto of the first four.[31] The argument is inevitably rendered uncertain because it depends on counting measures for locating phrase boundaries in a score in which the caesuras make the count unrepresentable to the ear. But more significant is the mere fact that the point is arguable. The struggle to draw the line between motto and motif proves that no line can be drawn. For so percussive a work, the musical contours remain disquietingly sinuous: the lyrical second subject of the first movement weaves in and out of its ascending and descending fourths, the triumphant ascending scales in the opening of the finale rise in waves of overlapping fourths, the eighth-note motif of the scherzo trio sounds its brief bass bursts in triple groups that resonate as § meter cutting away at the notated ¾. The work's beating, its *Schlag*, would like to persuade us that it is drawing an imaginative picture of a *Menschenschlag*, a race of (heroic) men, but every little tic upsets the large tock of its grand clock.[32]

Musical fantasy is incisive in the etymological sense: it cuts into and cuts away the complacencies of logic. For that reason, a fine account by Rainer Cadenbach has emphasized the destabilizing effects in the symphony.[33] He pairs it as part of a diptych with the *Pastoral* Symphony, expressing *Zeitvertreib*, or whiling, as opposed to the *Pastoral*'s endurance. Both symphonies employ the precise fretwork of fantasy to ruffle the smooth currents of time. There is one work, however, that has outdone even Beethoven, though it is not a work any of us have ever been privileged to hear, or ever will. That is the Septet by the impressionist composer Vinteuil that makes its appearance in the last installment of Proust's great novel. Here is the narrator's description of Vinteuil's meticulously precise fantasy: "This music seemed to me something truer than all known books. At moments I thought that this was due to the fact that, what we feel about life not being felt in the form of ideas, its literary, that is to say intellectual expression describes it, explains it, analyses it, but does not recompose it as does music, in which the sounds seem to follow the very movement of our being, to reproduce that extreme inner point of our sensations which is the part that gives us that peculiar exhilaration which we experience from time to time."[34] This is what I take Deleuze and Guattari also to mean in the brilliant pages on music in *A Thousand Plateaus*. "It is not really known," they write, "when music begins."[35] So it is with Beethoven's Fifth, which begins before the beginning, or with the *Midsummer Night's Dream* Overture, which is full of undertones and overtones but never wakes up into reality, or indeed with the *Pastoral* Symphony, which begins and remains in the middle of a shoreless flow. The machined voice, the Mozartean zigzag, the delirium of Schumann's piano works—all the effects of the diagonal that make, for Deleuze and Guattari, Schumann's mad cello concerto the archetype of musical freedom—these are the kinds of effects I have been trying to evoke, linking music to a different kind of meaning that might rescue society from the tyranny of its principles.[36]

CHAPTER 5

Whose Brahms Is It Anyway?

Observations on the Recorded Legacy of the Bb Piano Concerto, Op. 83

Walter Frisch

I

The relationship of Brahms to musical meaning and human values has perhaps never been imagined more vividly than in Hermann Hesse's 1927 novel *Steppenwolf*. In a fantasy theater the narrator Harry Haller encounters Mozart, who waves his arms to disclose a misty desert landscape in which a melancholy old man with a long beard trudges at the head of a line of ten thousand followers, all dressed in black. "Look, there's Brahms," says Mozart. "He is striving for redemption, but it will take him all his time." Haller realizes that the men in black are those who had to play "all those notes and parts in his scores which according to divine judgment were superfluous." "Too thickly orchestrated," Mozart remarks. "Too much material wasted."[1] Brahms's music is condemned as turgid and overladen; he is cast as a composer of morbid excess.

Although Hesse mentions the "notes and parts" of Brahms's scores, it is likely his disapproval is based not on the score but on the kinds of performances he would have heard in the early twentieth century. Brahms had become ponderous and slow not primarily because of what he put on the page but because of the way his works had come to be rendered in sound. Performance plays an essential role in the transmission of musical meaning and values from the composer to listener—and thus to posterity. It is a role still too little acknowledged by many writers who focus on the score as the principal bearer of significance.

Lawrence Kramer has written refreshingly about "the eternal dialogue of score and performance" as something to be nurtured in today's world of classical music. He urges "understanding performance as simultaneously an act of creation and reproduction, a process that animates the spirit embedded in the ideal form of the score while at the same time reshaping that spirit in the act of bringing it to life." "This is," he adds, "easy to say (what else would one say?) but difficult to do and challenging to think about." Kramer acknowledges, and seems to celebrate, how vastly different performances of the same score can be. As a wry entry for an imaginary handbook of music and performance, he gives the following: "A thirty-minute work can sometimes be performed in three—minutes or seconds." Kramer then comments, "Not all performances of a work need to be full or faithful to it, as long as *some* are, or may be."[2] Kramer's puckishly post-modern stance almost suggests that anything goes. But as listeners we sense (and he knows) that is not true. However much we struggle to articulate them, there are meanings and values embedded in a work—perhaps we should speak of a "horizon" of meanings, along the lines of Jauss—that some performances capture better than others.[3]

To explore this issue, this chapter takes a historical and critical look at performance traditions of a central work of the repertory, Brahms's B♭ Piano Concerto, op. 83, and specifically its third movement. In the case of the Andante, the "dialogue" between score and performance has been distinctive in several ways, if not unique. In the modern era, at least since the first recording of the piece in 1929 (around the same time as Hesse's novel), the movement seems never to have been played in a manner close to the one suggested by the score and other historical sources linked to Brahms. The Andante was conceived by Brahms in a classicizing spirit that became heavily distorted or romanticized across the twentieth century. How and why did the movement's horizon of meanings shift so drastically?

II

We begin with some background about the B♭ Concerto and its early performances. Brahms completed the work in the fall of 1881. He tried out the concerto, with Ignaz Brüll at a second piano, before a small audience of friends in Vienna, on October 8, 1881. He then played it in a private reading with Hans von Bülow and the Meiningen Orchestra ten days later, on October 17. The official premiere of the concerto took place on November 6 in Budapest, with Brahms as soloist and Alexander Erkel as conductor. Over the following three months, until February 22, Brahms played the concerto twenty-one more times with different orchestras and conductors across Germany, Austria, Switzerland, and Holland.[4]

Obviously, any investigation of a tradition or traditions of performance for the B♭ Concerto must thus begin with Brahms himself. He left no recordings of the work. But some eyewitness accounts and evidence from the autograph score of the concerto can provide at least a glimpse of what his performances may have been like. Bülow described Brahms's playing during the read-through in Meiningen as "inimitably beautiful—with a clarity, precision, and fullness that, as you know, the 'critics' will never acknowledge, but which really surprised me all the more."[5]

Bülow might have been "surprised" because by 1880 Brahms was no longer actively touring as a pianist and was not practicing regularly. Indeed, listeners often tended to praise the boldness and force of Brahms's playing of the B♭ Concerto while drawing attention—with varying degrees of tact—to its technical deficiencies. The critic reviewing the Vienna premiere of the concerto on December 26, 1881, for the *Musikalisches Wochenblatt* observed that Brahms had overcome the enormous technical difficulties of the work "with triumphant mastery, like a bold hero." He compared Brahms to "a musical Alexander cutting the inextricable Gordian knot with the sword. By aiming for powerful intensity of tone and by using the pedal, he helped himself and his listeners over many parts that are not masterable in the details because they are not conceived in an entirely pianistic manner."[6] In other words, Brahms fudged in many places.

A similar but more direct account comes from the English composer Charles Stanford, who heard Brahms perform the B♭ Concerto with Bülow in Berlin in January 1882 and who wrote in his memoir,

> His piano playing was not so much that of a finished pianist, as of a composer who despised virtuosity. The skips, which are many and perilous in the solo part, were accomplished regardless of accuracy, and it is no exaggeration to say that there were handfuls of wrong notes. The touch was somewhat hard and lacking in force-control; it was at its best in the slow movement, where he produced the true velvety quality, probably because he was not so hampered by his own difficulties. But never since have I

heard a rendering of the concerto, so complete in its outlook or so big in its interpretation. He took it for granted that the public knew that he had written the right notes, and did not worry himself over such little trifles as hitting the wrong ones.[7]

Stanford's report tends to bear out Marie Schumann's pithy description of Brahms's playing of the B♭ Concerto as a "spirited sketch," a *geistreiche Skizze*.[8]

In the autograph of the concerto, which was used by conductors for the initial season of performances and then served as the basis for the first edition, there are over twenty indications that Brahms added in pencil but later omitted as the piece was prepared for publication in the spring of 1882. These are almost exclusively markings for local changes in tempo— such as "animato," "poco sostenuto," "poco meno presto," or "in tempo."[9] Overall these markings suggest that Brahms played in a highly nuanced and expressive style and was willing to bend tempi, especially at structural moments.

Brahms provided a rationale for such markings in a letter about the Fourth Symphony written to Joseph Joachim of January 1886. This work was in its first season of prepublication performances, and, as with the concerto five years earlier, Brahms had entered into the score numerous smaller-scale tempo markings, which were not to appear in the published score. Brahms explained these as follows to Joachim, in remarks that could apply equally well to the B♭ Concerto:

> I have entered some tempo modifications in pencil into the score. They may well be useful, even necessary, for a first performance. Unfortunately, they often thereby find their way into print—with me and with others— where they mostly do not belong. Such exaggerations are only necessary as long as a work is unknown to the orchestra (or soloist). In that case, I often cannot do enough pushing forward and holding back, so that passionate or calm expression is produced more or less as I want it. Once a work has gotten into the blood stream, there should be no more talk of such things in my view, and the more one departs from this rule, the more inartistic I find the performing style.[10]

In other words, Brahms feels that such markings might be necessary when performers and listeners are familiarizing themselves with a new work. But frozen forever in the printed score, they could lead to a manner of playing too artificial, too calculated. Brahms's letter strikingly reinforces not only the great gap that lies between the notated score and its realization in performance but also the numerous possibilities of Kramer's "eternal dialogue."

III

The penciled markings in the autograph of the B♭ Concerto reveal a composer who wanted his works performed with rhythmic and temporal flexibility. Brahms's own metronome markings for the four movement of the B♭ Concerto, on the other hand, may be said to reveal a concern for how the work should flow on a larger scale. Brahms provided these figures to his publisher, Simrock, at the end of October 1881, after the trial performances but before the premiere, at the same time that he sent off the two-piano arrangement. When he sent the full score to Simrock at the end of March 1882, after the entire season of public performances, he saw no reason to revise or revoke the markings. They appeared in both the two-piano version and the full score, as follows:

I.   Allegro non troppo, $\downarrow$ = 92
II. Allegro appassionato, $\downarrow$ = 76
III. Andante, $\downarrow$ = 84
IV. Allegretto grazioso, $\downarrow$ = 104, then 132

   The metronome markings for the B♭ Concerto are among those that Brahms provided or approved for eight compositions at various points in his career. This number is, of course, a small portion of his total output, which already indicates that he had some ambivalence about metronome markings. Indeed, most of Brahms's recorded remarks on the subject are caustic or negative, as when he gave the following account of those occasions on which he provided metronome figures: only when "good friends have talked me into putting them there, for I myself have never believed that my blood and a mechanical instrument go well together."[11] In 1894 he withdrew the metronome markings that he had authorized to appear with the publication of the *German Requiem* in 1868.
   Yet we should not take these comments or actions at face value. Brahms clearly saw some practical benefits to metronome markings. Remarks he made in 1861 to Clara Schumann, who was contemplating metronome markings for some of Robert's works, suggest a somewhat more moderate view than the one expressed in the preceding paragraph: "You will naturally set the work aside for at least a year and scrutinize it from time to

time. Then you will mark them with fresh numbers each time and finally will have the best selection."[12]

Why was the B♭ Concerto one of the few works for which Brahms provided metronome markings? A likely reason is that it is the only large-scale orchestral work of Brahms's maturity in which he participated but that he did not himself conduct. As Robert Pascall has suggested, the markings would thus have served the very practical purpose of informing local conductors about Brahms's preferred speeds in advance of his arrival.[13]

Calculated mathematically from these metronome markings, the "ideal" duration of the concerto would amount to 40:02. Of course, this figure does not account for any smaller-scale shifts of tempo marked in the score, not to mention the kind of nuances that Brahms indicated in the autograph but then deleted. Nonetheless, an overall duration of about forty minutes is probably close to Brahms's original conception and to his early performances of the B♭ Concerto.

Figure 5.1 is a graphic representation of the total duration of the concerto on a selection of thirty-one recordings arranged chronologically from 1929, the very earliest, with Arthur Rubinstein, Albert Coates, and the London Symphony (on CD as BMG 09026 63001–2), to a more recent one from 1997, with Emanuel Ax, Bernard Haitink, and the Boston Symphony Orchestra (on CD as Sony SK 63229). Viewing the graph, we are immediately struck by a slowing trend across the recorded history of the

FIGURE 5.1. Brahms, Piano Concerto in B♭, op. 83, comparative recording durations.

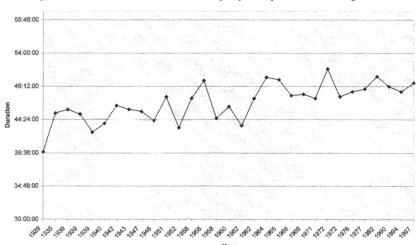

concerto.[14] With the exception of Rubinstein and Coates in 1929, no pianists and conductors get to the concerto's finish line within the forty minutes of the "ideal." Indeed, performers have gotten further and further away from it.

What are we to make of the slowing trend? First, we can observe that it is part of a general pattern in Brahms performances in the latter half of the twentieth century, really since World War II. Bernard Sherman and I have each demonstrated elsewhere how performances of the Brahms symphonies have slowed down considerably since the first generation of recordings made in the 1920s and 1930s.[15] The same also seems to be true of the First Piano Concerto. The infamous performance of that piece in 1962 by Glenn Gould, whose expansive tempi prompted a disclaimer from the conductor, Leonard Bernstein, and offended many critics, lasted 53:21.[16] That is indeed an eternity compared with the 39:07 of a Horowitz-Toscanini performance of 1935, and it is still considerably longer than Fleisher-Szell in 1958, at 46:48.[17] But Gould-Bernstein is in the same temporal universe as many later performances that have caused no scandals, such as Gilels-Jochum in 1972, at 51:43, and, more revealingly, Zimerman-Bernstein in 1984, at a whopping 54 minutes.[18] In this case, Bernstein seems to have lodged no protest at participating in an interpretation that exceeds in length his version with Gould. In short, when it comes to tempi in Brahms, we have become inured to what was so unusual just fifty years ago.

Not all standard-repertory composers have followed this slowing pattern. José Bowen has demonstrated that certain works by Mozart, Beethoven, Tchaikovsky, and Mahler have actually sped up in recordings—they take *less* time to perform than they did earlier in the twentieth century.[19] Why should Brahms get slower? My sense is that across the twentieth century there developed a sonic image of the ponderous, weighty Brahms—corresponding perhaps to the familiar visual image of the fat man with the beard and cigar—which has slowed up his music to the point where he himself would barely recognize it.

IV

The clearest discrepancy between the "ideal" and recorded timings of the B♭ Concerto is apparent in the slow movement, the Andante. The ideal duration for this movement would be 7:30.[20] (Another reminder: this timing does not reflect the many local changes of tempo that any performer, including Brahms, would introduce. But it is still likely to be close to Brahms's original conception.) In Table 5.1, I give timings for a dozen performances of the Andante, extending from Rubinstein in 1929 to Ax in 1997. The speediest version of the Andante, that of Rubinstein in 1929, comes in at 9:10, already well above the ideal timing. At the other end of the spectrum is the glacial Gilels-Jochum performance at 14:04.

Table 5.1 refers to four structural moments in the movement, which are illustrated in Example 5.1: (a) the opening cello solo with orchestra, (b) the beginning of the solo piano part, (c) the Più Adagio that acts as a transition or interlude, and (d) the return of the opening melody. (I should

TABLE 5.1. Brahms B-flat Concerto, op. 83—comparison of recorded speeds in Andante

Pianist/Date Duration	m. 1 Cello solo / orch.	m. 25 Solo entry (in tempo)	m. 59 Più Adagio	m. 71 Tempo I
Rubinstein 1929 9:10	♩ = 66	♩ = 69–76	♩ = 80–84	♩ = 72
Schnabel 1935 12:30	54	60	58	60
Ney 1939 13:18	56	54	50	56
Backhaus 1939 11:51	60	63	58–60	60
Horowitz 1939 10:27	72	72–74	56–62	69
Horowitz 1940 11:05	68	68	5066	
Fischer 1942 12:40	58	58	54–56	54
Solomon 1947 12:45	60	58–60	52	52
Rubinstein 1952 10:54	60–66	60–66	58–60	66
Fleisher 1962 12:55	60	54	54–56	54
Pollini 1971 12:50	56	60	50–52	58
Ax 1997 12:02	63–66	63	56	58–60

Brahms's Metronome Marking: ♩ = 84 (suggested speed for Più Adagio: ♩ = 63)
"Ideal" Duration: 7:30

EXAMPLE 5.1. Brahms Piano Concerto in B♭, op. 83, Four Passages in the Andante.

stress here that my readings, made with an electronic metronome, were not easy to establish. Each of these recordings fluctuates considerably in tempo from the very beginning—the cello soloists are often quite free in nuancing their melody, as are the pianists at measures 25 and 59.)

   Conductors and their cellists tend to begin the movement at well below ♩ = 84, and pianists follow their lead at the solo entry. Given the slow speed at which the movement normally begins, we should perhaps not be surprised how little slowing up there is at the Più Adagio. Of the performances listed in Table 5.1, only those of Horowitz and Toscanini come close to Brahms's own indications—not to the opening metronome marking but to the implied 25 percent reduction in speed between Andante and Più Adagio. In the 1939 recording, the Più Adagio begins some 22 percent slower than both the opening Andante and the solo entry. In the 1940 recording, the speed is reduced some 26 percent at the Più Adagio. At ♩ = 72, Toscanini's performance, although still 12 notches slower, is closer to Brahms's marking than any other recording.

The Rubinstein 1929 recording is, as already mentioned, the shortest overall. One of the most striking features of this performance, as can be seen from Table 5.1, is that Rubinstein and Coates actually *speed up* rather than slow down at the Più Adagio. This is not a practice that Rubinstein followed in his later recordings of the concerto. Coates's tempo at the return in measure 71 is, at ♩ = 72, close to Toscanini's initial tempo in the 1939 recording.

If we assume that Brahms meant his ♩ = 84 and his Più Adagio markings seriously, then no pianist-conductor team on record is playing the third movement of the concerto in the way that the composer intended and presumably played it in its premiere season. This phenomenon tends to corroborate what Fanny Davies said in 1905, in an era before any recordings of the work were made: that already at that time, Brahms's andantes were being taken too slowly.[21] The trend clearly continued throughout the century.

I believe that across the twentieth century the Andante of the B♭ Concerto was interpreted within what Margaret Notley in a recent article has called the "cult" of the adagio—that is, a tendency to value very slow movements as profound and weighty.[22] In casual exchange and in journalistic music criticism, any slow movement might have been called an adagio in the nineteenth century, as happened in the case of the B♭ Concerto, to which Billroth referred in a letter to Brahms as a "schwärmerisches Adagio."[23] But Brahms was quite careful in his scores to distinguish between adagio and andante. His instrumental slow movements may be said to be about equally divided between adagios and andantes, markings that often carry qualifiers that shift them a bit on the tempo spectrum.[24] The following list gives the metronome markings provided or approved by Brahms for all movements labeled either adagio or andante. In the two adagio movements, the basic pulse is in the low to mid-60s. In the andantes, which are more numerous, there is wider variation, dependent especially on the way the andante is qualified (with "con moto," "moderato," or "grazioso"). In the case of the four movements of the *German Requiem* for which Brahms eventually settled on German-language markings (first, second, fourth, and seventh), he had originally used the indication andante. In aggregate, as can be seen, the tempi of the andantes are considerably faster than the adagios. (The average of the metronome markings of all the andantes listed is 78.)

Adagio
Piano Trio No. 1 in B major, op. 8 (first version, 1854)
    III: Adagio non troppo, **C**, ♩ = 63
Rinaldo, op. 50
    III: Poco adagio, ¾, ♪ = 66

Andante
German Requiem, op. 45
    I: Ziemlich langsam und mit Ausdruck [originally Andante on
        Brahms's text sheet], **C**, ♩ = 80
   II: Langsam, marschmässig [originally Andante on Brahms's text
        sheet], 3/4, ♩ = 60
  III: Andante moderato **¢**, ♩ = **52**
  IV: Mässig bewegt [replaced by Andante in autograph], ¾, ♩. = 92
  VII. Feierlich [replaced Andante con moto in autograph], **C**, ♩ = 80
Rinaldo, op. 50
    X: Andante con moto e poco agitato, 6/8, ♩. = 76
  XII: Andante, **C**, ♩ = 69
Nänie, op. 82
    Andante, 6/8, ♩ = 100
Piano Concerto No. 2 in B-flat, op. 83
    III. Andante, 6/4, ♩ = 84
Piano Trio No. 3 in C Minor, op. 101
[markings recorded by Fanny Davies at a rehearsal with Brahms in 1890]
    III. Andante grazioso, ¾, ♩ = 72
    Quasi animato, 6/8, 6/8, ♩. = 96

Brahms's conception of andante seems to be pretty much in line with that given in an authoritative reference work of 1835, Schillings's *Encyclopädie der gesammten musikalischen Wissenschaften*, which describes *andante* as follows:

> In music this expression [andante] can refer to the heading of a movement, to the movement and the tempo, and also to the performance of it. . . . The

tempo occupies a middle ground between the fast and the truly slow. . . . Andante maintains at most times a relaxed character, restful and contented; its notes should thus neither drag nor blend into one another as much as in adagio, nor be as weightily performed; yet they should also not be as sharply accented and distinct as in an allegro. In an andante, everything is moderate, everything remains within the ordinary, even the loudness or accentuation of the notes.[25]

Even into the nineteenth century, then, andante connoted a fairly brisk tempo lying between allegro and adagio. Brahms clearly shared this attitude and the practice of what both Robert Pascall and Michael Musgrave have called "the classical fast andante."[26]

V

All this evidence suggests that Brahms's marking of $\quartnote = 84$ for the Andante of the B♭ Concerto is no anomaly. The movement's proper character— presumably as brought out by Brahms's playing at or near the indicated marking in the early performances—was recognized by Eduard Hanslick, who in his review of the Vienna premiere in December 1881 wrote, "This piece does not belong to those brooding, gloomier Andante movements of Brahms, in which (to paraphrase Schumann) a profundity full of mystery 'extinguishes the light from underground'; it is rather one of those rarer second kind of Andantes with a serenade-like, pleasing character."[27] Hanslick had heard Brahms play the B♭ Concerto at least twice, once during the two-piano tryout in Vienna on October 12 and then with the Vienna Philharmonic on December 26. He thus was presumably reporting on a quality of the movement as interpreted by the composer—an authentic quality, I think we can say—that seems to have disappeared from any performing tradition that we can trace today.

In interpreting this Andante as an adagio, pianists and conductors place it not just into a general "cult" of the adagio but specifically into the framework of the slow movement of the First Piano Concerto. This movement is also in ⁶⁄₄ meter, and there are certain similarities between the openings in that both feature accompanying lines that descend stepwise in quarter notes. But the theme of the Adagio of the First Concerto is hymnlike and solemn, very different from the Andante of the Second Concerto. The Adagio is, after all, the piece into which Brahms wrote "Benedictus qui venit in nomine Domine" in his autograph. In most recorded performances, the Adagio of the D-Minor Concerto is played with a quarter note at or below the mid-50s. That is the same tempo at which, as Table 5.1 shows, some of the Andantes of the B♭ Concerto settle in.

Played at or near the speed indicated by Brahms, the Andante of the B♭ Concerto would significantly alter not only the overall dimensions of the work as we now tend to hear and think of it but also its internal proportions. At forty or so "ideal" minutes, the concerto would not seem as outsized or significantly different from any of the other standard concertos of the nineteenth century. Moreover, the tauter dimensions would go some way toward justifying the unusual four-movement format, which Brahms clearly felt was integral to the concerto. When Billroth suggested omitting the Scherzo movement, Brahms replied that such a cut would be impossible: the first movement was "much too simple" (*gar zu simpel*), and he needed something "powerful and passionate" before the "likewise simple" (*ebenfalls einfach*) Andante.[28] There is of course a heavy dose of Brahmsian irony, as even Billroth realized, in calling the first movement of the B♭ Concerto "simple." Nor is the Andante exactly "*einfach*," but we might take that description as a bit of evidence for my argument as to its proper tempo and mood.

VI

My basic claim, then, is that the horizon of meanings of the Andante of the B♭ Concerto has morphed dramatically across almost 130 years, through the mediation of performance, recording, and reception by generations of listeners. Of course, Brahms is not unique in this regard. Musical meanings are never stable; they are continually being reshaped by values, as reflected by performance styles and preferences. But it is striking, perhaps even paradoxical, that the Andante, conceived by Brahms in a classicizing spirit, would so quickly become—and remain—romanticized and sentimentalized.

In the "eternal dialogue" between score and performance, failure to communicate set in very early. The process seems to have begun in Brahms's lifetime, and he was not happy about it. In 1895 he remarked grumpily about a performance of his First Symphony by Hans Richter and the Vienna Philharmonic, "Well, if my symphony were really such a dull thing, so grey and mezzoforte, like Richter plays it to people today, then they would be right to speak of the 'brooding [*grüblerisch*] Brahms.' That's how completely misunderstood everything was."[29] Here Brahms was commenting on the "hometown" conductor and orchestra strongly associated with his works, a team that had premiered his Second and Third Symphonies and was presumably very familiar with the composer's style and personal preferences. If Brahms had little satisfaction here, one can only imagine his feelings about performances beyond his earshot and his lifetime.

Despite his own best efforts, the brooding Brahms has remained with us. He is there in Hesse; he has been there throughout the twentieth century and into the twenty-first, in countless performances and recordings of the Andante of the B♭ Concerto. We have gotten accustomed to and, in my opinion, too comfortable with this situation. It is my hope that the evidence introduced in this essay can lead us to reenter the conversation among score, performance, recording, and listener, and to reexamine the musical and human values it reveals.

CHAPTER 6

The Civilizing Process

MUSIC AND THE AESTHETICS OF TIME-SPACE RELATIONS IN *THE GIRL OF THE GOLDEN WEST*

Richard Leppert

Getting Civilized/Going Natural

In 1907 Puccini made the first of two visits to New York; he had come to supervise the first performances of *Manon Lescaut* and *Madama Butterfly* at the Metropolitan Opera. He was also in search of a subject for his next project. Accordingly, while in the city, and despite his very limited English, he attended numerous plays, including three by David Belasco, whose *Madama Butterfly* he had seen staged in London in 1900. One of the Belasco productions caught his eye, *The Girl of the Golden West*, which is the general subject of this essay.[1] In particular, I am interested in exploring some of the ways that Belasco's play and Puccini's opera invest in modernist ideologies governing what Norbert Elias has called the civilizing process.[2] To get at the issue, I take a concentrated look at how both Belasco and Puccini envisioned time-space relations and with specific regard to how each understood his characters' place in history (hence time), place (hence space), and, above all, nature, which I consider as both a problem for, and opportunity within, the civilizing process.

In common parlance, we locate nature beyond history; yet the concept of nature is wholly historical, which is to say that nature is at heart a cultural construct.[3] As a concept, nature locates itself inside the parameters of the very thing to which it stands in opposition. Further, nature, in a dyadic relationship with culture, represents itself as a problem.

In *Dialectic of Enlightenment*, Theodor Adorno and Max Horkheimer argued that our historical relation to nature is one of conflict. As they put it, "What human beings seek to learn from nature is how to use it to dominate wholly both it and human beings."[4] They argued that the fundamental forms of domination organizing modernity had their roots in the primordial efforts of humans to survive in a nature—primordial totality—that they feared. Ironically, fearing nature expressed not least a fear of the human to the extent that people are not only *in* nature but also *of* nature; hence, the othering of nature also othered the self from itself.

And yet human beings lament the very separation from nature on which their identity is ultimately grounded. Thus, by the principle that Adorno and Horkheimer articulated, the designation of national parks, which first occurred during the heyday of the industrial revolution—signaling triumph over nature—directly responded to our fractured relation to nature. That is, the setting aside of small and as-yet "untamed" geographies signified less a nostalgic return to nature than a material acknowledgment of the permanence of the damage done to it. In the same way, contemporaneous salvage anthropology in essence picked among the graves and ruins to remember what "advanced man" had destroyed to become advanced.

Concomitantly, in *Aesthetic Theory*, Adorno staked out his position on natural beauty, which he regarded as the defining issue of aesthetics and a good deal more besides. Our longing for nature—for example, ecological regard, wilderness preservation, but also art, in Adorno's argument—is a projection of a lack that develops from our fraught relationship to nature.[5] The concept of nature in essence protests its relationship to culture, or, as Adorno put it, "The concept of natural beauty rubs on a wound."[6] Art is called upon to answer for natural beauty, in effect to substitute for it; art—wholly artifactual, that is, literally unnatural—perpetuates the attack on nature. And yet art does more, for it acknowledges the natural beauty that the human subject has otherwise degraded yet nonetheless desires in its nonextant "perfect" state; art reflects on this fact. Art, Adorno says, "want[s] to keep nature's promise. . . . What nature strives for in vain, artworks fulfill."[7]

Adorno once commented, "Whenever nature was not actually mastered, the image of its untamed condition terrified. This," he said, "explains the strange predilection of earlier centuries for symmetrical arrangements of nature"[8]—think French landscape architecture with its severe topiary or, in England, the contrived naturalism of Stourhead or Stowe, where "raw" nature was severely reorganized to appear, so to speak, more *suitably* natural. In other words, once human beings imagined they had mastered nature, it became their lost friend, only to be reimagined and fetishized.[9]

Belasco's play and Puccini's opera are situated within the Sierra Nevada mountains, perhaps the most dramatic landscape in the American West. The setting more or less constitutes a character in its own right, one of overwhelming power that shapes both action and people. Nature, that is, is the organizing metaphor of both the play and the opera; as Michel de Certeau remind us, metaphors "are spatial trajectories."[10] Both works, literally and figuratively, are also travel stories: literally so, to the extent that the characters are very much on the move, having traveled across the seas and the continent to get to California to participate in the Gold Rush; figuratively, to the extent that the characters journey toward moral redemption—though redemption is more a fundamental trope in Puccini's opera than in Belasco's play. The Sierra Nevada for Belasco and Puccini alike is a material site, inhabitable. It is likewise a psychic site, existing within the realm of the imagination as an ethereal reality.[11]

In the late nineteenth century in the United States, no landscape received greater attention than the West, particularly the mountain West of the Rockies and the Sierra Nevada especially. The California mountains claimed a place in the American imaginary, and not least because of the imposing challenge to cross them to get to the promised land. The fate of the Donner Party during the winter of 1846–47, whose history quickly passed into legend, drove home the point. The Gold Rush, which quickly followed the initial discovery in January 1848 at Sutter's Mill, fully established the Sierra Nevada in the forefront of national consciousness, creating new Western mythologies fueled by the promise of fortunes literally waiting to be scooped up from the gravels of the American River.

The actual mountains and their unimaginably gigantic trees produced particular awe (Figure 6.1), with Yosemite (early on known as Yo-Semite) serving as the focal point of the larger whole. Indeed, its visual splendors seemed to defy the human imagination, though hardly for wont of trying to come to terms with them. In 1864 Lincoln designated Yosemite as a wilderness preserve, the nation's first; it was made a national park in 1890. In the decades that followed, Yosemite was endlessly written about, painted, photographed, and of course visited as a major tourist attraction. Currier and Ives produced lithographs marking a sense of Yosemite's spa-

FIGURE 6.1. "The Mammoth Trees (Sequoia gigantica), California (Calaveras County)," chromolithograph published by A. J. Campbell, Cincinnati, c. 1860. (Library of Congress, Prints and Photographs Division, reproduction no. LC-USZ62-2514.)

tial vastness, just as photographers produced stereoscopes of views carefully selected to exploit the three-dimensional effects of the medium—a kind of vicarious substitute for the awe-inspiring reactions commonly experienced by visitors.[12] In the immediate aftermath of the Civil War, Yosemite took on greater significance as a site of healing and reconciliation—a park in place of a battlefield, in the parlance of Frederick Law Olmsted.[13] The writings of John Muir (1838–1914) in particular best expressed the spiritual impact of the landscape.[14]

The American West had its dystopian realities, as the fate of Custer demonstrated to a shocked nation in 1876, the news reaching the East, ironically, during the July 4 Centennial celebrations. But the promise of American singularity on the whole played well against inconvenient arguments to the contrary, made clear in the reception history of Frederick Jackson Turner's famous paper read to the American Historical Association in Chicago in 1893, "The Significance of the Frontier in American History":

> American social development has been continually beginning over again on the frontier. This perennial rebirth, this fluidity of American life, this

expansion westward with its new opportunities, its continuous touch with the simplicity of primitive society, furnish the forces dominating American character. The true point of view in the history of this nation is not the Atlantic coast, it is the Great West.[15]

The sublime drama of Turner's Great West was ably captured by painters, among whom Albert Bierstadt (1830–1902) had few equals, though his fame was short-lived and his critics, from the start, many.[16] From his hand came monumental imaginings of a Western Eden. As with Belasco and Puccini, three tropes in particular organize Bierstadt's visionary representations: monumentality, unimaginably vast space (the effect of both often amplified by the vast sizes of some of his canvases (Figure 6.2), the largest being nine and a half feet high and fifteen feet wide), and light (Figure 6.3). Each of these tropes served as metaphors for the untrammeled purity of a world in a state of nature and as signs of nature's redemptive agency for man after the fall from grace. In nationalist terms, these images visually certified claims to the mythologies of American singularity. Here was a landscape at once aged and at the seeming moment of its creation, a visible sign of the "divine endorsement of American progress."[17]

FIGURE 6.2. Albert Bierstadt (1830–1902), *Among the Sierra Nevada, California* (1868), oil on canvas. (Smithsonian American Art Museum, Washington, D.C., bequest of Helen Huntington Hull, granddaughter of William Brown Dinsmore, who acquired the painting in 1873 for "The Locusts," the family estate in Dutchess County, New York; 1977.107.1)

FIGURE 6.3. Albert Bierstadt (1830–1902), *Sunset in the Yosemite Valley* (1868), oil on canvas. (The Haggin Museum, Haggin Collection, Stockton, California.)

The West did not actually look like what Bierstadt painted, not least on account of the multiple perspectives encompassed in his canvases, a visually jarring effect that invites the eye to search out a compositional unity that does not in fact exist (this effect sorely irritated his contemporaneous critics, who regarded the violation of convention as mere incompetence). But whatever his shortcomings as a painter, Bierstadt pedagogically led viewers toward a particular way of seeing the Western mountains. In the words of Lee Clark Mitchell, Bierstadt "imagined the West as a dramatic (and therefore moral) terrain rather than a geographical one."[18] He envisioned a spectacular and visually magnetic Western sublime, whose results he put on display in exhibition galleries in the East and also made available in mass-produced prints.[19]

Anthropologist Mary Douglas points out that societies are imagined to have form, boundaries, and margins; in short, they have structure. But where society's energy concentrates is "in its margins and unstructured areas," precisely where "any structure of ideas is vulnerable."[20] It is precisely this vulnerability that Belasco and Puccini confront via the liminal terrain of the American West, specifically the imagined boundaries separating the civilization from its absence, and culture from nature.[21] Both men perceived the West as a space defined by its relation to time—historical time and the now-time of early twentieth-century modernity. Time, like nature, like space, as the product of history, is "a social institution."[22] Elias marks modern time as "the symbol of an inescapable and all-embracing compulsion."[23] Time in modernity has a life of its own; it reaches beyond our capacity to control it. Belasco and Puccini confronted modernity, despite the conservatism and even regression evident in their work. Their West was at once in the past, as a narrative of the Gold Rush, and a present, the literal reality of two worlds in stark opposition: the East of frenetic, ultramodern Midtown, and the West whose wildness was by then in *actuality* already well tamed apart from a few sanctioned sites set aside as national parks for eternal preservation.

Modernism, Stuart Hall has suggested, is "modernity experienced as trouble."[24] Belasco and Puccini were reluctant, conflicted modernists. Modernist Belasco virtually fetishized electricity for what it offered the theater; modernist Puccini, who collected fast cars and speedboats, experimented with post-Romantic sonorities learned from Debussy and Strauss. Belasco left California for New York as a young man and rarely returned to his wild Western roots; Puccini, whose life as an opera composer demanded endless journeys to urban centers, could never get back to his country estate fast enough to keep him happy.[25] Both men, in their lives and in their work, were deeply ambivalent about modernity; their ambivalence was manifested in the internal contradictions marking their respective settings of *The Girl of the Golden West*.

Belasco and Puccini both addressed the cultural displacements of modernity; both look back in time to a defining phenomenon of modernity, the American westward expansion and the formation of an imagined sublime. They envisioned a paradise, but a modern one in which presence is already marked by the promise of absence and even expulsion. Nevertheless, their narratives stage reconciliations, however momentary, of subject to object, man to woman, and culture to nature. Each seeks to bind what Adorno called nature's wound, though in the end the wound continues to bleed, precisely what guarantees their work a degree of historical, modernist authenticity.

The Girl of the Golden West was something of a cultural phenomenon in the early years of the twentieth century. The play itself was highly successful in the years following its 1905 opening. In 1911 Belasco produced a novel based on his play, a year following the premiere of Puccini's opera (Figure 6.4).[26] The book remained in print for some years thereafter and was resissued again in 2007. Its first printing included four color illustra-

FIGURE 6.4. David Belasco, *The Girl of the Golden West: Novelized from the Play* (New York: Grosset & Dunlap, 1911), cover illustration. (Private collection.)

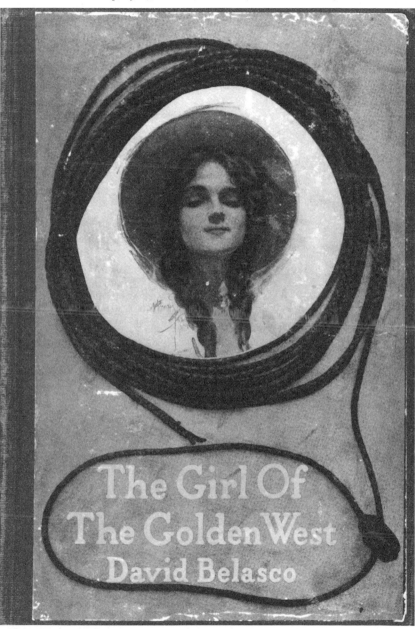

tions of important scenes; later printings replaced the illustrations with stills from a now-lost film of the same title released in 1923 (Figure 6.5). In fact, between 1915 and 1938, four American feature films followed in the wake of Belasco's play. The first, in five reels, shot in eight days in California in 1915, was by Cecil B. DeMille, then working only in his second year as a director.[27] The 1923 silent film in seven reels, directed by Edwin Carewe, starred popular actress Sylvia Breamer; this film was remade in 1930 with sound, in ten reels, with Ann Harding in the title role (Figure 6.6). The 1923 film had a popular music spin-off, a tune called "The Girl of the Olden West," (Figure 6.7), its cover sheet reproducing Breamer's face hovering over a mountainous landscape.[28] The 1938 film was a Nelson Eddy–Jeanette MacDonald musical, with a score by Sigmund Romberg.[29] (There were other Gold Rush films throughout this period, with Chaplin's 1925 film concerning the Yukon Klondike narrative being the best known.) In sum, *The Girl of the Golden West* spawned an opera, a novel, pop tunes, song recordings, sheet music,[30] and four films (five, counting a 1943 Italian version). It gave its name to a country music duo,

FIGURE 6.5. David Belasco, *The Girl of the Golden West: Novelized from the Play* (New York: Grosset & Dunlap, 1911; undated reprint), title page, and movie still of actress Sylvia Breamer as "The Girl" in 1923 film directed by Edwin Carewe. (Private collection.)

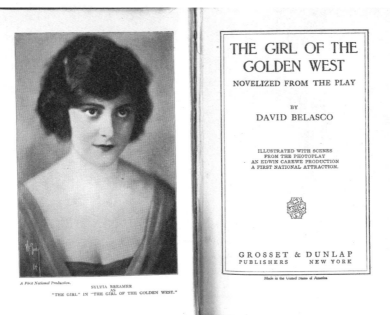

A First National Production.
SYLVIA BREAMER
AS
"THE GIRL" IN "THE GIRL OF THE GOLDEN WEST."

THE GIRL OF THE GOLDEN WEST
NOVELIZED FROM THE PLAY

BY
DAVID BELASCO

ILLUSTRATED WITH SCENES
FROM THE PHOTOPLAY
AN EDWIN CAREWE PRODUCTION
A FIRST NATIONAL ATTRACTION.

GROSSET & DUNLAP
PUBLISHERS   NEW YORK

Made in the United States of America

FIGURE 6.6. *The Girl of the Golden West* (1930), Vitaphone sound film directed by John Francis Dillon, First National Pictures, movie herald, 3.5 × 5 in. (Private collection.)

The Girls of the Golden West, Dolly and Millie Good, who achieved considerable fame in the 1930s. *The Girl of the Golden West* was also the subject of souvenir ephemera, including postcards and stereographs (Figure 6.8), Western paintings, and even a decorated metal fruit tin—objects that crop up from time to time on eBay. In brief, and this is my point, the subject touched something of a collective social nerve.

Belasco

David Belasco (1853–1931), born in San Francisco to immigrant parents, was involved in the theater throughout his childhood in the West. By the time he moved to New York in 1884, he was already widely experienced as an actor, prompter, and stage manager. In New York, where he remained until his death, he made his reputation as a producer, director, and playwright.[31]

First and foremost, Belasco specialized in a form of melodrama emphasizing naturalism. Indeed, every theatrical resource at his disposal was put to use in an effort to capture what he regarded as the essence of whatever place and time his plays represented. His often hoary plays, now notable

FIGURE 6.7. "The Girl of the Olden West," sheet-music cover; lyrics by Haven
Gillespie, music by Egbert van Alstyne and Charles L. Cooke (New York and Detroit:
Jerome H. Remick, 1923). (Private collection.)

FIGURE 6.8. "A Girl from the Golden West," stereocard, 1906, copyright by E. W. Kelley. (Library of Congress, Prints and Photographs Division, reproduction no. LC-USZ62-47727.)

for the strikingly old-fashioned tropes conventional to melodrama, were staged and acted out with the precision afforded by the most modern of stage technology, itself infected with an acute awareness of photographic and cinematic indexicality. Indeed, his special effects (and there were many) were as good, or better, than those in period movies. His painted backdrops sometimes moved, not very different from what audiences experienced with the painted scenery of early cinema. Belasco's wind devices replicated blizzards, produced howls, and blew window curtains. He used lighting to effect fire that was indistinguishable from the real thing—so threatening that authorities were once called to investigate.[32] He even attended to the olfactory. In one play set in a forest, he sprinkled pine needles on the stage so that when the actors moved about, crushing the needles, the scent would waft into the auditorium.[33]

The printed scene descriptions for each act of *The Girl of the Golden West* run to as many as five pages. The play's electrical plot occupies eight pages of precise settings and cues. The list of properties requires seventeen pages in all, enumerated in nearly exasperating detail.[34] Thus, devices and materials for the act 2 snow storm, requiring a full page of instructions, provide the flavor of his concern for naturalism. The list includes wind machines, an air tank used to produce a "large shriek of wind," another with whistle attachments "for canyon effect of wind," and a "cluster of whistles attached to pipe and running to bellows under [the] stage." To further effect howling wind, he calls for an electric fan to blow both the curtains of the bed canopy and some tissue paper stored under the bed. He lists rock salt to effect sleet, to be used with "two snow effect appliances," the salt to be blown against the cabin windows so that it can be both seen and heard. The instructions call for two offstage piles of snow, presumably flour, to be set in front of two fans; the snow will be blown into the crevices between the cabin's log walls. Other snow reservoirs are placed elsewhere. And when Sheriff Rance brushes snow off his overcoat, some of it landing in the fireplace, a hissing sound is to be made. And so on. These and other storm effects in the second act required thirty-two stagehands to activate, all of it coordinated by a conductor who could be seen by the each member of the stage crew.

Music was integral to Belasco productions. "If the play has a musical accompaniment," he wrote, "I read it to the composer I have engaged, indicating its moods and feelings. He must interpret every scene and speech as if he were writing the score for a song."[35] Belasco incorporated a great deal of music into *The Girl of the Golden West*, a combination of on- and offstage singing of thirteen old songs (including "Camptown Races," "O Susannah," "The Days of 49," "Sonora Slim," "Echoes of Home," "Clementine of '49," and "Ole Dan Tucker"),[36] employing two tenors, a baritone, and a bass, sometimes in costume onstage and at other times in the pit. An orchestra played a prelude (171 bars) at the start and also provided accompaniment to the male quartet between acts. Accompaniments were provided by the string orchestra, as well as by banjo and guitar, either solo or with orchestra. There are parts for other instruments as well, though their use was more restricted: flute, clarinet, cornet, trombone, two mandolins, accordion, piano, and drums. Numerous brief musical cues occur throughout. The play's original music was composed by William Wallace Furst (1852–1917), who also arranged orchestral versions of some of the old tunes.[37] Between acts, song medleys were performed.

The Girl of the Golden West, in four acts, tells the story of a California mining camp during the Gold Rush. Called Cloudy Mountain, the settlement is populated solely by men, apart from one young woman, who until well into the play is simply referred to only as Girl. Her name is Minnie. She runs the Polka saloon, the setting for the first act. Minnie is undereducated, virginal, and either soft or hard, as her situation requires. She has a heart of gold and a ready trigger finger. Everyone loves her, and several of the boys are in love with her. The Girl, while saddled with the clichés of the domesticized professional virgin, is in other respects very much of the New Woman mold: self-reliant, fearless, and readily adaptable to changing situations. The local law, in the person of the sheriff, Jack Rance, intends to have her as his wife. He is the play's heavy. The Girl's (eventual) love interest is the road agent Ramerrez, a bad guy with his own heart of gold, who introduces himself to Minnie as Dick Johnson in act 1, immediately sparking her libido. He first comes off as something of a dandy; he drinks his whiskey with water, which marks him as unmanly in the eyes of the miners, who take their drink straight up. His half-Mexican parentage renders him an Other. Belasco nonetheless represents him as a man of moral integrity, despite his profession and his ethnic heritage, which counted for little at the turn of the century.[38] Minnie, played by the famous actress Blanche Bates, whom Belasco especially favored, mothers the men and guards their gold. Act 1 (Figure 6.9), which begins at midnight, establishes Minnie's role in the camp. Johnson, intending to rob the gold, cases the joint but sees Minnie and plies for different treasure. Act 2 opens in the mountains, in the Girl's log cabin an hour later, at one o'clock in the morning. Dick comes courting. A storm ensues, the full force hitting just as the pair kiss for the first time. Soon thereafter, Rance and his posse arrive looking for Ramerrez, having learned of Johnson's real identity, and suspecting him to be with the Girl. Minnie gambles at poker for Johnson's life (Figure 6.10). If she loses, the sheriff gets Johnson for a hanging and Minnie for his wife. The Girl wins, but only by cheating.

Act 3, set in the saloon's adjacent dance hall a few days later, involves the recapture of Ramerrez and the passing of sentence for his execution by hanging. Minnie, coming in on the scene moments before Dick is to be killed, pleads for his life and wins over the miners. Act 4, about a week later, is set on "The boundless prairies of the West." Little more than a tableau, the scene lasts only a couple of minutes, during which the re-

FIGURE 6.9. *The Girl of the Golden West* (1905–6), by David Belasco, act 1. (Billy Rose Theatre Division, The New York Public Library for the Performing Arts, Astor, Lenox, and Tilden Foundations.)

FIGURE 6.10. *The Girl of the Golden West* (1905–6), by David Belasco, act 2. (Billy Rose Theatre Division, The New York Public Library for the Performing Arts, Astor, Lenox, and Tilden Foundations.)

united lovers bid final farewell to the Sierra Nevada and California as they head east for their uncertain future.

The Girl of the Golden West opened at the new Belasco Theatre in Pittsburgh on 3 October 1905 and in New York at the Belasco on 14 November of the same year; it played for 224 performances. It was mounted again on Broadway during the 1906–7 season with Bates still in the title role; it was this staging that Puccini witnessed. Thereafter, for three years, the play was extensively toured in the United States in dozens of towns and cities from the East Coast to the Midwest.[39] It was also performed internationally, as far distant as Tasmania in 1909.

The remarks that follow are largely confined to two brief episodes from the play: its wordless opening, accompanied only by music, and its close, also with music, in the brief act 4 epilogue. What interests me is Belasco's evocation of nature, which I will connect to my larger concern with time and space relations.

Picture Perfect

The representation of nature, which literally bookends the play, is constituted as an allegorical sublime within and against which the characters measure their existence. The play opens with house lights up during an upbeat musical prelude provided by the pit orchestra. The stage is hung with a painted curtain, illuminated by footlights (Figure 6.11), representing a scene with large evergreens in the foreground and mountains at the back. A brilliant sunset shows just above a ridge of mountain peaks, its impact heightened by a spotlight. Near the end of the prelude, four bars into the last section, marked *cantabile* (a $\frac{3}{4}$ moderato, and serving as the Girl's motive), the house goes dark and the prelude draws to a close, segueing to music in a quite different mood, an *andante misterioso*, played by muted strings. After four bars, the curtain is raised in darkness, in preparation for what Belasco called the "First Picture." The music continues until the play proper begins.

The First Picture moves from day to night; the sunburst is gone, replaced by a moon transparency, and soon followed by the ascent of an exactly described panorama. Here, in excerpt, is how Belasco describes it (unfortunately, no photographs seem to exist, although the production was otherwise extensively documented):

> In the far distance a wild range of the Sierras peaks. . . . Near R., on a mountain, a cabin is seen, a winding trail coming up to it. We see that it is

FIGURE 6.11. *The Girl of the Golden West* (1905–6), by David Belasco, act curtain. (Billy Rose Theatre Division, The New York Public Library for the Performing Arts, Astor, Lenox, and Tilden Foundations.)

cloudy about the mountain. The mountains behind this cabin continue to a great height. . . . It is night and the moon hangs low over the mountain peaks. The scene is flooded with moonlight, contrasting oddly with the cavernous shadows. . . . The sky is very blue and cold. The snow gleams white on the highest peaks. Here and there pines, firs, and manzineta bushes show green. All is wild, savage, ominous. In certain places the mountains are very jagged—one deep sheer ravine is suggested, the purple mists rising up from the bottom. There is a faint light twinkling in the cabin of the GIRL. As this first impression gradually moves up out of view of the audience:

SECOND PICTURE: The exterior of the "Polka" saloon . . .[40]

Belasco's two "pictures" are, of course, moving panoramas painted on canvas. Panoramas had already been used in the U.S. theater for decades, but the canvas rolls were conventionally at the back of the stage, not at the front, and the movement was normally lateral. Belasco's panorama rolls vertically, rising slowly from the stage floor, just behind the stage apron, revealing the described scene little by little, and in precise coordination with lighting cues, such as the light showing from inside the little cabin. The effect was striking: the scene rises from the stage floor, but what it gradually reveals is what in cinematic terms would be a tilt down. That is, we first see the mountainous peaks, after which the view slowly descends to the valley in which the Cloudy Mountain camp is located.[41]

The act curtain and subsequent panorama are critically important to the allegory that organizes the play's narrative. What becomes apparent by the end of the play is that the sun marks several interlocking tropes. Fundamentally, Belasco's use of sunlight works to reverse time. It rolls history backward. The play opens with a metaphorical setting sun, mirroring Frederick Jackson Turner's then-recent proclamations about the closing of the American frontier. It registers an ending and, accordingly, a new uncertain day to follow. As mentioned earlier, the play opens at midnight and its second act continues an hour later, at one o'clock in the morning. Act 3 is set in the morning; it is brightly illuminated but metaphorically dark, the mood lightening only when the hanging is averted; and this in turn leads to the epilogue, in which Belasco's handling of light matters far more than the short scene's very few words.

Act 4 is at sunrise, at once completing the reversal of time while alluding to new life and a hoped-for better future. But this ending nonetheless reiterates a profound uncertainty. To be sure, the lovers face the sunrise, but they are moving against the tide of American history as laid out by Turner; they are heading east, away from the new and toward the old.[42] More about this presently.

The opening panorama compresses time, just as it constitutes a journey. It begins, so to speak, in the clouds and drops to the mountain peaks; only gradually does it admit a human being, indirectly via the Girl's cabin, and all she represents. It eventually "arrives" by leaving the sublime for something of the ridiculous, a mining camp in societal gender disorder, a perverse family: one Girl and her all-male brood.[43]

Belasco invokes loss, history, and remembering before the curtain opens by means of a text that he quotes in the play's program and again as his novel's epigraph. The modernity of his subject is less its account of a localized version of manifest destiny and more its insistence on society's nonentities, people who perhaps were less forgotten and more never remembered in the first place, people as it were "known only to God":

> In those strange days, people coming from God knows where, joined forces in that far Western land, and, according to the rude custom of the camp,

their very names were soon lost and unrecorded, and here they struggled, laughed, gambled, cursed, killed, loved and worked out their strange destinies in a manner incredible to us to-day. Of one thing only are we sure—they lived![44]

Thus, before the curtain goes up, Belasco evokes a kind of freeze-frame in a look back on the young nation's still younger days. His epigraph acknowledges loss (this is conventional to melodramas) and posits the West in 1905 as a site of enormous distance, but one less in miles than in time, hence history. Time consciousness, that is, girds the primeval nature that will shortly unfold to a troubled modernity defined by human anonymity, greed, and violence, which together seem to trump the allusions to pleasures and happiness. In brief, time and nature are in conflict. What the panorama and the epigraph together reinforce is a sense of loss, which the epigraph especially overdetermines. The Gold Rush, a mere fifty years in the past at the time of the play, presents itself as lost in the mists of legend. It can now only be imagined. By 1905 the West was well familiar to most Americans, but Belasco's invocation pushes it back into a territory of the unfamiliar, as though it were a foreign geography. In brief, Belasco sought first to estrange the now familiar, then to allegorize it and to render it thereafter precise via a material naturalism, only in the end once more to throw all of it back into uncertainty, in a kind of *Misterioso* complaint against the very modernity that he otherwise technologically fetishized.[45]

Lighting Out

Belasco's act 4 two-minute epilogue marks the departure of the lovers onto what Belasco describes as "the boundless prairies of the West. On the way East, at the dawn of a day about a week later."[46] Act 4 is a looking back at paradise following the lovers' self-imposed expulsion. The setting carried heavy weight for Belasco, despite its brevity and brief text, evident not least in the number of photographs Belasco had shot of it, proportionally much larger than those taken of the other, far longer acts.

The dialogue is little more than an afterthought, giving excuse for the scenery, the accompanying music, and, above all, the lighting. The music is a reprise of the tune "Old Dog Tray," first heard at the play's start and one that Puccini was to make good use of as well, so far as the text is concerned, though he chose a different melody. It is a song about the loss of home. In act 1, it is the home back East that has been left; at the end, it is the West, which is to suggest that there *is* no home.

The principal "character" of act 4 is light, on which Belasco lavished a great deal of attention and, for that matter, money.[47] He understood light as a kind of hermeneutic medium marking the passage of time through which changes are enacted—changes in his characters and changes in the nature that surrounds and shapes them. He employed light with great subtlety as regards both intensities and colors, which he conventionally carefully blended. Belasco's light is never static. In order to effect nuanced change he used extreme care in both the placement and types of lighting. The result resonates with Bierstadt; for Belasco and Bierstadt alike, light is at once expressive, dramatic, and apparently symbolic, however vaguely, an abstract entity that serves to define a kind of spiritual essence of both men's sense of the Western landscape.

As dawn breaks, the Girl tells her lover that the foothills are growing fainter, that soon they will be invisible. "That," she says, "was the Promised Land." Dick, rather less convincingly, assures her, "The promised land is always ahead," a remark that is coordinated with the first glimmer of the rising sun seen on the foothills' foliage. All the while, from first curtain of the act and via a series of four gauze scrims rising one after another, the scene very gradually lightens, the sky blues, clouds roll slowly across the sky (projected from a stereopticon cloud machine), and shadows begin to form (Figure 6.12). The final, fourth gauze remains in place, keeping the scene in a kind of soft haze. Nowhere else in the play does Belasco call for this effect. By employing it here, the naturalism so consistently employed to this point throughout the play is retired; in its place, allegory is visually referenced as both time and space begin to be distanced. History retreats, as we are reminded less of the past and more of loss, even as a new day dawns. The scrim emphasizes the allegorical function of the scene's lighting, a modern expulsion from the promised land, intermixed with the American myth of dynamic striving, but tinged with more regret than any convincing sign of conventional optimism about lighting out for the territory. As the first rays break above the hills, the Girl acknowledges the new day: "The dawn is breaking in the East—far away—fair and clear," she intones. The lovers in turn acknowledge "A new life!" And then the Girl speaks her last lines as she moves to embrace Johnson one final time as the curtain falls: "Oh, my mountains—I'm leaving you—Oh, my California, I'm leaving you—Oh, my lovely West—my Sierras!—I'm leaving you!" Then turning to her

FIGURE 6.12. *The Girl of the Golden West* (1905–6), by David Belasco, act 4 (epilogue). (Billy Rose Theatre Division, The New York Public Library for the Performing Arts, Astor, Lenox, and Tilden Foundations.)

lover, she closes, "O, my—my home."[48] Minnie's arm outstretched toward the distant mountains is her final reach back for what she has surrendered.[49]

The ambiguity of the play's ending is made clearer in Belasco's novel. Acknowledging the personal paradise of the couple's mutual love, in the same breath Belasco describes their location "at the edge of the merciless desert, stretching away like a world without end."[50] "The Girl had ever been a lover of nature. All her life the mystery and silences of the high mountains had appealed to her soul; but never until now had she realized the marvelous beauty and glory of the great plains. And yet, though her eyes shone with the wonder of it all, there was an unmistakably sad and reminiscent note in [her] voice."[51] As she looks back on the faded view of the distant mountains, and as she acknowledges the need to look ahead and not back, her tone is one of "resignation." She thinks of all she has left, the people and the place, and thinks of them, as she puts it, "like shadows movin' in a dream—like shadows I've dreamt of."[52] Her words account for Belasco's use of the final scrim, keeping things hazy to the play's end.

FIGURE 6.13. Giacomo Puccini, *The Girl of the Golden West* (Milan: G. Ricordi, 1910), piano-vocal score, cover illustration. (Private collection.)

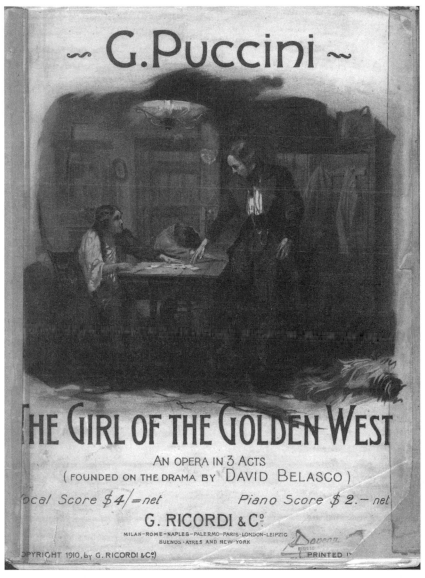

Puccini's Acoustic West

La fanciulla del West (Figure 6.13) was the first world premiere in the history of the Metropolitan Opera, with music by the foremost living Italian composer.[53] The stakes were high for all concerned; accordingly, no stone was left unturned to assure both notice and success. Once the opera was secured for the Met (it was not a commission), the company's publicity apparatus was set in high gear, beginning already in May 1910, nearly nine months before the 10 December opening, the result being stories in many of the New York dailies.[54] The first performances, with Emmy Destinn, Caruso, and Pasquale Amato in the principal roles, and Toscanini conducting, were a stunning success, with dozens of curtain calls for the cast and conductor, as well as for Puccini and Belasco, who had coached the acting of the principals and chorus.[55]

La fanciulla del West is an instantiation of the West of the imagination, though not with regard to a sonoric invocation of natural sounds but instead addressing nature's abstract temporal-spatial dimension in a state of crisis. The natural space—indeed, the natural paradise—of Puccini's West, like Belasco's, is mediated by the rawest form of cultural modernity, registered in class distinction, ethnic and racial tension, economic destitution, jealousy, hatred, loneliness, greed, violence, and injustice. That is, in this opera the eternal sameness of a would-be perfect nature is confronted by modern history. The limitless *space* of nature meets modern *time*. This is the opera's modernity and of course its problem.

Music has long played an important role in myriad practices associated with cultural and ethical assessments of time and its use or abuse. Music itself functions as a timing device, to work either with or against the clock time that in modernity so completely controls people's lives. Experienced *in* time and, in essence, *of* time, music invites a heightened experience of, but also an engagement with, temporality. Adorno once suggested that music has time as its problem and that it has the responsibility to "act upon time, not lose itself to it."[56] In *La fanciulla del West*, Puccini addresses time's impact on the civilizing process. The lengthy "Preliminary Note" appended to both the libretto and the score describes the opera as "a drama of love and of moral redemption against a dark and vast background of primitive characters and untrammeled nature."[57] The opera, that is, works toward a reconciliation, but one, as it turns out, with a considerable price to pay.

Modernity emerged through the conjunction of space and time recognized as interrelated parameters for development—dynamism supplanting stasis. Since music is by definition both a temporal and a spatial art, it is hardly surprising that it was early and often called on to represent modernity—often to cheer modernity onward but sometimes to engage it critically. One response, often in protest, was the valorization of nature, increasingly placed in binary opposition to culture and especially evident in the music of the nineteenth century, the music, that is, that accompanied the industrial revolution and the hegemony of industrial capitalism.

Puccini noted that he intended his music as an evocation of the California primeval forest—where stand the giant sequoias and the highest mountain on the continent outside Alaska—none of which he had ever seen (he knew the Sierra Nevada from pictures; indeed, for the third act he supplied his librettist a postcard and photographs of the gigantic trees).[58] For Puccini, the West was experienced only at the greatest geographical and psychic distance, which itself may well have helped to provoke his fascination for it, alongside the challenge to invoke in sound a sense of its vastness as well as its seeming untamed essence—as it were, space remaining in the State of Nature.

In *La fanciulla del West*, Puccini had to deal with the seeming boundlessness of pristine Western Nature for the better part of two and a half hours, since everything that happens in the opera in one way or another is determined by this overwhelming setting; indeed, the characters themselves are transformed by the locale, which is largely foreign to them—until, at the end, the setting metaphorically morphs, as it were, into the homeland that the lovers must leave, and very much against their will.

La fanciulla del West is different from Puccini's other mature works in that it begins with a one-minute prelude of thirty-four bars. Within that time frame Puccini introduces several tropes that govern the whole, foremost among which is an evocation less of nature than of nature's force, and its force in relation to human beings. The prelude constitutes a musical struggle, which in the end instantiates resolution but only in the final triumphant chord that is introduced with an abruptness that does not fully convince.

Marked *allegro non troppo, con fuoco*, the prelude begins almost brutally, a *fortissimo* with upward sweeping arpeggios, wind- and stormlike, climaxing on augmented chords held with fermatas, then to fall back, only to repeat, in quick succession, all of it very un-Puccini-like, a kind of sonic calling card telling his auditors that what they are going to hear is not Puccini as usual. The prelude alternates among three musical ideas; the second, a whole-tone motif, is associated with the lover's first kiss (act 2, rehearsal no. 27, measure 3 and thereafter),[59] and it is this motif that gyrates in competition with the opening chords (Example 6.1). The third motif, whose entrance is somewhat jarring, in syncopated cakewalk rhythm, is heard only three measures prior to the final chord; later it sounds again with the first appearance of Dick Johnson (Example 6.2).

EXAMPLE 6.1. Giacomo Puccini, *The Girl of the Golden West* (*La fanciulla del West*) (Milan: G. Ricordi, 1911), piano-vocal score, opening of prelude.

The first two motifs unite nature with the Girl, less in competition and more to show what is immanent to both: strength, uncertainty, change-ability, and forces that cannot be contained.[60] Into this alliance comes the man, rhythmically swaggering, a smart-ass know-it-all who, in a confron-tation with both nature and the Girl, will himself be remade, be redeemed.

Everything about the prelude projects multiple acoustic instabilit-ies—of nature, character, experience, and emotion.[61] The *tutti* ending, marked *violento*, ends on a C-major chord with considerable finality, which turns out to be ironic. No such musical triumph ends the opera. The final chord of act 3, a barely audible E-major triad, played only by the first and

EXAMPLE 6.2. Puccini, *Girl of the Golden West*, conclusion of prelude.

second violins and bass, proclaims nothing and evokes only uncertainty. (In like fashion, the opera's first act concludes on a C-major chord, with the addition of the second and seventh scale degrees; in three bars the final chord diminishes from *fortissimo* to the virtually inaudible, and in apt reflection of all that remains unresolved.)[62]

La fanciulla del West, more than any other opera that Puccini had previously written, is filled with dissonance, often with delayed resolutions or without resolution. Major and minor seconds and ninths are common, as are tritones. Vocal lines have wide tessituras (Minnie's is more than two octaves), and the vocal writing, especially for the Girl, is peppered with wide intervallic leaps. Vocal outbursts at high dynamic levels are common as well, and more so with Minnie than with her lover, though he too is assigned passages of great drama. All of this carries over into the orchestra, Puccini's largest prior to *Turandot*.

The orchestra essentially serves as another character, something like a Greek chorus, whose musical metaphors are registered in the score with a striking range of markings, and especially ones that indicate force, violence, and brutality, as Mosco Carner has duly noted: *allegro incisivo, allegro brutale, allegro feroce, come gridi* (like shouts), *con strazio* (tearing), *robusto, strepitoso* (noisy, boisterous), *staccatissimo, martellato* (hammerlike), *marcatissimo*, and so on.[63] In like fashion, tempos change frequently, and the shifts deliver a jolt.

In brief, *La fanciulla del West* is an opera whose modernity is marked by instability and rapid change; accordingly, there are relatively few moments when action stops for the commentary typical to arias. Indeed, the lack of conventional arias was a regular complaint in the opera's early reception: Puccini did not sound like Puccini was supposed to, evident in the fact that very few of the opera's "numbers," apart from "*Ch'ella mi creda*," have been individually recorded.[64]

Puccini unquestionably understood tonality as a kind of sonic geography, a historical map tracing modern subjectivity and desire. But in *La fanciulla del West*, he exploited tonal instabilities, laying bare his self-consciousness about the limits of conventionalized musical practice to represent the world. Sonically speaking, he recognized tonality's closing frontier and elected to head West, however tentatively, toward the outer boundary of the familiar, seeking the energy available at the margins of acoustic modernity.

The time was apparently ripe for this quest. Just a few years earlier, in 1905, Richard Strauss had done much the same thing in *Salome*, in which, however, the margins are sexual rather than geographical. As Lawrence

Kramer has suggested, modernity is the subtext of the exotic distance of *Salome*, which places the opera at "modernity's cutting edge." *La fanciulla del West* stakes out the same territory, and if its willingness to shock is not quite at Strauss's level (no severed heads), it is real nonetheless.[65]

Distance and Distancing

Time, critical to the cultural discourse of *La fanciulla del West*, is compressed. Whereas Belasco's play involved the passage of a week, Puccini's opera unfolds in twenty-four hours, but not a day in the Aristotelian sense of dramatic unities. Puccini's time compression is one manifesting the urgencies of what Walter Benjamin later coined *Jetztzeit*, a Now-Time that surpasses what is contained in the concept of *Gegenwart*.[66] The opera's time compression, in sync with the rapidity of change in modernity, is neither celebratory nor historicist.

Among the musical devices that define the opera's allegory, one in particular stands out. Puccini made the decision to evoke the vast California wilderness by producing for his audience a sense of distance, and by that means to articulate not only space but also—and crucially—time and memory. Puccini's West, above all, evokes time through space; it is this relation that controls his understanding of the West's essence—as was the case a generation later in the films of John Ford, albeit by means of the backdrop of Utah and Arizona's Monument Valley rather than the Sierra Nevada.

The opera's characters enter as if in a never-never land: when they arrive, they bring history with them; when they leave, history exits as well. What remains is a natural paradise, yet it is a paradise only so long as it is unpeopled: when it is only imagined or remembered. Puccini marks the phenomenological spatial excess that defines everything important about the opera by means of what I call the fade-in and fade-out. Repeatedly, his characters are heard well before they are seen on stage, and the voices are invariably on the move, as though making their way through the deep forest. Indeed, the opera's first voices come from offstage, what Puccini describes as *voci lontane*, distant voices, and to achieve this effect he sometimes altered what Belasco called for in the play and what he described in his novel. Thus, at the opera's start, and at a distance, the miners returning to camp late at night boisterously greet one another with hellos, and then one of them quotes a tuneful lament, also about distance—and loss: "*Là lontano, là lontan, quanto piangera!* . . ." (roughly: "Back home, far away, she'll cry for me"). This same trope is soon thereafter repeated, and amplified, in one of the opera's few real arias, *"Che faranno i vecchi miei."*[67] Choosing an aria form, one whose character is strikingly simple and folk-like, in an opera that otherwise virtually abandons conventional arias, marks a past, a history—here musical—that the opera itself musically supersedes. The aria is the most strikingly old-fashioned music in the entire opera, a nostalgic sonic look-back. It is sung, *andante tranquillo*, by the camp minstrel, one Jake Wallace, a character based on a camp singer whom Belasco knew from his youth in California.[68] In the play, Jake Wallace is inside the Polka saloon when he sings his song.[69] In the opera, by contrast, Jake starts the song as he approaches slowly from offstage. He is physically distant from the homely saloon, and what he sings immediately marks *lontano*, in a slow-moving and sorrowful lament about faraway home, sad parents, and a faithful dog that might no longer recognize him. Before long, the rest of the men echo the lament in chorus, the previous hard-edged boisterousness turned soft (act 1, rehearsal nos. 20–22). The loss, that is, is general just as the distance is overwhelming, to the point that one of the miners, young Larkens, breaks down crying. The song's sentiment, its *lontano*, its distance, marks a general condition. What begins the opera, as it turns out, is precisely what ends it as well.[70]

Turning in Circles

By the opera's end, Minnie is a woman, no longer the child of nature who in act 2 tells Dick about her innocent life in the mountains, galloping her pony among the flowers—flora that in fact do not grow in the Sierra Nevada (Belasco gets the plants right; Puccini's librettist cluelessly substitutes jonquils and carnations, and for good measure adds jasmine and vanilla).[71] Minnie's morph, however, begins much earlier. In the first act, she and Dick come together physically for the first time in a dance, a ritual metaphor of love and lovemaking, in essence establishing a bond that will make a new home, later, if temporarily, staged in the second act, when the relationship is sealed with a fateful kiss, one duly and dramatically marked in the orchestra and by Minnie's high-C reaction (Example 6.3).

In the play, Minnie declines a waltz, saying she does not know how. Instead, she polkas, or as she puts it, "polkys."[72] William Furst, Belasco's composer, initiates a waltz tune at the first mention of that dance, only to break it off for the livelier and rather less romantic polka. Puccini dispenses altogether with the polka, writes a waltz, and alters the story further

EXAMPLE 6.3. Puccini, *Girl of the Golden West*, act 2, "Un bacio, un bacio almen!" mm. 1–10.

by having the Girl apologize that she has never once previously danced at all. She is nonetheless game and, to the accompaniment of the men singing along softly and clapping the rhythm, the pair comes together. The tune as first sounded, to which Minnie and Dick dance, is folksy and disarmingly simple—to a fault. As the miners chime along, even lightly tapping their feet as they sing and clap, the orchestra softly evokes the rhythms associated with the gliding and whirling movements common to the dance. Dick and Minnie literally turn in circles, the uncertain outcome of their "progress" thus duly marked, even though they cannot take their eyes off each other.

The waltz marks a future and potential. The tune's simplicity, like the budding relationship between the man and the woman, can become much more than it currently is, and the tune can be the acoustic vehicle for both producing and reflecting the change. The cultural associations between love and the waltz are soon thereafter exploited, as soon as the lovers-to-be are alone for the first time near the end of the act. Here the melody immediately gains the character necessary for advancing the relationship. It is first heard in the orchestra, with a sweet edge provided by seconds in quarter-note suspension. The waltz has become lovely and, in a word, poignant (Example 6.4, mm. 5–6). Soon thereafter, in a one-minute arietta, Dick sings the entire melody to Minnie, with a text that speaks of dancing, hearts, trembling, and strange joy. Taking the lead in the ritual dance of love, he acknowledges the thrill of sensing her heartbeats when they embraced. The tune, first heard in F major for the dancing, migrates to A major for the second iteration and finally to G♭ as the arietta. (Exam-

EXAMPLE 6.4. Puccini, *Girl of the Golden West*, act 1, waltz (second iteration), mm. 1–6.

ple 6.5). In Belasco's play, at the moment when the Girl sets eyes on Dick, her first utterance is an inarticulate "H'mp!" followed quickly by a single word: "Utopia!"[73] Puccini's waltz accomplishes the same effect, but rather more gradually.

Ambiguity

Distance is evoked throughout the opera, to its very conclusion. Thus, near the opera's end, Minnie rides into the scene astride a horse. Coming hurriedly from offstage, again vocally suggesting distance as well as time urgency, she is accompanied in the orchestra by a repeated staccato rhythm meant to resonate with the sounds of a galloping horse.[74] Her voice is audible well before she herself is visible; her voice dramatically excites the miners (act 3, rehearsal no. 29, m. 1, to rehearsal no. 31, m. 8). Sheriff Rance, sensing an impending rescue, repeatedly demands that Johnson be hanged immediately.

EXAMPLE 6.5. Puccini, *Girl of the Golden West*, act 1, waltz melody as arietta, "Quello che tacete me," mm. 1–6.

The rescue comes, of course, and that triggers a final *lontano*, but in this last instance, what has been near now becomes far; accordingly, sound little by little fades away to nothing. In other words, the opera is book-ended by two forms of distance and distanc*ing*. At the start, action and history, so to speak, come onstage for us to experience; sounds get louder, becoming increasingly audible. At the end, distance increases, and action ceases into a staged stasis once the lovers depart, their voices trailing off into the haze of history.

In each of the three acts, offstage voices reach our consciousness as if from nowhere, from great distances, slowly—ever so slowly—approaching the acoustic proscenium separating opera from audience. In one sense, the obvious one, they approach camp from working their staked claims, but in another sense, they approach as if being recalled from a faded memory of a time long past—spatial and temporal nostalgia in the heart of bustling 1910 Midtown, the epicenter of industrialized modernity in its prewar self-satisfied self-confidence. The gap between the New York setting of the world premiere and the scene onstage, in the first really major opera about America, carries a significant ideological burden.[75] The vastness of the opera's natural setting holds out the promise of an American paradise: eternal, without boundaries, a utopia of striking visual splendor—and this despite the fact that the old-growth forests of the Sierra Nevada had already long since been savaged. In other words, Puccini's West of the imagination, aesthetically speaking, provides modernity's rapaciousness with the deniability it ethically craved.[76]

The arrivals of the voices from the wilderness and from the past make their appearances, speak their peace—and then vocally fade away. Puccini's repeated use of motifs from "Echoes of Home" more or less constitutes the opera's defining leitmotif, the citation marking a perfect coincidence of time, space, and place, on the one hand, and memory in relation to loss, separation, and alienation, on the other.[77]

The third act of play is set in the dance hall attached to the Polka saloon. Puccini set his final act in a forested wilderness. (Roughly speaking, Puccini collapsed Belasco's third and fourth acts, eliminating much of the third.) But in this instance nature matters so much that an overdetermined invocation is essential (Figure 6.14). As Puccini put it to Giulio Ricordi, "I have a grand scenario in mind, a clearing in the great Californian forest, with colossal trees."[78]

The opera's ending, a departure, is, perforce, "happy." The scene opens at dawn and the sunrise, thus reversing the sunset with which the opera opened.[79] We hear Minnie well before we see her riding in, vocaliz-

FIGURE 6.14. Giacomo Puccini, *La fanciulla del West*, New York, Metropolitan Opera House (1910), act 3 finale. (Photo: The Metropolitan Opera Archives.)

ing her desperation and fury, Valkerie-like, in essence so as to ride off forever with her lover—as every operagoer knows all too well, Puccini conventionally killed off his sopranos, whereas no one actually dies in *La fanciulla del West*, which is odd for a Western. Sonora hands off Dick to Minnie, and, fittingly, to fragmentary strains in the orchestra from the act 1 waltz music (act 3, rehearsal no. 44, mm. 1–5). The lover's astride their horses slowly depart, their voices only very gradually fading as the dawn breaks. In short, the lovers move forward into time and history—but not so much with a sense of new beginnings. The audience is left less with a climax and more with the dynamic decay and inevitable disappearance of music itself. With the music's fading, as the miners lament Minnie's loss via a fragment of tune from Jake Wallace's act 1 "Old Dog Tray," the opera's own time fades into the timelessness of the vast forest that swallows up the departed lovers as they themselves head off into uncertainty, and in duet:

> Addio, mia dolce terra!
> Addio, mia California!
> Bei monti della Sierra, nevi, addio!

The distinctive and often dissonant rhythmic percussiveness that marks much of the opera, and which delineates the real time experienced by the characters—modernity's freneticism or something like that—fades into a virtually rhythmless drone in the orchestra's strings, as the lovers' voices trail off above this line. They fade, like time and like memory; next to nature they are nothing. Nonetheless, as they voice their goodbyes to their beloved California, what is striking is less the happy reuniting of the young lovers—that fact seems rather an afterthought—and far more the sense that their mutual terrestrial salvation comes with a bill attached: their expulsion from a natural paradise that they had experienced in a perpetual state of paradox if not dialectical contradiction.[80] All that is left are the aged trees, timeless like the mountains.[81]

The grand allegory Puccini alleges represents the civilizing process, which is notably akin to what some years later Horkheimer and Adorno articulated as the defining moment of Western consciousness of what it was to be human. To be human—that is, to be civilized—they suggested had been worked out at considerable cost. As they put it,

> At the moment when human beings cut themselves off from the consciousness of themselves as nature, all the purposes for which they keep themselves alive—social progress, the heightening of material and intellectual forces, indeed, consciousness itself—become void, and the enthronement of the means as the end, which in late capitalism is taking on the character of overt madness, is already detectable in the earliest history of subjectivity. The human being's mastery of itself, on which the self is founded, practically always involves the annihilation of the subject in whose service that mastery is maintained.[82]

Puccini's opera and, for that matter, Belasco's play acknowledge the reality that the civilizing process is not a guarantee of progress. Puccini's Sierra Nevada itself reflects a wish rather than a reality. The forests of his imagination have not already been clear-cut, as was in fact the case; the landscape has not been mined for all it could give up in favor of the closing of the frontier. In one sense, of course, both Puccini and Belasco acknowledge this reality, if indirectly. They make their characters leave the promised land, thereby preserving the dialectic: Nature-Culture, barbaric-civilized, binaries whose collapse can be thought but cannot, so it seems, be realized in modernity.

CHAPTER 7

A Farewell, a Femme Fatale, and a Film

THREE AWKWARD MOMENTS
IN TWENTIETH-CENTURY MUSIC

Peter Franklin

Having chosen to write about three of my favorite musical works—all of them lacking canonic authority, but all, I believe, rich in meaning and human value—I find myself up against the problematic mismatch between personal taste and History. Taking another look, recently, at the prologue to Lawrence Kramer's *Opera and Modern Culture*, I was led to wonder if I were not simply slipping into the role of Don Giovanni in Kramer's allegorical reading of that operatic antihero: defying a form of institutionalized Authority in search of ferocious reserves of musical subjectivity that no authority can touch, only to find myself investing these objects with the "implausible significance" of which Kramer speaks.[1] Was I, like Opera in his account, trying "to retrieve the transcendental value of the abnorm in proximity to the norm . . . without a remainder"?[2] The pieces I want to speak about are in a sense all remainders, residues. They are "beyond the regime of the norm" and only arguably closer to what Kramer calls "best examples."[3] All three of the works I discuss inspire complex questions about their multimediated status as "works" at all. The authoritative narrative of musical modernism has thus tended to flow over and around them. I will nevertheless proceed, accepting that I may prove less of a Don Giovanni than a sort of musicological Don Quixote.

Part of the trouble is that we musicologists have always "done" musical Modernism so well—and I refer to the narrower, style-historical meaning of that term. We have always relied on those knowing smiles of complicit superiority when we rehearse mutually comforting stories about the scandals and misunderstandings that attended performances of Modernism's canonic masterpieces. There was *Le Sacre du Printemps*, of course, and those items programmed by Schoenberg in his Vienna "*Skandalkonzert*" of 1913. Yes, as we embroider the tale, people then really *did* hit each other on the nose and call each other names. As if *we* would do such things: we, the unshockable allies of The New, the advanced who can take anything in our stride. Yet in the name of mutually reinforcing open-mindedness we nevertheless persist in closing ourselves vehemently off from other manifestations of "twentieth-century music" that still inspire scorn, unease, or even outrage for reasons that are of more than merely historiographical interest.

My examples here are an embarrassing symphony, an even more embarrassing (and probably justly "forgotten") opera, and a simply *shocking* arrangement of Wagner ("My *dear*," the connoisseur exclaims, "you simply cannot *imagine*!"). The mitigation of the horror of it all by a little parodic camping up of our affection for varieties of old kitsch is probably appropriate to my list of dramatis personae: at least two undone men and one undone woman, balanced by two femmes fatales and an homme fatale.

Some of these characters were victims or creations of the tawdry and increasingly popular imaginative realm in which they mostly fade and die—albeit to music of extraordinary beauty that appears either to have lost faith with or lost comprehension of what Julian Johnson has boldly reaffirmed as "the higher spiritual and intellectual function of art."[4] Two of my examples must be located retrospectively in historical corners of the popular Other, where the conventional binaries of the discourse of European high art have always raised ghosts and monsters of gender trouble from the multimediated "impurity" of popular aestheticism hostile to "art." Forget the "difficult listening hour"; we are heading for murky and rather mucky territory. But it is a richly populated territory, and no less rich, perhaps, in what Susan McClary (in her essay "Terminal Prestige") calls intelligence of a kind that inhabits and is provoked by the music I shall speak of: an intelligence "that accepts the experience of the body—dance, sexuality, feelings of depression and elation—as integral parts of human knowledge that accrue value precisely as they are shared and confirmed publicly."[5]

The awkwardness of my awkward moments, then, is conditioned by a knowledge about art that might threaten our very belief in art, even as it affirms our fatal attraction. The situation is close to the one that Nietzsche observed, both in himself and in German culture, as a consequence of the "hypnotic tricks" of Wagnerism.[6] The first of these moments takes me back to Mahler, more specifically to late Mahler. Franz Schreker follows in the second moment, to be followed in the third by that shockingly "bad" Wagner—or his Hollywood double.

The Mahler story takes little telling. The official narrative of musical Modernism finds pared-down chamberlike sonorities and a renunciation of romantic-metaphysical epiphanies in Mahler's later works, which may have anticipated or inspired the Expressionism with which Schoenberg supposedly shocked the Viennese bourgeoisie (most of whom never heard it) in or around 1909. Here is Mahler the historiographical Transitional Phenomenon.

I have all but given up on a quest to draw attention to the peculiarities of Schoenberg's own never less than generously ambivalent attitude toward Mahler, particularly as expressed in the long essay, originating in 1912, which became the second item in *Style and Idea* in 1951.[7] The text is a web of barely concealed put-downs and bombastically convoluted encomiums. Schoenberg's own reliance on the tropes of romantic-metaphysical idealism is most marked when he touches on the Tenth Symphony. Having briefly described the "most strange" Ninth and its "objective, almost passionless statements of a beauty which becomes perceptible only to one who can dispense with animal warmth and feels at home in spiritual coolness,"[8] he addresses its successor as follows:

> We shall know as little about what his Tenth . . . would have said as we know about Beethoven's or Bruckner's. It seems that the Ninth was a limit. He who wants to go beyond it must pass away. It seems as if something might be imparted to us in the Tenth which we ought not yet to know, for which we are not yet ready. Those who have written a Ninth stand too near to the hereafter. Perhaps the riddles of this world would be solved, if one of those who knew them were to write a Tenth. And that is probably not to take place.
>
> We are still to remain in a darkness which will be illuminated only fitfully by the light of genius.[9]

And people mock *Wagner's* prose! Behind this metaphysical and theoretical smokescreen lay a work that Schoenberg and his circle would probably have seen all too much of between the wars. The score of the Tenth was actually displayed in a glass case in Alma Mahler's apartment in Vienna, open at a page bearing some of the notorious annotations in which Mahler addressed her by name[10]—annotations that have consistently inspired more embarrassment than postrevelatory awe and that were (and remain) airbrushed out of the translated (and expurgated) versions of Alma's *Memories and Letters of Gustav Mahler*.[11] Nor were the annotations reproduced in the otherwise fine Faber score of Deryck Cooke's painstaking decipherment and orchestration of the manuscript material, which even includes transcribed sketches of the sections where Mahler failed to complete his own full score.[12] Only in the extraordinary 1924 facsimile that Alma herself published are we offered the full, multimediated text.[13] This facsimile faithfully reproduced, on loose bifolia, the colors of Mahler's blue crayon, the blots and the crossings out, and the striking and often painful-to-read annotations, such as those on the last page of the last movement: "To live for you! To die for you! Almschi!" (*Für dich sterben! Für dich leben! Almschi!*).

Schoenberg the modernist foretold unearthly mysteries in Mahler's Tenth; the reality must have been not a little embarrassing for the supersensual superhero and swimmer in boiling oceans in search of cool pleasures.[14] At the moment just referred to, Mahler's score—both as inscribed text and in performance—speaks of earthly pain at the *loss* of sensuality. What we encounter here is something approaching an unscripted diegetic cry from within a musical texture "working itself out," as we say, toward a "logical" major cadence that—whatever its logic or lack thereof—signifies a kind of death of the spirit as much as the spirit's redemption.

But that cry was not exactly unscripted. It was born of a key motivic element of the Finale's introduction (first heard in the middle of the earlier "Purgatorio" movement and annotated with an exclamatory "*Erbarmen!*"—Have mercy!). When Mahler changed his mind about the key in which he wanted the Finale to end, he wrote out the closing pages in transposition, apparently with the inscribed annotations in exactly the same places. This is music that is undoing itself as "art"—as the fabricator of grandiose illusions and visionary reconciliations—even as it goes through the comforting motions of formalized artistic rhetoric. It seems to transcribe and perform the double discourse of protestation and self-consolation that may speak of a broken spirit: perhaps that of the man whom Alma would find weeping on the floor of his composing hut and on the landing outside her bedroom door.

What Schoenberg energetically shrouds in his prose, Alma would reveal to all comers in that paradoxical display case: a work that seemed to "see through"[15] the symphony as viable public theater in sound and to reclaim it for the privacy of a subjective meditation, or even a personal communication about the impossibility (as Adorno might have put it) of the very thing that it is. This was not emotion recollected in tranquility so much as emotion performed in extremis. Here Mahler seems to renounce Beethoven-Hero status and almost to court one of the key tropes of anti-Semitic criticism of his music: that it was gesturally overdemonstrative and thus out of control. Not only that: the music's evidently desperate eloquence is not, in a traditional sense, resolved or fully "finished." Higher, "difficult" modernists such as Pierre Boulez still refuse to perform realizations of this music that make audible what we can nevertheless hear by eye—not the "mind's eye" but, if one might so put it, the body's eye, as it slowly dances with the music into oblivion.

My language has perhaps rather too deliberately echoed that of Thomas Mann's *Dr. Faustus* in its invocation of self-destructive doubleness. Yet I do not necessarily seek to endorse the kind of parodistically inclined unmasking by which Adrian Leverkühn debunks Wagner's rhetorical trickery in the supposedly sublime Prelude to act 3 of *Die Meistersinger*.[16] I am more interested in Mahler's refusal to offer Music a way out of the impasse of realizing that it could not do what the Romantics thought it could and what Mahler himself sometimes hoped it could: the impasse, that is, of realizing that it cannot *really* reveal or transcend or resolve anything.

Perfecting some of the most persuasive ways of *appearing* to do such things, while advertising their status precisely *as* appearance, Mahler produced music that is as widely consumed as any comparable product of the European fin de siècle. Out of it Modernism was born, as we were always told in those stories that granted Mahler's music at best a maternal role, "transitional" to the Difficult Listening Hour where all music had been heading all along. That this music is so readily comprehended and consumed by untrained listeners who lack musical "literacy" raises awkward questions indeed. Those questions lead me to my second awkward moment: another Viennese moment whose awkwardness, and even "awfulness" to some people, had not a little to do with its dramatization of turbidly erotic musings about music's doubleness, linked even more specifically than Mahler's to gender and sexuality.

The second awkward moment involves Franz Schreker's opera *Das Spielwerk und die Prinzessin*, dedicated to Alma Mahler and first produced in Vienna and Frankfurt in 1913. That was the year of Schoenberg's *Skandal-*

konzert in the Musikvereinsaal, the year Webern had released the pithy expletive "Bagage!" (rabble/scum) at the Viennese philistines who were always on hand, like film extras, to be shocked by the difficult, *progressive* Good and True.[17] Schreker was an associate of Schoenberg and the nascent Second Viennese School, but his supposed naiveté, vulgarity, and (damn it) popularity got up the noses of more elegant aesthetes such as Berg and others of Schoenberg's circle. But they need not have worried. *Das Spielwerk*, following in the wake of the widespread success of Schreker's *Der ferne Klang* in 1912, seems to have shocked not only the bourgeoisie but also the journalistic establishment. Critics either damned it for its arid and intellectualized modernity or implicitly scorned it for its unmanly indulgence in, precisely, "Klang": in sonority, timbre, musical theater tricks, and decadent eroticism.[18] (Szymanowski, like other younger romantic modernists, nevertheless loved it and went to all five performances.)[19]

Das Spielwerk und die Prinzessin is a sort of allegorical Märchenspiel, set "near a medieval town." It went a sizeable step beyond *Der ferne Klang*'s morality tale of a male artist whose idealistic delusions bring about the descent into prostitution of his abandoned girlfriend, Grethe, the opera's multiply "undone" heroine (she survives to be reconciled with the repentant Fritz, only to have him die in her arms, having realized that the source and essence of his longed-for "distant sound" was in Grethe herself). This was heady stuff, but Schreker's next opera was to be a Grand Guignol monument to a version of the self-contradictory aesthetic doubleness that lay at the heart of Mahler's Tenth Symphony.

Das Spielwerk und die Prinzessin was, characteristically for Schreker, inspired by a fleeting fancy. He was struck by a newspaper article about a famous Spanish violinist who had returned to his hometown to be greeted by a nocturnal gathering of its inhabitants, who had come bearing torches.[20] What, he then seems to have mused, if they had actually brought those torches to burn down the musician's ancestral home, to silence him and his art? What might have been the reason for this bizarrely projected hostility?

The opera, with Schreker's own libretto and epigraph from Nietzsche's *Also sprach Zarathustra*,[21] provides its answer in part by turning the musician into two related characters. The first is Meister Florian, an old inventor who has created an extraordinary and complex musical machine—the "Spielwerk"—whose delicate membranes and myriad components vibrate in sympathy with human love and longing. But Florian's mysterious assistant, Wolf, has added other components that both respond to and arouse baser, more destructive urges. As if giving voice to the Schopenhauerian

"Will" that pulsates and "vibrates" (as Schreker's original foreword put it) within both Nature and the human heart, the Spielwerk, once aroused to and even *by* music, is both Apollonian and Dionysian. Its sounds can inspire the round-dance of loving social cohesion *and* the destructive Dionysian orgies that are favored by the demonic Princess—as fatale a femme as ever the fin de siècle created.

Two young men complete the weird cast of main characters, along with Old Liese, Meister Florian's former wife and the mother of his son (the second, and openly Oedipal, avatar of the Spanish violinist). The son's wasted and ailing form is the pretext for the preludial tableau in the opera's first version, in which four shadowy figures prepare a stretcher for him. He is a violinist who has been able to "awaken" both the Spielwerk and the Princess, thus drawing out the erotic implications of musical stimulation. The Princess's infatuation with him is also an infatuation with the music they quite literally had made together via the Spielwerk, which "lit up" the entire town and seduced the populace into joining the Princess's self-destructive festivities.

Drained of his Will, along with what Brigadier General Ripper in *Dr. Strangelove* would have called his "precious bodily fluids," by the Princess, Meister Florian's son is dying. The Princess is left in disconsolate frustration until another good-looking young man appears on the scene, a sort of flute-playing Siegfried whose naive aim is to redeem the Princess and bring her "down to earth" by playing a different kind of music, simpler and more harmonious, to heal both her depraved soul and the town's body politic. But his ability to restart the Spielwerk means that he also restarts its "darker" side. The climax finds him intervening in the apocalyptic orgy that the Princess has devised and at the climax of which she plans to have herself immolated along with the Spielwerk. In a sense, the lad succeeds, but not before the Spielwerk has indeed been burnt, along with Meister Florian's cottage, where it resides. In it, his ostensibly dead son has risen up to add a ghostly violin obbligato to the wondrous polyphony of Music's end.

The opera's first version left the townsfolk muttering a prayer for forgiveness beneath the smoke from the fire, the Princess and her new "redeeming" lover having disappeared into the castle on the hill. In the revised one-act version of 1920,[22] the Spielwerk is spared so that we can dwell longer on Florian's cottage, which in both versions becomes translucent. In the cottage, we see Old Liese stilling the ghostly, postmortem musical ecstasy of her son, which is now given substance by an extraordinary solo violin line. Liese's solution is to sing a kind of lullaby in which she brings her son's soul to rest, silencing at last both his violin and the Spielwerk.

The two versions (or three if we count the composer's own edited performance in a 1932 recording)[23] speak to each other in fascinating ways. In the first version, an extended orchestral interlude presages the ecstatic love-duet of the boy and the Princess, an example of the kind of highly sexual post-Wagnerian *Liebesszene* for which Schreker became notorious (and which now curses Schreker sopranos with the unerotic directorial requirement to suddenly heave down their knickers at or near one of the multiple climaxes). In the 1920 revision, as represented by the edited version that Schreker recorded, the lovers' duet has been joined by a chorus of enthralled townsfolk who have been seduced by the transfiguring fantasy of "phosphorescent mists" and the "thousand distant lights of eternal kingdoms." The townsfolk are spared the darker turn taken by the duet's first version at its conclusion, where the lovers had sung, "Heiah, we journey / into blessed expanses! / Heiah, we wander / into the sunset! / But then comes the morning's / chill awakening, / ah—then we are / already long dead."[24] In place of this dark climax, Schreker gives us the wonderful threnody of the dead son's fiddle as a prelude to the lullaby sung by his mother. The old "fallen woman" (she had left Florian for Wolf, his dark assistant) has taken center stage, we recall, to bring the opera to a post-Oedipal close, like some aging avatar of Brünnhilde. "Calm yourself, old man, I'll put him to rest," she says to Florian, who has become deranged by the spectral fiddling of his dead son, giving the lie to any fantasy of redemption in what he now sees as a dance of death. Liese's lullaby begins "sleep my child, ah, rest in peace" and ends,

> The Spielwerk's sound shivers into silence:
> The primeval song of Death and Birth,—
> A gentle transfiguration of agonizing instinct,—
> The Song of Love.[25]

However we read this ending, this is an essay in post-Wagnerian self-indulgence that seems to come with its own health warning and notes from Dr. Freud. It might almost have been a work imagined *by* Thomas Mann in *Faustus*-mode, except that his high-bourgeois taste did not grant him easy access to the works of romantic modernism that seemed most to draw on and in turn cater to the popular imagination. For related phenomena one might think of Rachmaninoff, of Puccini, or of Erich Wolfgang Korngold, not to mention other works by Schreker himself, at least up to the mid-1920s. At that point popular opera was being eclipsed by operetta revivals and the musical, or supplanted by the new, more genuinely "mass" art form of film. The climax of *Das Spielwerk und die Prinzessin* is awkward not least because both its style and its idea were about to be appropriated by the movies.

Appropriately, we cross the Atlantic to Hollywood for the last of my awkward moments in twentieth-century music, albeit with ears usefully acclimatized to the period grain of the dead boy's violin in Schreker's recording of his protocinematic score for *Das Spielwerk*. No less appropriately, perhaps, European authorial identity, even of the compromised and self-compromising masculine kind that we have encountered in Mahler and the self-indulgent Schreker, blur and multiply in the work I want to consider. My title describes it as a film, but in reality the "work" in question is a troubling cover version (as we might say) of the grandest of all nineteenth-century love-deaths: an operatic fantasy by Franz Waxman derived from Wagner's *Tristan* but recast, perhaps revealed, as a concerto—a classical power-piece for a male virtuoso and his pianist friend: a double concerto for two men.

Readers who know their '40s movies will realize that I am speaking of Jean Negulesco's 1946 *Humoresque*, based on a story by the fascinating woman writer Fanny Hurst. It has not surprisingly interested feminist commentators on film such as Mary Ann Doane,[26] but it merits cherishing no less by New Musicologists with subversive suspicions about twentieth-century Modernism and the modernist reliance on romantically idealistic constructions of Classical Music. The attendant gender trouble and, indeed, sexual violence have been linked by Lawrence Kramer to the fundamental "pathology of modern subjectivity."[27] *Humoresque* (a case study if ever there was one) merits a whole chapter in some unwritten history of mid-twentieth-century music.

Whereas Mahler became embarrassing and Schreker was mocked both by the Nazis as a composer of "sexual pathology" and by devotees of the Second Viennese School as a purveyor of kitsch and adolescent musicosexual reveries,[28] Waxman's *Tristan and Isolde Fantasy* was recently denounced to me by a prominent British composer as *"utterly* dreadful." This music is remarkable not least for being situated in a multiauthored cinematic production that proves to be a shockingly direct and apposite critique of its operatic model, whose emblematic historiographical role as the initiator of the European musical-modernist project I have already referred to. It is as if Hurst or Waxman or Negulesco or Joan Crawford (or all of them) had somehow come across spectral advance copies of more recent work by our own McClary, Leppert, or Kramer.

For readers unfamiliar with the film: Negulesco's MGM melodrama involves Joan Crawford in the leading role of Helen Wright, a wealthy metropolitan socialite and self-willed femme fatale. Helen collects adoring and occasionally talented young men like so many trophies after eyeing them through the emblematic spectacles that claim for her a perversely empowering gaze.[29] Piercing the cigarette smoke that always shrouds her, her gaze seems to emphasize the threatening masculinity of her character and role. But this excess also marks her decadence and "unnatural" way-wardness, which signal her required downfall as the film's narrative un-folds.

That narrative has, in fact, been running for some time before Wright even appears. It has been telling the rags-to-riches story of an overdeter-minedly masculine violinist, played by John Garfield like a street-wise boxer or gangster (early in the film a partygoer tells him he looks like a prizefighter). This character seems to have taken on board (in another time warp) Mary Ann Doane's ideas about the demasculinizing effect of love stories and of Art. At least he seems forearmed against "contamina-tion" by the former and energetically counters the "femininity" of the latter by resolutely refusing lyrical excess in any area of his private or pro-fessional life other than playing the violin.[30] In this refusal he is assisted by his friend and mentor, the pianist Sid Jeffers, played by Oscar Levant as the satirical, ironic Fool of the piece who verbally subverts what his virtuo-sic piano playing relentlessly asserts (along with his sexually ambiguous air as the unattached insider-outsider who tells Garfield to attend Helen Wright's party with his hair mussed—"you look pretty that way").[31]

The virtuosity of both men earns the respect that, according to Doane, music can attract as a culturally sanctioned feminized activity. Yet Garfield, as Paul Boray, emphasizes even more than Levant does the athletic and artisanal aspect of performative virtuosity. He specializes in bravura show-stoppers and concert arrangements of popular classics and opera that seem designed to dazzle in the old Lisztian, nineteenth-century manner. What is more, the implication that he is appropriating an often more specifically feminized construction of performance is consistently, if negatively, stressed by the extent to which the Joan Crawford character is denied any practical musical ability, any musical "voice." She only listens, and looks—and listens while looking (see Figures 7.1 and 7.2).

It is the emphatic nature of that denial of musicality that paradoxically renders both Crawford's role and her performance as an actress so threat-

FIGURE 7.1. *Humoresque* (1946). Helen Wright approaches Paul Boray as she hears him play for the first time.

ening to the patriarchal construction of high-culture classical music as a romantic mission and idealized vocation. And it is this threat that will bring us back to Wagner and the supreme romantic music drama that is the instrument of Crawford's final downfall. She approaches this end via an inexorable transformation: from masculinized Maecenas to overdeterminedly feminized woman-in-love—*hopelessly* in love, of course, since Garfield is too committed to his career and his "art" to allow himself anything more than sex without romantic "commitment." Such commitment would have entailed his contamination by the very love stories that it is his purpose to resist, even as his art may inspire them.

I have pointed out that Paul Boray's "art" is primarily affiliated with the virtuoso tradition and with nineteenth-century performance on both the concert platform and the operatic stage. The diegetic concert performances that punctuate and structure the film remain mostly distinct from its relatively limited original underscore, which is conventionally associated with subjective experience, typically with Helen's. It is, however, the film's two operatic fantasies that thematize the issue of performativity, not simply as masculine display but more curiously as an appropriation of female performances and female voices. This appropriation points to the deeper symptomatology of Paul Boray's complex and disturbed psychol-

FIGURE 7.2. *Humoresque* (1946). Paul Boray plays the Lalo *Symphony Espagnole* [*sic*].

ogy, behind which lurks a terrifyingly powerful Freudian mother (played magnificently by Ruth Nelson).

Paul's ethnic affinity with gypsy violin playing (we assume the family is Hungarian in origin) seems naturally to express itself in a penchant for Iberian-flavored concert items. The first big public performance after the emerging crisis in Paul's now explicitly sexual affair with Helen Wright is significant. She has started to break cocktail glasses and become given to compromisingly refeminizing lines about herself, such as "What good is a woman if she's of no *use* to anyone?" By the point when she agrees to love Paul "without the grand opera," Helen finds herself in a contest for who can muster the most intense and expressively significant gaze at him. During a concert in which Paul is the soloist in Lalo's *Symphony Espagnole* [*sic*], Helen, her face partly in shadow, passionately watches her lover from a box, while from the seats below Paul's former girlfriend Gina, his admiring father, and his ever-watchful mother all register their attention in different ways. Gina proves unequal to the strain and rushes out in tears before the end, as if admitting defeat by Helen (see Figures 7.3–7.5).

Still more significant, however, is the rehearsal for a concerto-like fantasia on themes from Bizet's *Carmen*, at which Helen is the sole spectator. On this occasion her sense of exclusion from "his" world of music—he rebuffs her attempt to contact him through a message delivered by a stage-

FIGURE 7.3. *Humoresque* (1946). Helen, listening to the Lalo performance.

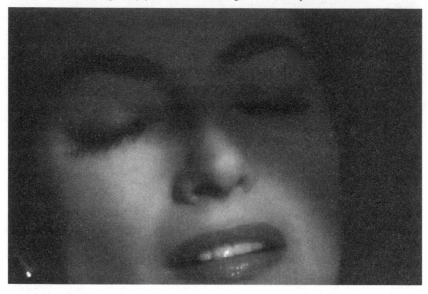

FIGURE 7.4. *Humoresque* (1946). Gina watches Helen listening to the Lalo performance.

hand—is emphasized by the fact that the central part of the scene is dominated by his appropriation of Carmen's notoriously seductive "Habañera."[32] The episode, like the film overall, is ripe for a "queer" reading. This movie had started by pitting an attractive male violinist against a discursively masculinized woman patron. Now, as the woman heads for her discursive punishment, she is confounded by that same male violinist, who specializes in appropriating the voices of doomed operatic heroines with whom *she* should be empathizing. But this episode is still only a foretaste. It is Paul's final and most outrageous appropriation of a woman's operatic voice that seals Helen's fate while also revealing, to the gaze, all the psychological and sociocultural implications of the Great Work he plays.

Presented as Paul Boray's "own" arrangement, the *Tristan* fantasy is outrageous on more than one level. As a condensation of the opera into a single musical movement, it follows the Lisztian model of the operatic fantasia. But by turning the fantasia into a kind of double concerto for violin *and* piano (played by Sid Jeffers), Negulesco and/or Franz Waxman emphasized the homosocial (if not homosexual) relationship of the foregrounded performers. The fantasy also appears to be offered to us as "pure music," something representing the overarching spiritual Good that Paul's mother had long ago implicitly invoked when she had sternly not

FIGURE 7.5. *Humoresque* (1946). Paul's mother, listening to the Lalo performance.

his artistic "work" *against* the temptation of sexual pleasure with Helen, the "married woman" (and a failed married woman at that, as Mrs. Boray resonantly impressed on Helen when the latter came to the family shop to talk to her).

On the day of the concert Mrs. Boray arrives ostentatiously late in the box for the *Tristan* fantasy. She has now reached and herself appropriated the "power" location that was once Helen's. She glows with a motherly pride that luxuriates in the normative sociocultural meaning of the great music she now hears being performed by her hero-son. Far away, Helen herself is hearing another music altogether—in 'a manner arguably much closer to the nineteenth-century musical "mother tongue" of Wagnerian intoxication. To hear what she hears, we need a retrospective detour.

Friedrich Nietzsche, in *The Birth of Tragedy* (1872), had imagined the verbal and theatrical elements in the third act of *Tristan und Isolde* as little more than a defense against being overcome by a nontheatrical, "purely musical" performance. Summoning up "those who, immediately related to music, have in it, as it were, their motherly womb, and are related to things almost exclusively through unconscious musical relations,"[33] he puts his conjecture as a rhetorical question: "To these genuine musicians I direct the question whether they can imagine a human being who would be able to perceive the third act . . . without any aid of word or image, purely as a tremendous symphonic movement, without expiring in a spasmodic unharnessing of all the wings of the soul?"[34] Carolyn Abbate has found Nietzsche here to be making "large claims for music": "Music is granted security of meaning, transcendent force, even a pre-lapsarian virtue."[35] The claims are certainly large, but they are not, I argue, of the idealist or idealized kind that Abbate seems to imagine. They certainly have nothing to do with "pre-lapsarian virtue." By decontextualizing Nietzsche's statement about the music of *Tristan*, and by failing to address just what that "spasmodic unharnessing" is all about, Abbate misrepresents what Nietzsche is actually saying, not least the unhistorical and uncritical assumption she makes about that phrase "tremendous symphonic movement."

A good deal of subversive wisdom, along with the seeds of Nietzsche's later polemical rejection of Wagner, had been packed into that phrase. Nietzsche was offering a negative evaluation of what (for him) was the dangerously Dionysian and feminized character of Wagner's albeit incomparable music, as opposed to something inspiring "the simplest political feelings" and a "manly desire to fight." To fight what? Presumably the implicitly feminine inclination to those "orgies" of so-called Dionysian liberation? And that, as Nietzsche well knew from personal experience, was what the ungrounded, untexted "symphonic" music could do if one shut one's eyes and gave oneself up to *Tristan*'s act 3 without the redeeming catharsis of its tragic text and stage performance. The language of revelatory romantic ecstasy portrays the "unharnessing" of the wings of the soul as a spasmodic, and by implication involuntary, flight from individuation into some orgiastic expiration deeply threatening to the very politics of nation and patriotism that Nietzsche later, appropriately enough, accused Wagner of espousing in a perverted manner.

Much could be said about the importance of this section of *The Birth of Tragedy* for an understanding not only of Nietzsche's subsequent disaffection from Wagner but also of the inner dialectic that possibly drove Wagner's own struggle with Dionysian-orgiastic Eros, the force that threatened to undo some of the heroes of his music dramas (Tannhäuser, Parsifal) and promised to redeem others (Siegmund, Siegfried). What Nietzsche's remarks tell us about how we might read the conclusion of *Tristan*'s act 3 has fascinating repercussions for how that reading might bear on our interpretation of Modernism's battle with Hollywood film music.

Film music has all too often been vaguely associated with Wagner and his leitmotifs without the slightest attention to the nature of Wagner's music or to the ways in which it was received. Wagner himself ventriloquizes a lesson about this association through the female singer whose last words in *Tristan*'s act 3 are a description of the "bliss" of submission to the "surging swell" of sound that engulfs her, and us, yet that she alone "hears" as emanating from the beloved man who lies dead in her arms:

> Are they clouds
> of delicious perfumes?
> As they swell
> and roar around me
> shall I breathe,
> shall I listen?
> Shall I sip,
> plunge beneath
> in sweet fragrances
> to breathe my last?[36]

Isolde's words bring us back to Joan Crawford listening, as Helen Wright, to the live radio broadcast of her lover's *Tristan* arrangement, in the concert from which she has judiciously absented herself. She has returned to her beach house to nurse the wounds inflicted by Paul's mother's denunciation of her and by her still faithful husband's sad, gentlemanly advice. She has had a hurried, interrupted, and unsatisfactory phone conversation with Paul before he went on stage. Now, as the *Tristan* concerto plays over the radio, she pours herself the drink whose empty glass will smash the windowpane that holds and restricts her image. Only then, as Paul and Sid work through the music of fatal portent toward the "Liebestod"—here signifying the death of *love* as much as any love of death—only then does she walk out onto the terrace, her hair blown by the sea breeze. She picks up a handbill for the concert, the music of which now follows her down onto the beach as subjective underscore, with no reduction in volume level even though she leaves the radio ever farther behind her (see Figures 7.6 and 7.7).

Denied the voice of Isolde that Paul has appropriated (as the "Liebestod" itself now unfolds), Helen pauses after passing a man walking his dog. The moonlight is on the sea, and her head is filled with the sound of the breaking waves and with Wagner's music, the music with which the Great Composer drowned his fantasy image of Mathilde Wesendonck, in whose arms he imagined himself dying.[37] Crawford's face, streaked with tears, fills the screen until she seems, frighteningly, almost to walk out of it

FIGURE 7.6. *Humoresque* (1946). Helen, on the beach, "hears" Paul's performance of the *Tristan Fantasy*.

FIGURE 7.7. *Humoresque* (1946). Helen walks toward the sea.

toward us. But then we see what she sees: the crashing waves into which she strides as the final climax of the music breaks over our heads (see Figures 7.8 and 7.9). The kitsch image of bubbles rising as we sink into a fantasy aquarium resonates uncomfortably with the newly reheard cadential trickery of spritualizing "redemption."

Perhaps no serious Wagnerian *can* take the ending of *Humoresque* seriously. And yet here we have a film heroine who really "listens"—in the sense of Madame von Meck's protestation that she would "die for listening" to Tchaikovsky's Fourth Symphony—and the music she listens to will, both literally and figuratively, kill her. "I *hate* music!" Helen had proclaimed at the end of a romantic balcony scene with Paul. And just as her cinematic death inspires a secret horror of recognition in the musicians who feel obliged to scorn it, as they must scorn Waxman's "sacrilegious" arrangement, so this undone woman resists revisionist musicological redemption as "triumphant in voice" as resolutely as she seems to embrace and understand the music in which she drowns.

The next morning, on the beach with Sid and the policemen, Paul distractedly regresses to pubertal confusion: "Why do I have to shave every day?" he mutters incoherently to his absent but triumphant mother. The final scene has him assuring Sid that he is not "running away," but the closing shot of him setting out along a big city street that stretches every-

Figure 7.8. *Humoresque* (1946). Helen's final close-up at the sea's edge.

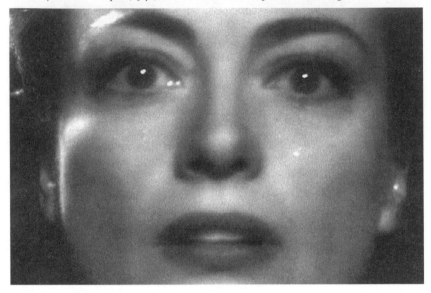

Figure 7.9. *Humoresque* (1946). As she walks into the waves, we see through Helen's eyes.

where and nowhere is as enigmatic as the triumphant return of the mind-lessly cheerful skipping motif of Dvořák's "Humoresque" in the closing credits. All too uncompromisingly does this close remind us of the poten-tial heartlessness of the formal closure strategies of "music itself." Yes, it is more than awkward. It is utterly and wonderfully dreadful.

So my three awkward moments: First, a revelation of impersonal Truth that turns out to be a deeply personal figuring of the irreconcilable tension between lived psychological pain and an aesthetic discourse that might "contain" or soothe such pain with harmonious "resolution." Then, a re-gressively "self-indulgent" protocinematic opera that proposes a strikingly ambivalent reading of the very post-Romantic music that it exemplifies. And finally, a film featuring a shameful reworking of Wagner's *Tristan* that seems by chance to have articulated something about Great Music that anticipated New Musicology by three or four decades.

None of these moments changes the Modernist Narrative, exactly; it is too late for that. In some ways they confirm and shadow that narrative, but they do so in what had become an accessibly complex vernacular lan-guage. With no investment in notions of progress, they offer a model of decline. They also remind us that beneath the heavy stone of the Modern-ist Narrative and its masterpieces there lies a partly hidden network of competing and contradictory stories, and music, in which meaning and human values were no less passionately in play.

CHAPTER 8

"Pour Out . . . Forgiveness Like a Wine"

CAN MUSIC "SAY AN EXISTENCE IS WRONG"?

Walter Bernhart

It has been claimed that the dreadful wolf's-glen scene from Weber's *Der Freischütz* of 1821 marked a decisive departure in the presentation of villainy on the opera stage, introducing a new musical vocabulary for representing evil: tremolos, trills, bassless diminished chords, chromaticism, eerie pianissimo pizzicatos in the double basses, unisono playing, low clarinets, gloomy drumrolls, obsessive repetitions, and the like. In a stimulating paper on "villains, outsiders, and failures in opera," Stefan Kunze finds no evidence of the representation of true villainy in opera prior to Samiel and Caspar in *Der Freischütz*. Negative characters in earlier works—from Monteverdi's Poppea and Nero through Metastasio's Vitellia to Mozart's Elettra, Osmin, and Queen of the Night—are in their essence manifestations of great passion,[1] and passions are nothing negative by nature but only turn negative when brought to extremes. This characterization is even true for Beethoven's Pizarro, who is not essentially bad but equally only driven by his emotions, which, admittedly, are excessively forced up into a blind rage of revenge. Kunze asserts that early heroic operas of the eighteenth century did not have villains as protagonists as, at the time, it was unthinkable to represent evil through music because harmony was considered the essence of music, and evil contradicts harmony.[2] The element of "ideality," which in eighteenth-century views was adjoined to a person or action by music, "reduces the reality of evil."[3] As a consequence, when evil was meant to appear onstage, music tended to fall silent. A telling example is Bouilly and Gaveaux's *Léonore ou L'amour conjugal* of 1789 (the forerunner to Beethoven's *Fidelio*), in which Pizarro significantly appears as a speaking part only.

From Samiel and Caspar onward, however, negativity, no longer a product of excessive emotion, becomes the manifestation of inescapable and malicious fate, a product of hell, whether in the shape of the Nibelungs (Alberich and Hagen), of Scarpia, or of Iago.[4] Iago appears as the representation of "essential evil," but according to Kunze, his music breaks with the traditional romantic "evil" vocabulary, as I have just characterized it, and suggests his perverted creed by a "dissociation of musical texture."[5] Yet generally, to follow Kunze a little longer, the presentation of evil remained problematic throughout the nineteenth century. Even Meyerbeer's Robert le Diable is no real "devil" but rather wavers between good and evil, only to be redeemed by mere serendipity.

Kunze did not continue his survey into the twentieth century, when the depiction of evil in opera became even more problematic. A general corrosion of ethical standards and the horrendous experience of mass evil may have been responsible. What can be observed is that criminals or representatives of evil increasingly became protagonists of twentieth-century operas. In what follows, I concentrate on relevant operas by Hans Werner Henze, Paul Hindemith, and Benjamin Britten. However, to begin with a central point, the characters in these operas do not necessarily appear to be evil and are clearly presented in an ambivalent light.

A prime example is Hans Werner Henze's *Elegy for Young Lovers*, written in collaboration with W. H. Auden and Chester Kallman and premiered in its German version in 1961. Together with the libretto of *The Rake's Progress* by the same authors, it is the finest post-Hofmannsthal opera libretto, and in spite of the octogenarian composer's unbroken productivity, the *Elegy* is still Henze's most attractive and most often produced stage work. The story is quickly told. The central figure is Gregor Mittenhofer, a famous elderly poet, who spends his summer vacation in the Austrian Alps, where he hopes to find inspiration for his poetry in the visions of an elderly woman, "mad" Hilda Mack. After forty years, she is still waiting for her fiancé to return from an excursion into the glaciers, where he meant to get her some edelweiss for their wedding. Gregor has a young lover with him, Elisabeth Zimmer, who unsurprisingly falls in love with a further guest who arrives, the young Toni. Elisabeth and Toni are the young lovers of the opera's title, and the elegy is for their tragic

death. The circumstances of their death and of the writing of that elegy
are the central concerns of the opera and of our discussion here. Gregor,
deceptively magnanimous, surrenders Elisabeth to Toni but asks as a favor
that, before getting married, they bring him some edelweiss (again) from
the glaciers because he expects poetic inspiration from the flower. He
hopes for this inspiration because Hilda's visions as a source of inspiration
for his work have come to an end, for Maurer, the mountain guide, has
found her fiancé's mummified body in the glacier. The discovery cures
Hilda of her madness, and she starts a normal life, wanting to see *The
Merry Widow*. Gregor, however, is warned by the guide that a blizzard is
coming up, yet he denies that anyone is on the mountain, as Toni and
Elisabeth in fact are. The "young lovers" die in the blizzard (musically
represented by a furioso orchestral interlude), but only after they have
pledged their eternal love. (Characteristically, Henze dropped the *Aida*-
like scene in his own later productions of the opera.) Gregor is now able
to write his "elegy." At the end of the opera, the elegy is delivered before
a prestigious Viennese audience to great acclamation. Yet we do not hear
any words spoken or sung. What we actually hear are the vocalizing voices
of all the people who have contributed to the making of the poem, a poem
that we are meant to believe is a truly great artistic achievement.

Gregor Mittenhofer is the product of Auden and Kallman's desire to
represent the prototypical Romantic artist-hero as a character of mythic
stature, a quality indispensable for an opera's central figure in their view.[6]
Models for Gregor were Stefan George, William Butler Yeats, Richard
Wagner, Rainer Maria Rilke, and Gabriele D'Annunzio.[7] Dietrich Fischer-
Dieskau, for whom the role was written, appeared onstage in a mask, suggesting both Yeats and Strindberg.[8] All these artists were self-serving "ge-
niuses," "Masters," "Herrenmenschen," and it is clear that Auden, self-
critically, also had himself in mind when he conceived of Mittenhofer.[9]
Reading the opera's libretto reveals quite unmistakably that the figure of
this artist-hero is there seen in purely negative terms. This comes out even
more directly in the first draft of the text, in which, for example, Elisabeth
deplores Gregor's "utter selfishness," "the Great Bard" is ironically
scorned, and Toni exclaims, "Master! The word makes me sick." Toni also
calls the "Poet" (as yet without a name in the draft) "You devil!" remind-
ing one of the well-known ending of Henry James's *The Turn of the Screw*.
The ridiculousness of the genius pose of the Poet satirically emerges when
Hilda says about him, "Goethe-woethe must be quite upset" or "You can
use that, too, if you like, Virgiletto." The Romantic cult of inspiration is
equally ridiculed when the Poet explains to Toni and Elisabeth why he

wants the edelweiss: "I have always found that sleeping with some under my pillow inspired my dreams."[10]

However, this satirical and sharply critical view of the devilish artist-hero in the libretto, who sends people to death for his poetic inspiration, has not been identified as such by all critics of the opera. Some saw in Mittenhofer "an admirable character," detected no "spiteful discrediting" of the genius, even observed a "resurrection" of the myth of the "untethered *Künstlergenie*."[11] This position was authoritatively backed up by Henze himself when he talked about "leaving open the question of guilt" and concluded his remarks on the opera of 1962 (the date is significant) by alluding to a telling passage from an Auden poem, which the title of this chapter quotes:[12]

> You alone, alone, imaginary song,
> Are unable to say an existence is wrong,
> And pour out your forgiveness like a wine.[13]

This passage is taken from a sonnet called "The Composer," which Auden wrote in 1938 with Benjamin Britten in mind, and it expresses Auden's Kierkegaardian conviction at the time that the Beautiful and the Good, or the Aesthetic and the Ethical, were strictly separate. Only song, as a prototypical representative of the aesthetic, shows the spontaneous immediacy of emotional expression, is pure presence and actuality without reflection, and as such is not subjected to the historical process and is independent of everyday social experience with all its ethical claims.[14] The younger Henze of 1962, who Hanspeter Krellmann has called the "Cimarosa of the 20th century" and who, to take the words of Auden and Kallman, had "tender, beautiful noises" in mind when he thought about the opera that later became his *Elegy*, was attracted by the idea of the ethical indifference of free-floating artificial forms.[15] This idea comes out in Henze's reference to Auden's poem and in his own early forgiving appraisal of Mittenhofer, in spite of what the libretto manifestly says.

Yet the sensational "political turn" in Henze's life, which took place in the later 1960s, led the composer himself radically to reinterpret Mittenhofer. His newly acquired left-wing social commitment made unbearable to him the notion that an artist—even a great one—should be judged by different ethical standards than "normal" people were, and he now saw Mittenhofer as "the accused poet," a "daunting Dracula,"[16] and he asserted, "I very much like the denunciation of the 'artist as a hero.'"[17]

It is of particular interest not only that Henze changed his opinion of Mittenhofer as a character representing the artist-hero type but that he extended his reevaluation into a rereading of his own music. By using the quotation from Auden's poem "The Composer," he had earlier claimed that thanks to the music, Mittenhofer stands uncondemned. The music functions as an agency that redeems the "evil" character, "pouring out forgiveness." As Edward Mendelson has noted, Auden's point of comparison ("like a wine") alludes to the redemptive power of the Eucharist.[18] Yet the "reformed" later Henze saw "denunciation" and "sarcasm" in his music and detected in it a *jugendstil*-like weaving and whispering of alienated nature."[19]

In the article of 1975, Henze also discusses musical details of his opera in an attempt to demonstrate how the music itself suggests condemnation and criticism of the "evilness" of Mittenhofer. When the poet first appears on the stage, we hear (in Henze's words) "thudding tam-tam beats," "piano and harp arpeggios," and, most intriguingly, a "whining flexatone" that "creates an atmosphere of Gothic films."[20] The flexatone, a variant of the singing saw, can be heard two more times: in act 2, when Mittenhofer "half consciously, half unconsciously is planning his crime—the music already debunks him,"[21] and again in act 3, "when the crime is actually committed."[22] This last occasion, the actual murder, is from a moral perspective the most decisive moment in the whole opera. The relevant scene starts off with Maurer, the mountain guide, warning Mittenhofer of the oncoming blizzard and asking him whether anyone is out on the mountain, which the poet denies. This is the moment of the actual crime, of Mittenhofer's murderous lie, and it is marked by "the metallic clatter of a heavy object."[23] Carolina, the poet's secretary, is present and deeply shocked because she knows that Elisabeth and Toni are on the mountain. Mittenhofer notices her "shivering" and "dreadful looks" and interprets them with characteristic deception as a sign of overwork and suggests to her a "change of scene."[24] In other words, he wants to send her off.

Carolina is exasperated—she does not know where to go—and Mittenhofer mollifies her by saying, "I meant no harm." This is a significant remark, as the German version, the one Henze actually set to music, says, "es war nicht bös gemeint," "böse" being a word that is twice repeated. The word means "wicked" or "evil," but "böse sein" is also used colloquially in the sense of "to be cross" or "angry." This is crucial because in the scene a truly "evil" man ("ein böser Mensch") is deceptively playing a social role, a situation that Carolina obviously realizes. And it is precisely at this point that the flexatone is heard, though only for two bars when the sky darkens and it begins to snow (indicated by the stage directions), signaling the impending death of Toni and Elisabeth (Example 8.1).

EXAMPLE 8.1. Hans Werner Henze, *Elegy for Young Lovers*, Act 3, mm. 367–71. (German text with literal English translation.)

EXAMPLE 8.1 *(cont'd.)*

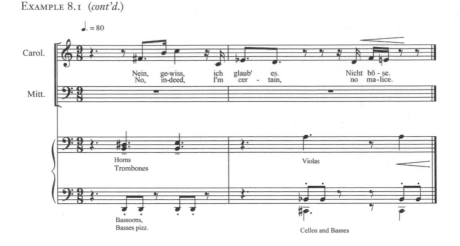

Carolina becomes extremely nervous and starts making a fire in the stove, staging a "miniature-*Götterdämmerung*."[25] Mittenhofer comments on this action, talking "to himself" in a passage that shows him in an unusual fashion, wearing no mask and giving expression to his true thinking, his infernal "Credo," reminiscent of Iago's Credo in Verdi's opera (Example 8.2).

What is the position and function of music in the fascinating scene of "evil" described here? Most significantly, at the very moment of the actual vicious deed, that is, when the murderous lie is articulated, the music itself is silent, precisely as if the sensual allure of music would otherwise avert attention from the monstrosity of the deed. What we do hear—apart from the words—is one of the "real-life sounds" in the opera that always appear when chaos arises, as Henze observes,[26] in this case, the dropping of the heavy metallic object (which arguably indicates Carolina's shock). The only musical element that Henze discusses with reference to "evil" in his opera is the whining, creepy flexatone (m. 367). This is quite an unexpected point of reference because, first, the sound of the instrument can hardly be heard and, second, it appears at a moment in which the disaster is ominously anticipated (the snow begins to fall) but that is not in itself significant from a moral point of view. A full-fledged musically assisted expression of evil can be found only later at Mittenhofer's "Credo," which uses some traditional means of describing villainy, such as deadly gloom and sheer power of sound, and which conspicuously suggests high emotional intensity (and high emotional intensity conventionally numbs the ethical sense). It is characteristic that Henze, in his later attempt of 1975

EXAMPLE 8.2. Hans Werner Henze, *Elegy for Young Lovers*, Act 3, mm. 374–83. (German text with Auden and Kallman's English original.)

to draw attention to the denunciatory, crime-disclosing function of his music in the murder scene, talks about the hardly noticeable flexatone and not about this big orchestral outburst: evil appears in a deceptively subtle shape, not with stamping feet.

Similarly subtle is the way in which the composer later reinterpreted other passages of his music. The final scene of the opera, when Mittenhofer reads his elegy in public, shows "very beautiful music," as Auden put it in 1968.[27] Henze himself had commented on the scene in 1962 by paraphrasing Auden's phrase "pour out your forgiveness like a wine." Yet in 1975, again radically reinterpreting his own music, he wrote that "the final scene of the opera opens our eyes to the atrociousness" of the selfish, murderous artist-hero[28] and that we need to be aware of the "inverted commas put around the crystalline sound world" of this music.[29] In the composer's own later view, the "beauty" of the final music, the wordless ensemble of six voices representing the remarkable poetic achievement of Mittenhofer's elegy, needs to be heard as a sinister reflection of the viciousness of the poet who wrote it. In this reading, the music becomes highly ambiguous as it subtly mirrors the willful deception of the criminal artist.

Another impressive criminal artist who found operatic representation in the twentieth century is Cardillac in Paul Hindemith's eponymous opera, which in this respect can meaningfully be compared to Henze's *Elegy for Young Lovers*. Cardillac, the famous goldsmith from E. T. A. Hoffmann's tale "Das Fräulein von Scudery," is another representative of the Romantic artist-hero. Again a person deeply at odds with the social world around him claims that his artistic excellence justifies radically independent moral standards. He is a demonic character who notoriously kills those people who buy his artworks because he feels totally unable to part with his great artistic products. Hindemith's opera came out in two versions, in 1926 and 1952, the latter with a heavily revised text but, interestingly, without substantially revised music. In the first version, as in Henze's early reading of Gregor Mittenhofer, Cardillac appears as a fascinating hero, full of dignity, a superhuman man who despite his evildoings is "forgiven." He dies heroically transfigured as a victim of the small-mindedness and Philistinism around him. But just as the late politically and socially committed Henze reinterpreted Mittenhofer, so the mature Hindemith of 1952 reconceived Cardillac in terms of his own heightened social consciousness and thus presented him as an irresponsible, calculating liar who wickedly covers up his murderous activities.[30]

In order to discuss the role of music in the presentation of this evil character, the ending of act 1 of the opera can serve as a demonstration (Example 8.3). At this point, when a Cavalier presents a piece of jewelry to his beloved Lady (the minor characters of the opera have no names), Cardillac suddenly appears batlike from the dark and stabs him to death. We hear but two flutes, until the score indicates, "The music stops!" (*Die Musik setzt aus!*) The subsequent lengthy stage direction tells us what happens on the stage: only the Lady sees the intruder, but because she is

EXAMPLE 8.3. Paul Hindemith, *Cardillac*, Act 1, conclusion.

Während der letzten Bewegungen ist hinter in der Fensteröffnung eine schwarze,

Die Musik setzt aus!

maskierte Gestalt aufgetaucht, steht gross im Fenster, überblickt das Zimmer. Dann, während beide in Liebesvergessenheits versunken sind, ist jener mit einem Satz ins Zimmer hinein gesprungen, lautlos auf dem weichen Teppich. Er bleibt starr hinten stehen. Der Kavalier indessen hat den Kopf gehoben, öffnet lansam die Augenlider der Geliebten. Der Fremde, wie ein Raubtier schleichen, ist im Bogen nach vorne rechts gekommen; er lauert. Die Dame hebt langsam den Oberkörper in ermattetem Glück.--Plötlich sieht sie dem Fremden. Träumt sie? Wacht sie? Bewegung eines taumelden irrsinnigen Entsetzens, sie ist stumm vor Schreken. Der Kavalier fasst ihre Bewegung als eine letzte Angst vor der Liebe auf und umarmt sie. Sie ihrerseits umschlingt ihm ganz, um ihm mit dem Armen zu schützen.-- Der Fremde ist dicht an das Bett gekommen. Mit der einen Hand ergreift er den Gürtel, mit der andern zückt er einem Dolch in die Höhe und stösst ihn in das Genick des Kavaliers.-- Die Dame schreit voller Entsetzen laut auf. Der Kavalier--tot--gleitet vom Bett herab. Die Dame sink ohmächtig in die Kissen.

Raubvogelhafte Flucht des Mörders -- Mantel gespreizt wie Flüugel--dursch das Fenster in den Garten.

"dumbstruck by fright" (*stumm vor Schrecken*), she only "cries out loud in horror" (*schreit voller Entsetzen laut auf*) and "slumps aswoon into the cushions" (*sinkt ohnmächtig in die Kissen*) when the stranger draws his dagger and thrusts it into the Cavalier's neck. It is only after these dramatic events that the music starts again, when the score says, "Raptorlike flight of the murderer" (*Raubvogelhafte Flucht des Mörders*).

It is significant that the murder and the Lady's reaction to it are accompanied by a long break in the music.[31] Thus, the concluding dramatic music of the act does not illustrate the murder itself but the murderer's subsequent flight.[32] The situation both parallels the murder scene in *Elegy for Young Lovers* and suggests another parallel to Henze's opera, in this case a parallel between its "elegy" ending and passages from Benjamin Britten's *The Turn of the Screw*.

Britten's opera, based on Henry James's famous novel, is the most significant product of the composer's lifelong obsession with childlike innocence and its secret subversion and loss through hidden corrupting forces. Whatever the biographical sources of this obsession may be, it can be traced in a great number of Britten's works, in many of his songs and operas.[33] But rarely has it found as impressive a manifestation as in the music of *The Turn of the Screw*. Closely following James's text, the opera centrally addresses the ambivalence of innocence, indeed the very question of whether there *is* innocence or not. Peter Quint, the dead former valet at Bly, the gorgeous country house, is the evil force that is thought to corrupt Miles and Flora, the two children in the charge of the inexperienced new Governess. The questions of whether Quint or the nameless Governess is evil, whether Quint exists at all or is only a product of the Governess's hallucinations, whether the children are corrupted by Quint or by the Governess or are not corrupted at all—all these questions are left open in the novel, according to James's own intentions. It was a challenge to Britten to convey this ambivalence of evil in his music, and an investigation of two short passages from the opera may be able to show how Britten dealt with the problem. One scene is Quint's melismatic siren song from act 1 in which the valet (echoed by the celesta) wickedly tempts Miles (Example 8.4). Or this is at least what the Governess thinks he is doing when she cries out, just before Quint's scene starts, that the children are "Lost! Lost! Lost!" (seven times repeated).[34]

The other scene is the one in which Miles sings his "Malo" song (act 1, scene 6; the song later makes fragmentary reappearances):

Malo: I would rather be
Malo: in an apple-tree
Malo: than a naughty boy
Malo: in adversity.[35]

The song is based on an old joke that makes use of the multiple ambiguity of the Latin *malo* ("I prefer," "I choose," "apple," "crime," "injury," "evil"): the absurd sentence "Malo malo malo malo" might be translated

EXAMPLE 8.4. Benjamin Britten, *The Turn of the Screw*, Act 1, "At Night" (Quint's melismas).

"I would rather be in an apple-tree than a naughty boy in adversity." The suggestion is that Miles refers to himself as "a naughty boy . . . in adversity" thus echoing the ambiguity of *malo*, but with an edge: the primary meaning of "naughty" is disobedient, not evil, but in context it suggests the primary disobedience of another "naughty boy" who figuratively fell from an apple tree, namely Adam; and "naughty" also carries a sexual connotation that may carry over into Miles's relationship with Quint. The point in our context is that Miles may suggest that he is evil, but not necessarily; he may very well only be playful and harmless.

When one considers the music of these two songs, it is essential to observe that the music clearly dominates over the text. The verbal side is only of marginal interest: Quint's melismas are pure vocalizations on the name "Miles," and Miles's enigmatic words in the "Malo" song distract little from the melic quality of his song. Despite their different textures, both songs are "beautiful" by any common standard. They appear as cases of what Lawrence Kramer has called "songfulness," as they have a typical "indefinable" aesthetic quality and "gratifying intimacy." Miles's song has it in particularly high measure. Quint's high voice and "melismatic undulation" are signs of male "songfulness," as Kramer observes. Kramer also makes the essential point that the beauty of songfulness rests in "the positive quality of singing-in-itself: just singing." It is a medium for attaining "unattainable bliss." Kramer demonstrates this "blissful" quality of songfulness by analysing Schubert's "Heidenröslein," yet he adds a riveting story about the use that Alfred Hitchcock made of the song in his film *Lifeboat*. A captive German U-boat's captain deceptively lulls the crew of the Allied Forces into cosy conviviality by singing the song. He goes on to commit a merciless murder, which draws from Kramer the insightful comment on "the danger inherent in all *volkstümlich* innocence."[36]

The comment also applies to Quint's and Miles's songs from Britten's *The Turn of the Screw*, as it does to the "beautiful" vocalized ending of Henze's *Elegy for Young Lovers*. The ambivalence to be noticed in the reception of these vocal utterances—are they merely "beautiful" or do they at the same time suggest the presence of evil?—depends entirely on the observing mind. In Kramer's words, "voice brings the music into a space of potential or virtual meaning even [or, possibly, particularly] when actual meaning is left hanging." Equally illuminating is Kramer's observation that "songfulness is a fusion of vocal and musical utterance *judged to be . . .* pleasurable . . . independent of verbal content." It may very well be "judged" not "pleasurable," in which case quite a different "potential meaning" emerges.[37]

Thus, in my discussion of the presentation of evil in twentieth-century opera, we have come to a point where I may hazard a few summarizing observations. Henry James, discussing *The Turn of the Screw* in his preface to the New York edition of 1909, gives the following advice: "Make him [the reader] *think* the evil . . . and you are released from weak specifications." What one needs, according to James, is a "thin" story, one that leaves things unsaid, vague and unexplained, the "shadow of a shadow." In the modern guise, evil does no longer step onto the stage with a cleft foot snarling spiteful words and openly acting out dreadful deeds, "announced," as James puts it, "by the hot breath of the Pit."[38] Modern evil tends to appear in disguise, as a cunning and deceptive agency. It asks the perceiver to penetrate the veil in order to recognize its very existence. It finds its expression in subtle calculation and cold-hearted double-dealing, asking for subtleness and sophistication on the perceiver's side to realize its destructive power. This is why ambivalence and opacity are its dominant features.

How does music deal with this situation? Evil that openly appeared on the stage, as Caspar or Iago did, gave music an opportunity to describe and to illustrate it more or less directly. But evil of the cunningly deceptive kind can no longer be unabashedly illustrated by the kind of musical vocabulary developed in the nineteenth century. The wish to express the enigmatic ambivalence of innocence and evil asks for a different musical language, and it has in significant cases been found in the beauty and simplicity of vocalized songs whose mere "songfulness" leaves it up to the listener to become aware of the underlying ambivalence. The musical instruments that usually accompany such songs in the operas discussed are the flute, bells, harp, and celesta, instruments that traditionally suggested the "heavenly" sphere but that here become possible voices from hell. So the question asked at first—can music "say an existence is wrong"?—can be answered in the affirmative only if and when the experiencing mind (with the help of conventional devices) is willing to read music in these terms. This is so even when the music may superficially seem to say something different. All the same, music tends to act, as Kierkegaard and Auden say, "pouring out forgiveness," or, as Kramer expresses it so disarmingly, "songs, in their songfulness," despite their latent dangerousness, "remain stubbornly and disconcertingly beautiful."[39] Thus, wise composers who, when their dramatic texts expect them to show unquestionable evil, wish to evade the musical power of "forgiveness" do the only reasonable thing to do in such a situation. They stop the music.

INTRODUCTION
Lawrence Kramer

1. For more on this subject, see the introductions to my *Critical Musicology and the Responsibility of Response*, Ashgate Contemporary Thinkers in Critical Musicology (Aldershot, U.K.: Ashgate, 2006), pp. ix–xvi, and to Richard Leppert's *Sound Judgment* (2007) in the same series. The disciplinary change began in the late 1980s; for a general survey through 2001, see Alastair Williams, *Constructing Musicology* (Aldershot, U.K.: Ashgate, 2001); and for one through 2005, David Beard and Kenneth Gloag, *Musicology: The Key Concepts* (London: Routledge, 2005).

2. On the capacity of music to anticipate cultural and social change, see Jacques Attali, *Noise*, trans. Brian Massumi (Minneapolis: University of Minnesota Press, 1985).

3. From "Gerontion," in T. S. Eliot, *Collected Poems: 1909–1962* (New York: Harcourt, Brace, and World, 1963), p. 30. On what I am calling nostalgic irony, see Walter Frisch, *German Modernism* (Berkeley: University of California Press, 2005), pp. 186–213. The term "infinite irony" is from Wayne C. Booth, *A Rhetoric of Irony* (Chicago: University of Chicago Press, 1974).

4. Judith Butler, *Giving an Account of Oneself* (New York: Fordham University Press, 2005), pp. 36–40.

5. See Jacques Lacan, *The Four Fundamental Concepts of Psychoanalysis: The Seminar of Jacques Lacan, Book XI*, ed. Jacques-Alain Miller, trans. Alan Sheridan (New York: Norton, 1998), pp. 53–64; and Slavoj Zizek, *Looking Awry: An Introduction to Jacques Lacan through Popular Culture* (Cambridge, Mass.: MIT Press, 1992), pp. 1–38.

6. Hans-Georg Gadamer, *Truth and Method*, 2nd rev. ed., trans. Joel Weisheimer and Donald G. Marshall (1960; New York: Continuum, 1989), pp. 303–4.

7. On these and other usages, see Esteban Buch, *Beethoven's Ninth: A Political History*, trans. Richard Miller (Chicago: University of Chicago Press, 2004); on the European Anthem in particular, see Caryl Clark, "Forging Iden-

tity: Beethoven's 'Ode' as European Anthem," *Critical Inquiry* 23 (1997): 789–807.

8. Michel Foucault, "The Subject and Power," *Critical Inquiry* 8 (1982): 777–95.

1. *DUE ROSE*, DUE VOLTE: A STUDY OF EARLY MODERN SUBJECTIVITIES
Susan McClary

1. See in particular his most recent book, *Why Classical Music Still Matters* (Berkeley: University of California Press, 2007).

2. For the Italian both here and in the examples, I am using the version in Robert Durling, *Petrarch's Lyric Poems* (Cambridge, Mass.: Harvard University Press, 1976), p. 407. The English translation draws on a number of available printed versions but ultimately is my own.

3. Nancy Vickers, "Diana Described: Scattered Woman and Scattered Rhyme," *Critical Inquiry* 8 (1981): 265–70.

4. Alfred Einstein, *The Italian Madrigal*, 3 vols., trans. Alexander H. Krappe, Roger H. Sessions, and Oliver Strunk (Princeton, N.J.: Princeton University Press, 1949), p. 534.

5. See María Rosa Menocal, *Shards of Love: Exile and the Origins of the Lyric* (Durham, N.C.: Duke University Press, 1994).

6. For an extensive discussion of the theoretical framework within which these pieces operate, see my *Modal Subjectivities: Self-Fashioning in the Italian Madrigal* (Berkeley: University of California Press, 2004).

7. Einstein, *Italian Madrigal*, p. 534.

8. Ibid., p. 643.

9. For a discussion of Arcadelt's madrigal, see McClary, *Modal Subjectivities*, chap. 3.

10. For more on this allusion, see Anthony Pryer, "Monteverdi, Two Sonnets, and a Letter," *Early Music* (August 1997): 367.

11. See Carolyn Abbate, "Music—Drastic or Gnostic?" *Critical Inquiry* 30 (2004): 505–37. See also my *Reading Music* (London: Ashgate, 2007).

12. Giovanni Maria Artusi, *L'Artusi, ovvero Delle imperfezioni della moderna musica* (1600).

13. Menocal, *Shards of Love*.

14. See my *Conventional Wisdom: The Content of Musical Form* (Berkeley: University of California Press, 2000).

15. See McClary, *Modal Subjectivities*, especially the chapters on Arcadelt and Willaert, both of whom produced their extraordinary expressive effects within the constraints of modal propriety.

16. See Thomas K. Nelson, "The Fantasy of Absolute Music" (Ph.D. dissertation, University of Minnesota, 1998).

17. Ernesto Sabato, *On Heroes and Tombs*, trans. Helen R. Lane (Boston: David R. Godine, 1981), pp. 22–23.

18. Here and elsewhere in my discussion of early modernity, I am influenced by the work of my recent advisee Ljubica Ilic; see her "Music and Modernity: Investigating the Boundaries" (Ph.D. dissertation, UCLA, 2007).

19. See Abbate, "Music—Drastic or Gnostic?"

20. See Artusi, L'Artusi and Vincenzo Galilei, *Dialogo della musica antica e della moderna* (1581).

2. SUBLIME EXPERIENCE AND IRONIC ACTION: E. T. A. HOFFMANN AND THE USE OF MUSIC FOR LIFE
Keith Chapin

1. "Welcher Künstler hat sich sonst um die politischen Ereignisse des Tages bekümmert—er lebte nur in seiner Kunst, und nur in ihr schritt er durch das Leben; eine verhängnisvolle schwere Zeit hatte den Menschen mit eiserner Faust ergriffen, und der Schmerz preßt ihm Laute aus, die ihm sonst fremd waren." E. T. A. Hoffmann, *Fantasie- und Nachtstücke*, 6th ed. (Düsseldorf: Artemis & Winkler, 1996), p. 55. All translations are mine unless otherwise noted.

2. Rüdiger Safranski, *E. T. A. Hoffmann: Das Leben eines skeptischen Phantasten* (Munich: Hanser, 1984), pp. 425–35, 455–71; Holly Watkins, "From the Mine to the Shrine: The Critical Origins of Musical Depth," *19th-Century Music* 27 (2004): 192.

3. Stephen C. Rumph, "A Kingdom Not of This World: The Political Context of E. T. A. Hoffmann's Beethoven Criticism," *19th-Century Music* 19 (1995): 50–67; Stephen C. Rumph, *Beethoven after Napoleon: Political Romanticism in the Late Works* (Berkeley: University of California Press, 2004), chap. 1.

4. Documents relating to Hoffmann's legal career appear in E. T. A. Hoffmann, *Briefwechsel*, ed. Hans von Müller and Friedrich Schnapp, 3 vols. (Munich: Winkler, 1967), vol. 3. The following overview is based on Safranski, *Hoffmann*, pp. 455–70; Alfred Hoffmann, *E. T. A. Hoffmann: Leben und Arbeit eines preussischen Richters* (Baden-Baden: Nomos, 1990); Hartmut Mangold, "'Heillose Willkühr': Rechtsstaatliche Vorstellungen und rechtspraktische Erfahrungen E. T. A. Hoffmanns in den Jahren der preußisschen Restauration," in *E. T. A. Hoffmann: Neue Wege der Forschung*, ed. Hartmut Steinecke (Darmstadt: Wissenschaftliche Buchgesellschaft, 2006), pp. 97–108.

5. Abigail Chantler has cited Hoffmann's enthusiastic letter to Hippel of 7 July 1814 as proof of his sympathies with the Prussian state. However, Hoffmann wrote the letter to assuage the doubts of prospective employers that he would be up to a post. Hippel noted on the letter that it had been written "to be shown around." Hoffmann, *Briefwechsel*, 1:474–75; Abigail Chantler, *E.T.A. Hoffmann's Musical Aesthetics* (Aldershot, U.K.: Ashgate, 2006), p. 173.

6. See Hoffman to Hitzig, 2 September 1814, in Hoffmann, *Briefwechsel*, 1:482–84.

7. The king's order is reproduced in Friedrich Schnapp, ed., *E. T. A. Hoffmann in Aufzeichnungen seiner Freunde und Bekannten* (Munich: Winkler, 1974), p. 494.

8. "Anstatt sie zu eröfnen [*sic*], hat die Commission auf den flüchtigen, actenwidrigen Vortrag des Decernenten ihn von der Untersuchung freigesprochen und entlassen." Ibid., p. 510.

9. The many official letters from Hoffmann's pen appear in volume 3 of Hoffmann, *Briefwechsel*.

10. Hoffman to Kircheisen, 18 May 1820, in ibid, 3:197–98.

11. "Wie Du mich kennst, magst Du Dir wohl meine *Stimmung* denken, als sich vor meinen Augen ein ganzes Gewebe heilloser Willkühr, frecher Nichtachtung aller Gesetze, persönlicher Animosität, entwickelte!" Ibid., 2:263.

12. Mangold, "Heillose Willkühr," p. 106.

13. E.g., E. T. A. Hoffmann, *Die Elixiere des Teufels. Lebens-Ansichten des Katers Murr*, 7th ed. (Düsseldorf: Artemis & Winkler, 1997), pp. 506–9.

14. "Die schnöde, ja sündliche Tapferkeit eines verhärteten Gemüts." E. T. A. Hoffmann, *Späte Werke*, ed. Friedrich Schnapp (Munich: Winkler, 1965), p. 593.

15. Ibid., pp. 751–53.

16. Mangold, "Heillose Willkühr," pp. 101–3.

17. Ibid., p. 97.

18. Traditionally, the Prussian king had the right to pardon and to affirm legal decisions. Over the eighteenth century, however, Prussian kings gradually limited their powers. In 1752, Frederick the Great wrote, "I have decided never to interfere in the workings of a legal proceeding, for in the courts of law the law should speak and the ruler should remain silent." ("Ich habe mich entschlossen, niemals in den Lauf eines gerichtlichen Verfahrens einzugreifen; denn in den Gerichtshöfen sollen die Gesetze sprechen und der Herrscher soll schweigen.") Cited in Hoffmann, *E. T. A. Hoffmann: Leben und Arbeit eines preussischen Richters*, p. 120.

19. Heinrich Heine, *Heinrich Heine's Sämmtliche Werke*, ed. Adolf Strodtmann, Rechtmäßige Original-Ausgabe, 21 vols. (Hamburg: Hoffmann und Campe, 1862), 13:48.

20. The standard survey on phases in the history of irony is Ernst Behler, *Klassische Ironie, Romantische Ironie, Tragische Ironie: Zum Ursprung dieser Begriffe* (Darmstadt: Wissenschaftliche Buchgesellschaft, 1972).

21. The distinction merged seventeenth-century moralists' distinctions between truth and opinion with Kant's distinction between the noumenal and

phenomenal realms. Skeptical about the claims of reason and human freedom, the Romantics reversed Kant's placement of agency. For Kant, human beings had free will in the noumenal realm, but in the phenomenal realm they were caught in rational causal chains that determined their actions. The Romantics associated the realm of the noumenon with forces (often metaphysical) that determined human action, and the phenomenal realm with the place where human beings could act and control their actions.

22. Gary Handwerk and Ernst Behler have rightly noted that the step is not large from Schlegel's dreams about a universal language to postmodern arguments about the degree to which discourse and symbolic orders inform human action. Gary J. Handwerk, *Irony and Ethics in Narrative: From Schlegel to Lacan* (New Haven, Conn.: Yale University Press, 1985), p. 3; Ernst Behler, *Irony and the Discourse of Modernity* (Seattle: University of Washington Press, 1990).

23. "Die Natur verfolgt, ihrer Kinder Schicksal erwägend und bestimmend, ihren eignen dunkeln, unerforschlichen Weg, und das, was Konvenienz, was im beengten Leben geltende Meinungen und Rücksichten als wahre Tendenz des Seins feststellen wollen ist ihr nur das vorwitzige Spiel sich weise dünkender betörter Kinder. Aber der kurzsichtige Mensch findet oft in dem Widerspruch der Überzeugung seines Geistes mit jenem dunkeln Walten der unerforschlichen Macht, die ihn erst an ihrem mütterlichen Busen gehegt und gepflegt und ihn dann verlassen, eine brillane Ironie, und diese Ironie erfüllt ihn mit Grausen und Entsetzen, weil sie sein eignes Ich zu vernichten droht." Hoffmann, *Späte Werke*, p. 549.

24. "'Und immer werden Sie,' erwiderte die Benzon, 'mit dieser phantastischen Überspanntheit, mit dieser herzzerschneidenden Ironie nichts anstiften als Unruhe-Verwirrung—völlige Dissonanz aller konventionellen Verhältnisse, wie sie nun einmal bestehen.'" Hoffmann, *Lebens-Ansichten*, p. 351.

25. "Die Ironie, welche, indem sie das Menschliche mit dem Tier in Konflikt setzt, den Menschen mit seinem ärmlichen Tun und Treiben verhöhnt, wohnt nur in einem tiefen Geiste, und so enthüllen Callots aus Tier und Mensch geschaffene groteske Gestalten dem ernsten, tiefer eindringenden Beschauer alle die geheimen Andeutungen, die unter dem Schleier der Skurrilität verborgen liegen." Hoffmann, *Fantasie- und Nachtstücke*, pp. 12–3.

26. Friedrich Schlegel, *Lucinde and the Fragments*, trans. Peter Firchow (Minneapolis: University of Minnesota Press, 1971), p. 167; Schlegel, *Kritische Schriften und Fragmente: Studienausgabe*, ed. Ernst Behler and Hans Eichner, 6 vols. (Paderborn: Schöningh, 1988), 2:109.

27. Behler, for instance, finds the pendular motion between enthusiasm and skepticism to be the primal motive of Schlegel's thought on irony, but he

finds three different ways that this motive is developed. Behler, *Klassische Ironie*, p. 67.

28. "Opfre den Grazien, heißt, wenn es einem Philosophen gesagt wird, so viel als: Schaffe dir Ironie und bilde dich zur Urbanität." Schlegel, Athenäums-Fragment No. 431, in *Kritische Schriften*, 2:154.

29. See David E. Wellbery, "Stimmung," in *Ästhetische Grundbegriffe: Historisches Wörterbuch in sieben Bänden*, ed. Karlheinz Barck (Stuttgart: Metzler, 2000–2005), 5:703–33, esp. pp. 704–12.

30. "Der Fremde [Kreisler] hatte sich, sowie die Prinzessin zu sprechen begann, rasch zu ihr gewendet, und schaute ihr jetzt in die Augen, aber sein ganzes Antlitz schien ein andres worden.—Vertilgt war der Ausdruck schwermütiger Sehnsucht, vertilgt jede Spur des tief im Innersten aufgeregten Gemüts, ein toll verzerrtes Lächeln steigerte den Ausdruck bitterer Ironie bis zum Possierlichen, bis zum Skurrilen." Hoffmann, *Die Elixiere des Teufels. Lebens-Ansichten des Katers Murr*, p. 342.

31. "Er ging sonderbar lächelnd an den Tisch, Anselmus stand schweigend auf, der Archivarius sah ihn noch immer so wie in höhnendem Spott lächelnd an, kaum hatte er aber in die Abschrift geblickt, als das Lächeln in dem tiefen feierlichen Ernst unterging, zu dem sich alle Muskeln des Gesichts verzogen." Hoffmann, *Fantasie- und Nachtstücke*, pp. 216–17.

32. Lawrence Kramer, "The Mysteries of Animation: History, Analysis and Musical Subjectivity," *Music Analysis* 20, no. 2 (2001): 156–68.

33. "Er trennt sein Ich von dem innern Reich der Töne und gebietet darüber als unumschränkter Herr." E. T. A. Hoffmann, *Schriften zur Musik, Nachlese*, ed. Friedrich Schnapp (Munich: Winkler, 1963), p. 37.

34. "Die Musik schließt dem Menschen ein unbekanntes Reich auf"; "es ist wahrhafte Musik aus der andern Welt (*musica dell'altro mondo*)," both in ibid., pp. 34, 215.

35. Thomas Weiskel, *The Romantic Sublime: Studies in the Structure and Psychology of Transcendence* (Baltimore: Johns Hopkins University Press, 1976), pp. 23–24.

36. The ambiguity regarding the temporality of the moment is common to German critical thought. Berthold Hoeckner has teased out relationships between individual moments, entire works, and, more spectacularly, the historical "moment" of German music from Beethoven through Schoenberg. Berthold Hoeckner, *Programming the Absolute: Nineteenth-Century German Music and the Hermeneutics of the Moment* (Princeton, N.J.: Princeton University Press, 2002).

37. Carl Dahlhaus, "E. T. A. Hoffmanns Beethoven-Kritik und die Ästhetik des Erhabenen," in *Klassische und romantische Musikästhetik* (Laaber: Laaber-Verlag, 1988), p. 108.

38. "Seine [Haydn's] Symphonie führt uns in unabsehbare, grüne Haine, in ein lustiges, buntes Gewühl glücklicher Menschen. . . . In die Tiefe des Geisterreichs führt uns Mozart." Hoffmann, *Schriften zur Musik*, p. 35.

39. Mark Evan Bonds has surveyed the ways that Hoffmann distinguished Mozart and Haydn from Beethoven: here the categories of rhetoric, there those of philosophy. It is important to note, however, that Hoffmann ascribed the same basic operation of severance to the experience of the music of all three composers. Indeed, Hoffmann took pains to insist on the commonality: "*So* Beethoven's instrumental music opens to us *as well* the realm of the terrible and the immeasurable." ("So öffnet uns auch Beethovens Instrumentalmusik das Reich des Ungeheueren und Unermeßlichen.") After all, his intent was at least as much to claim a status for Beethoven already enjoyed by Haydn and Mozart as it was to explicate the particularities of the new composer on the block. Ibid., 36 (emphasis added); Mark Evan Bonds, *Music as Thought: Listening to the Symphony in the Age of Beethoven* (Princeton, N.J.: Princeton University Press, 2006), pp. 35–37.

40. "Glühende Strahlen schießen durch dieses Reiches tiefe Nacht, und wir werden Riesenschatten gewahr, die auf- und abwogen, enger und enger uns einschließen, und alles in uns vernichten, nur nicht den Schmerz der unendlichen Sehnsucht, in welcher jede Lust, die, schnell in jauchzenden Tönen emporgestiegen, hinsinkt und untergeht, und nur in diesem Schmerz, der, Liebe, Hoffnung, Freude in sich verzehrend, aber nicht zerstörend, unsre Brust mit einem vollstimmigen Zusammenklänge aller Leidenschaften zersprengen will, leben wir fort und sind entzückte Geisterseher." Hoffmann, *Schriften zur Musik*, p. 36.

41. Ibid., p. 34.

42. The distinction goes back to Aristotle, but it was given an expression that had great influence on Hoffmann's generation by Friedrich Schiller in his review of Matthisson's poetry (1794). Schiller argued that music provides an outer "analogy" to the inner movements of the spirit. Friedrich Schiller, *Sämtliche Werke in 5 Bänden*, ed. Peter-André Alt, Albert Meier, and Wolfgang Riedel (Munich: Hanser, 2004), 5:998–99. Christian Friedrich Michaelis, for example, worked the distinction into his second version of *Ueber den Geist der Tonkunst* (1800). Good recent discussions of the distinction include Charles Rosen, *The Romantic Generation* (Cambridge, Mass.: Harvard University Press, 1995), pp. 127–28; Karol Berger, *A Theory of Art* (Oxford: Oxford University Press, 2000), pp. 204–6; Jenefer Robinson, *Deeper than Reason: Emotion and Its Role in Literature, Music, and Art* (Oxford, U.K.: Clarendon, 2005), pp. 5–27, esp. 19.

43. Bonds has also noted that Hoffmann, following Jean Paul, distinguished levels of sublimity (*Music as Thought*, pp. 48–50).

44. "Haydn faßt das Menschliche im menschlichen Leben romantisch auf; er ist kommensurabler für die Mehrzahl. Mozart nimmt das Übermenschliche, das Wunderbare, welches im innern Geiste wohnt, in Anspruch." Hoffmann, *Schriften zur Musik*, p. 36.

45. Edmund Burke, *A Philosophical Enquiry into the Sublime and the Beautiful and Other Pre-Revolutionary Writings*, ed. David Womersley (London: Penguin, 1998), part 1, sections 5–6 (pp. 85–87).

46. Hoffmann thus took up the *Empfindsamkeit* (sensibility) ideal of the bonding power of music, but he respected the insights that Wackenroder and Tieck gained as they noted the failure of that ideal. On the crisis of *Empfindsamkeit* in Wackenroder, see Barbara Naumann, *Musikalisches Ideen-Instrument: Das Musikalische in Poetik und Sprachtheorie der Frühromantik* (Stuttgart: Metzler, 1990).

47. In Hoffman's enthusiasm for the fugue, for example, he never engaged in the hope that the fugue could represent an entire society, as Forkel did in the *Allgemeine Geschichte der Musik*.

48. To describe the emphatic experience that pulls an individual away from everyday events, Western thinkers have been imaginative both with their descriptive terms and with their explanatory philosophies. The terms include "harmony," "the sublime," "presence," "situatedness" (*Geborgenheit*), and "attunement" (*Stimmung*). The explanations refer to divine or metaphysical orders (Ancient and Christian thinkers), rational and moral orders (Kant and Schiller), nature (Goethe and other Romantic natural supernaturalists), unconscious drives common to all human beings (Freud), the life-worlds that surround individual human beings (Heidegger and Blumenberg), the shock of an encounter with the symbolic representation of a social order defined by linguistic and social convention (Lacan), or simply the fact of existence (Lyotard). For a discussion of such issues with respect to Hoffmann, see also Lawrence Kramer, "Saving the Ordinary: Beethoven's 'Ghost' Trio and the Wheel of History," *Beethoven Forum* 12, no. 1 (2005): 50–81.

49. Joseph Kerman, "*Tändelnde Lazzi*: On Beethoven's Trio in D Major, Opus 70, No. 1," in *Slavonic and Western Music: Essays for Gerald Abraham*, ed. Malcolm H. Brown and Roland J. Wiley (Ann Arbor, Mich.: UMI Research Press, 1985), pp. 109–22.

50. Robin Wallace, *Beethoven's Critics: Aesthetic Dilemmas and Resolutions during the Composer's Lifetime* (Cambridge: Cambridge University Press, 1986), p. 24; Stephen C. Rumph, *Beethoven after Napoleon: Political Romanticism in the Late Works* (Berkeley: University of California Press, 2004), pp. 27–31.

51. Jacob de Ruiter, *Der Charakterbegriff in der Musik: Studien zur deutschen Ästhetik der Instrumentalmusik 1740–1850* (Stuttgart: Franz Steiner, 1989), pp. 266–68; Werner Keil, "Hoffmann, Erst Theodor Amadeus (Wilhelm)," in

Musik in Geschichte und Gegenwart, 2nd ed., ed. Ludwig Finscher (Kassel: Bären-reiter, 1994–2007), Personenteil 9, col. 120.

52. "Seine schriftstellerischen Arbeiten, denen er zuweilen noch die Stunden der Erholung und der Muße widmet, tun seinem Fleiße keinen Ein-trag und die üppige, zum Komischen hinneigende Phantasie, die in derselben vorherrschend ist, kontrastirt auf eine merkwürdige Art mit der kalten Ruhe, und mit dem Ernst, womit er als *Richter* an die Arbeit geht." In Schnapp, ed., *E. T. A. Hoffmann in Aufzeichnungen,* p. 459 (emphasis in the original).

53. Hoffmann, *Briefwechsel,* 2:263.

54. E. T. A. Hoffmann, *Die Serapions-Brüder,* 5th ed. (Düsseldorf: Artemis & Winkler, 1995), p. 95.

55. See Keith Chapin, "Lost in Quotation: Nuances behind E. T. A. Hoff-mann's Programmatic Statements," *19th-Century Music* 30, no. 1 (2006): 54.

56. "Da ich nicht einsehe, wehalb der Geist zu seinem Leben der Form des Endlichen bedarf d.h. warum außer Gott d.h. der Seeligkeit der Geister noch was anders ist, so ist mir der Inhalt und der Zweck der Natur und des menschlichen Lebens leer und völlig gehaltlos, daher kann ich nicht thätig sein für die bloße Verbesserung des menschlichen Zustandes, sondern ich werde meine ganze Kraft auf die Vernichtung der Natur und des mensch-lichen Lebens verwenden dadurch, daß ich die Idee der Geisterseeligkeit, des wahren geistigen Lebens (d.h. negativ die Vernichtung alles Endlichen oder alles Wechsels) folglich der Freiheit in mir zu entwickeln und zu verwirklichen strebe, so daß alsdann nach dieser Arbeit die Aufhebung dieses Lebens nicht mehr ist, als der Triumph über die Form, das Ja zur Seeligkeit, indem nämlich alles Endliche selbst in sein Wesen, die Seeligkeit übergehen muß, so daß, was ist, nichts als Gott ist." Quoted in E. T. A. Hoffmann, *Juristische Arbeiten,* ed. Friedrich Schnapp (Munich: Winkler, 1973), p. 172.

57. Behler notes that the mysticism was important to one of three different concepts of irony that Schlegel developed in the *Athanäums-Fragmente* and also that this concept of irony was the one he increasingly turned to in his later career. Behler, *Klassische Ironie,* pp. 69–70.

58. "Ist die innere Ueberzeugung von Recht und Unrecht ohne Rüksicht auf Gesetz und bürgerliche Ordnung die einzige Norm alles Handelns, ist eben jene Ueberzeugung das Forum vor das der Mensch die Thaten seiner Brüder zu ziehen und zu richten sich befugt achtet, glaubt er, daß wenn nur nach jener Ueberzeugung der Zweck recht und gut ist, auch jedes Mittel ihn zu erreichen erlaubt sci, hält er jeden, der dem im eignen Innern recht befun-denen widerstrebt des Todes schuldig und sich selbst berechtigt diesen Aus-spruch der innern Gesinnung auszuführen, so sind alle Bande der menschlichen Geselschaft zerrissen, und in Unthaten jeder Art muß sich dann das wüste Treiben eines fanatischen Wahnsinns, der in sich selbst den über

alles waltenden richtenden Gott erkennen will, offenbaren." Hoffmann, *Juristische Arbeiten*, p. 173.

59. Kramer, "Mysteries of Animation," pp. 162–63.

3. THE DEVOTED EAR: MUSIC AS CONTEMPLATION
Lawrence Kramer

1. This formulation echoes "purposiveness without purpose," one of the traits by which Kant defines the beautiful; see Sec. 1, Bk. 1, nos. 10–11 of his *Critique of the Power of Judgment*, ed. Paul Guyer, trans. Paul Guyer and Eric Matthews (Cambridge: Cambridge University Press, 2000), pp. 105–6.

2. Lord Byron, *Childe Harold's Pilgrimage*, Canto the Third, sec. LXV, ll. 1–6, in *Byron's Poetry*, ed. Frank D. McConnell (New York: Norton, 1978), p. 65.

3. *The Shorter Poems of Robert Browning*, ed. William Clyde Devane (New York: Appleton, Century, Crofts, 1934), p. 38.

4. For the memorial culture that sprang up around Haydn—even before he died—see Matthew Head, "A Music with 'No Past'? Archaeologies of Joseph Haydn and *The Creation*," *19th-Century Music* 23 (2000): 191–217.

5. On the meanings found in this movement and the history of their transformations, see the second chapter of my *Musical Meaning: Toward a Critical History* (Berkeley: University of California Press, 2001), pp. 29–50.

6. See my *Music and Poetry: The Nineteenth Century and After* (Berkeley: University of California Press, 1984), pp. 60–75 (op. 59, no. 1), and *Music as Cultural Practice: 1800–1900* (Berkeley: University of California Press, 1990), pp. 31–33 (op 59, no. 2).

7. See Scott Burnham, *Beethoven Hero* (Princeton, N.J.: Princeton University Press, 1995).

8. Friedrich Nietzsche, *On the Genealogy of Morals*, Second Essay, sec. 1, in *On the Genealogy of Morals and Ecce Homo*, trans. Walter Kaufmann (New York: Random House, 1969), p. 57–58.

9. W. B. Yeats, epigraph to "Responsibilities," in *Collected Poems* (New York: Macmillan, 1967), p. 112.

10. *Lyceum Fragments*, no. 42, in *German Romantic Criticism*, ed. Leslie Willson (New York: Continuum, 1982), p. 115 (translation slightly modified).

11. See Slavoj Žižek and F. W. J. von Schelling, *The Abyss of Freedom/The Ages of the World* (Ann Arbor: University of Michigan Press, 1997), pp. 80–81; and Slavoj Žižek, *Looking Awry: An Introduction to Jacques Lacan through Popular Culture* (Cambridge, Mass.: MIT Press, 1992), p. 128. For more on the musical sinthome, see my "Odradek Analysis: Reflections on Musical Ontology," *Music Analysis* 23 (2004): 287–309.

12. Richard Taruskin, "Speed Bumps," *19th-Century Music* 29 (2005): 185–207.

13. Judith Butler, *Excitable Speech: A Politics of the Performative* (New York: Routledge, 1997), p. 36.

14. From the preface to *Prometheus Unbound*, in *Shelley's Poetry and Prose*, ed. Donald H. Reiman and Sharon B. Powers (New York: Norton, 1977), p. 135.

15. On Bergson's concept of *durée* and musical modernism, see Michael Klein, "Debussy's *L'isle joyeuse* as Territorial Assemblage," *19th-Century Music* 31 (2007): 41–48.

16. On monuments, ruins, and the *siste, viator* tradition, see Geoffrey Hartman, "Wordsworth, Inscriptions, and Romantic Nature Poetry," in *Beyond Formalism: Literary Essays, 1958–1970* (New Haven, Conn.: Yale University Press, 1970), pp. 206–30; and my "Chopin at the Funeral: Episodes in the History of Modern Death," *Journal of the American Musicological Society* 54 (2001): 97–126.

17. T. S. Eliot, "The Dry Salvages," sec. V, ll. 18–19, in *Collected Poems: 1909–1962* (New York: Harcourt, Brace, and World, 1963), p. 198.

18. G. W. F. Hegel, "The Unhappy Consciousness," in *The Phenomenology of Spirit*, trans. A. V. Miller (Oxford: Oxford University Press, 1977), p. 131.

19. On the spiritual and musical logic of the conclusion to *Parsifal*, see David Lewin, "Amfortas's Prayer to Titurel and the Role of D in *Parsifal*: The Tonal Spaces of the Drama and the Enharmonic C♯/B," *19th-Century Music* 7 (1984): 336–49; and my "The Talking Wound and the Foolish Question: Symbolization in *Parsifal*," *Opera Quarterly* (2007): 108–19. The D slowly metamorphoses into D♭, the subdominant of A♭; Lewin suggests that the opera tends to equate D with D♭ throughout.

20. Walter Frisch, *German Modernism* (Berkeley: University of California Press, 2005), pp. 186–213.

21. On the idea of distance in Romantic music, see Berthold Hoeckner, "Schumann and Romantic Distance," *Journal of the American Musicological Society* 50 (1997): 191–212.

4. MUSIC AND FANTASY
Marshall Brown

1. Lawrence Kramer, *Why Classical Music Still Matters* (Berkeley: University of California Press, 2007), pp. 197, 200.

2. Eduard Hanslick, *Vom musikalisch Schönen: Ein Beitrag zur Revision der Ästhetik der Tonkunst* (Wiesbaden: Breitkopf & Härtel, 1966), pp. 7–8.

3. Lawrence Kramer, "Hands On, Lights Off: The 'Moonlight' Sonata and the Birth of Sex at the Piano," in *Musical Meaning: Toward a Critical History* (Berkeley: University of California Press, 2002), pp. 29–50.

4. Immanuel Kant, *Anthropologie in pragmatischer Hinsicht*, §28, B80. Quotations from Kant (ignoring Kant's typographical emphases) are cited in the

text, in standard form: by section number and by page number in the original editions (B = second edition). Section numbers in the *Anthropology* diverge in different editions. Unattributed translations are mine throughout the chapter.

5. The information concerning Kant's knowledge of music is assembled in Hermann Güttler, "Kant und sein musikalischer Umkreis," in *Beethoven-Zentenarfeier: Internationaler musikhistorischer Kongress*, ed. Guido Adler (Vienna: Universal, 1927), pp. 217–21.

6. In general, as I have argued in *The Gothic Text* (Stanford, Calif.: Stanford University Press, 2005), pp. 69–104, I look in Kant's writings toward places that "push toward the margins of his thought and hint at the poetic vision that is chastely excluded from his rational discourse, perhaps even from his conscious thought" (71).

7. Paul Guyer offers a fine description of the difficulties surrounding imagination in "The Harmony of the Faculties Revisited," in *Values of Beauty: Historical Essays in Aesthetics* (Cambridge: Cambridge University Press, 2005), pp. 77–109. But in the desire to systematize Kant's account (and despite his musical title), Guyer elides the productive tensions. He claims that judgment presumes a concept and that Kantian "aesthetic judgments . . . are about particular objects, which can only be individuated by means of such concepts" (95). But how determinate can Kant's notion of "the parrot, the hummingbird, the bird of paradise" have been (*Critique of Judgment*, §16, B49) way up there in the North?

8. Guyer, "Harmony of the Faculties," p. 79. See David Wellbery, "Stimmung," in *Ästhetische Grundbegriffe*, ed. Karlheinz Barck et al., 7 vols. (Stuttgart: Metzler, 2003), 5:703–33, stressing the musical resonance of the term, especially in Kant; on *proportionierte Stimmung*, see p. 709.

9. For summaries of most of the important eighteenth-century writers on the physics of music, consult the pages on "Musik" listed in the index of Joachim Gessinger, *Auge & Ohr: Studien zur Erforschung der Sprache am Menschen, 1700–1850* (Berlin: de Gruyter, 1994).

10. Charles Rosen, *Sonata Forms* (New York: Norton, 1980), pp. 310, 314.

11. Charles Rosen, *The Romantic Generation* (Cambridge, Mass.: Harvard University Press, 1995); John Daverio, *Nineteenth-Century Music and the German Romantic Ideology* (New York: Schirmer, 1993), p. 46.

12. Joseph Kerman, *The Beethoven Quartets* (New York: Knopf, 1967), p. 121.

13. For very suggestive speculations about irony and about Beethoven's endings, see Daniel K. L. Chua, *Absolute Music and the Construction of Meaning* (Cambridge: Cambridge University Press, 1999), pp. 199–217 and 257–86, respectively.

14. Jean-Pierre Richard, *L'Univers imaginaire de Mallarmé* (Paris: Seuil, 1961), p. 569.

15. David Code, "Hearing Debussy Reading Mallarmé: Music 'après Wagner' in the 'Prélude à l'après-midi d'un faune,'" *Journal of the American Musicological Society* 54 (2001): 493–554; David Code, "The Formal Rhythms of Mallarmé's Faun," *Representations* 86 (Spring 2004): 73–119; Elizabeth McCombie, *Mallarmé and Debussy: Unheard Music, Unseen Text* (Oxford: Oxford University Press, 2003), an admirable project, though of limited value in the execution.

16. On the music of decadence, see Yopie Prins, "Sappho Recomposed: A Song Cycle by Granville and Helen Bantock," in *The Figure of Music in Nineteenth-Century Poetry*, ed. Phyllis Weliver (Aldershot, U.K.: Ashgate, 2005), pp. 230–58. The essay relates the Bantocks' songs to Verlaine's "Art poétique"; my quotations come from Helen Bantock's song text, Carolyn Abbate, and a tribute by Kennedy Scott included in Myrrha Bantock's memoir of her parents, quoted by Prins, pp. 254, 255, 258. On unheard melodies and structuration, see my essay "Unheard Melodies: The Force of Form," in *Turning Points: Essays in the History of Cultural Expressions* (Stanford, Calif.: Stanford University Press, 1997), pp. 239–67.

17. I take my cue concerning the symphonic poem from Carl Dahlhaus: see the essays grouped under the title "Aporien der Programmusik," in *Klassische und romantische Musikästhetik* (Laaber: Laaber, 1988), pp. 365–413. In English, see Carl Dahlhaus, *Esthetics of Music*, trans. William W. Austin (Cambridge: Cambridge University Press, 1982), pp. 57–63, arguing that Liszt's works are progressive in intention but regressive in method.

18. See Carl Dahlhaus, "Lieder ohne Worte," in *Klassische und romantische Musikästhetik*, pp. 140–44, relating to Hanslick and Liszt a well-known letter by Mendelssohn claiming that music portrays feelings more precisely than words can.

19. See Alexander Main, "Liszt after Lamartine: 'Les Préludes,'" *Music and Letters* 60 (1979): 130–48.

20. Verlaine's *Sagesse* (a volume almost entirely devoid of the *rimes impaires* recommended in "Art poétique") has several music-related examples of the sanctimonious tone into which he often fell: see number 16, beginning "Ecoutez la chanson bien douce"; and then in number 19, "Et j'ai revu l'enfant unique," see the line "Et tout mon sang chrétien chanta la Chanson pure."

21. Lawrence Kramer, *Music as Cultural Practice, 1800–1900* (Berkeley: University of California Press, 1990), pp. 102–34.

22. Rosen, *Sonata Forms*, 261; Rosen, *Romantic Generation*, 583.

23. Rudolf Stephan comments briefly but pointedly on the equivalence of major and minor in Mendelssohn in "Über Mendelssohns Kontrapunkt: Vorläufige Bermerkungen," in *Vom musikalischen Denken: Gesammlete Vorträge*, ed.

Rainer Damm and Andreas Traub (Mainz: Schott, 1985), pp. 57–58. Stephan
wants to defend Mendelssohn from the charge of superficiality, but my
account would set the accents differently: the value of surfaces is precisely
what was sought by a widespread nineteenth-century culture of refinement.

24. Lawrence Kramer, *Franz Schubert: Sexuality, Subjectivity, Song* (Cambridge: Cambridge University Press, 1998), pp. 5, 38, 131, 141. Kramer associates scoring with the Lacanian Real, manifested through "disclosure . . . by
means of an incongruity" (ibid., p. 131). Another pun with related impact but
antithetical gestation is "jamming," in Lawrence Kramer, *After the Lovedeath:
Sexual Violence and the Making of Culture* (Berkeley: University of California
Press, 1997), pp. 60. Jamming harmonizes with the improvisational conduct
of *After the Lovedeath*, but the dialectic of score and performance remains fundamental to Kramer's conception of classical music, which "always addresses
the listener against the possibility or memory of other note-for-note renditions" (*Why Classical Music Still Matters*, p. 82). Yet another version of musical
fantasy, this time drawn from Wittgenstein, is "lighting up" (*Aufleuchten*), in
Lawrence Kramer, *Opera and Modern Culture: Wagner and Strauss* (Berkeley:
University of California Press, 2004), pp. 70–71. Kramer here links lighting
to hermeneutic perspective; it is important to keep in mind that *Aufleuchten*
implies light flaring from within, not from the interpreter's searchlight, which
would call for the transitive form *Beleuchtung*. Mendelssohn's ophicleide flares
from within the work, just as do the "loud cymbal clashes" in the prelude to
Lohengrin (ibid., p. 71). Of course, the scoring can be further highlighted or
else downplayed in performance.

While using these notes to record my infinite debt to Kramer's work, I
should also pay tribute to his generosity of spirit by recording my finite reser-
vation. Scoring, after all, hurts. What Kramer says about Schubert seems to
apply generally to his own work: "affirmative moments are rare," and "the
fullness of counternormative subjectivity is more often attained in the arena
of pain" (*Franz Schubert*, p. 128). Joy is inevitably *jouissance* and hence
orgasmic: sensual pleasure is "visceral," indeed "literally visceral"; it "ripples
throughout the whole body" to overcome the risk of being "skeletal, literally
superficial, without the addition of the inner voices"; and (quoting Ligeti on
Chopin), it is "felt as a tactile shape, as a succession of muscular exertions"
(*Why Classical Music Still Matters*, pp. 74, 78, 153, 162). This body without
surface does not dance (the late Nietzsche, admirer of Bizet, seems not to
figure in Kramer's pantheon); its joy is too earnest for delight. In Kramer's
accounts, so far as I can see, though play and irony can detoxify a tumescent
masculinity (*After the Lovedeath*, p. 122), they become civilizing ends only in
Mendelssohn, who offers "uninhibited play in which social and bodily energies merge and circulate" (Lawrence Kramer, *Classical Music and Postmodern*

Knowledge [Berkeley: University of California Press, 1995], p. 139). Yet even in the work here under discussion, Mendelssohn's cantata *Die erste Walpurgisnacht*, the joy is "inextricable from the nightmare image of its other" and "claims . . . that patriarchy can humanize itself by recasting that nightmare as a midsummer night's dream" (ibid., p. 141). I suppose that in this spirit one might etymologize Mendelssohn's ophicleide to interpret it as a threateningly patriarchal snake in the grass, but to my ear it's a hoot.

All the same, I cannot imagine a richer conception of intimacy than Kramer's songfulness, when "voice addresses itself in its sensuous and vibratory fullness to the body of the listener, thereby offering both material pleasure and an incitement to fantasy" (Lawrence Kramer, "Beyond Words and Music: An Essay on Songfulness," in *Musical Meaning* [see note 3], p. 54).

25. For Bloch's critique of formalism, see Ernst Bloch, *Geist der Utopie: Zweite Fassung* (Suhrkamp: Frankfurt, 1964), pp. 146–52. Bloch is not an anti-formalist but regards form as an epiphenomenal sedimentation of the artistic essence, which is will.

26. On cheerfulness, a cardinal principle of German classicism, see Harald Weinrich, *Kleine Literaturgeschichte der Heiterkeit* (Munich: Beck, 2001). *Heiterkeit* mixes the Latin qualities *serenitas* and *hilaritas*, which perfectly encompass the spirit of Mendelssohn.

27. See in particular Lawrence Kramer, *Music and Poetry: The Nineteenth Century and After* (Berkeley: University of California Press, 1984), pp. 234–41; also see Joseph Kerman, "Taking the Fifth," in *Write All These Down: Essays on Music* (Berkeley: University of California Press, 1994), pp. 207–16, arguing that the symphony moves from thematic-universal "thought" to motivic-contemporary "deed"; Peter Gülke, *Zur Neuausgabe der Sinfonie Nr. 5 von Ludwig van Beethoven: Werk und Edition* (Leipzig: Peters, 1978), pp. 49–71.

28. Although arguably an extreme case, the ambiguities in the Fifth Symphony are also representative of Beethoven's "new path," as analyzed by Carl Dahlhaus in *Ludwig van Beethoven: Approaches to His Music*, trans. Mary Whittall (Oxford, U.K.: Clarendon, 1991), pp. 166–80. So, commenting on the D-Minor Piano Sonata, op. 31, no. 2, Dahlhaus writes, "Nearly all the formal sections occupy a twilight world, in which it is difficult or impossible to make pronouncements about their functions." And he draws the conclusion, "the ambiguity should be perceived as an artistic factor—an attribute of the thing itself, not a failure of analysis" (ibid., p. 170).

29. Kerman, "Taking the Fifth," pp. 207–16. Scott Burnham says that the first movement "eschew[s] preamble" (*Beethoven Hero* [Princeton, N.J.: Princeton University Press, 1995], p. 33), yet the whole opening section is "an opening," with "tonics that act as points of departure rather than points of arrival and closure" (ibid., p. 39). The symphony, that is, lacking a preface,

keeps on starting, all the way to the coda in the last movement that keeps on beginning to end (well described by Burnham on pp. 57–59). More generically, introductions are problematized in Peter Gülke, "Introduktion als Widerspruch im System: Zur Dialektik von Thema und Prozesualität bei Beethoven," *Deutsches Jahrbuch der Musikwissenschaft* 40 (1969): 5–40, though I find this essay less accessible than the later essay by Gülke, cited in note 27.

30. For suggestive literary readings, see Susan J. Wolfson, *The Questioning Presence: Wordsworth, Keats, and the Interrogative Mode in Romantic Poetry* (Ithaca, N.Y.: Cornell University Press, 1996).

31. Heinrich Schenker, *Beethoven: Fünfte Sinfonie* (Vienna: Universal, 1969).

32. I am alluding here not so much to Frank Kermode's well-known account of the stabilizing tic-tock of narrative form in *The Sense of an Ending: Studies in the Theory of Fiction* (Oxford: Oxford University Press, 1966), pp. 44–46, as to the correction that motivates Stuart Sherman's wise and witty *Telling Time: Clocks, Diaries, and English Diurnal Form, 1660–1785* (Chicago: University of Chicago Press, 1996), pp. 9–11.

33. Rainer Cadenbach, "5. Symphonie c-Moll op. 67," in *Beethoven: Interpretationen seiner Werke*, ed. Albrecht Riethmüller, Carl Dahlhaus, and Alexander L. Ringer (Laaber: Laaber, 1994), pp. 486–502.

34. Marcel Proust, *Remembrance of Things Past*, trans. C. K. Scott Moncrieff, Terence Kilmartin, and Andreas Mayor (New York: Vintage, 1981), 3:381. In *Proust musicien* (Paris: Bourgois, 1984), Jean-Jacques Nattiez quotes this passage (on pp. 137–38) toward the climax of his argument linking music in Proust with Schopenhauerian timelessness. Suffice it to say that *ivresse* (here translated "exhilaration") is the French equivalent to a Nietzschean term, *Rausch*, and is incompatible with Schopenhauer's aesthetics.

35. Gilles Deleuze and Félix Guattari, *A Thousand Plateaus*, trans. Brian Massumi (Minneapolis: University of Minnesota Press, 1987), p. 300.

36. Many thanks to Larry Kramer for the occasion for this essay and to Keith Chapin for invaluable bibliographic and musical advice.

5. WHOSE BRAHMS IS IT ANYWAY?: OBSERVATIONS ON THE RECORDED
LEGACY OF THE B♭ PIANO CONCERTO, OP. 83
Walter Frisch

1. Hermann Hesse, *Steppenwolf* (Cutchogue, NY: Buccaneer Books, 1976), p. 232.

2. Lawrence Kramer, *Why Classical Music Still Matters* (Berkeley: University of California Press, 2007), pp. 71, 79, 85.

3. Hans Robert Jauss, *Toward an Aesthetics of Reception*, trans. Timothy Bathi (Minneapolis: University of Minnesota Press, 1982), pp. 22ff.

4. The most helpful summary of the genesis and early performing history of the concerto is in Ulrich Mahlert, *Johannes Brahms: Klavierkonzert B-Dur Op. 83* (Munich: Fink, 1994). Although Mahlert is good at reporting the facts and assembling the relevant documents, his speculations based on the evidence often lead him astray.

5. Hans von Bülow to Hermann Wolff, October 20, 1881, in Mahlert, *Johannes Brahms*, pp. 110–11. All translations are my own unless otherwise noted.

6. The full sentence reads, "So war es bei der Erstaufführung seines neues Concertes, wo Brahms in glücklichster Stimmung die von ihm selbst in diesem Werke aufgegebenen enormen technischen Schwierigkeiten theils mit siegender Meisterschaft wie ein muthvoller Held bewältigte, theils auch—ein musikalischer Alexander den unlösbaren gordischen Knoten gleichsam mit dem Schwerte zerhauend—durch kraftvollste Steigerung im Tone und Pedalgebrauch über manche in den Details unüberwindliche, weil nicht ganz claviergemäss gedachte Partie sich und dem Auditorium hinüberhalf." *Musikalisches Wochenblatt* 13 (1882): 40.

7. Quoted in Michael Musgrave, *A Brahms Reader* (New Haven, Conn.: Yale University Press, 2000), p. 125. Musgrave mistakenly gives the date and location of the performance as the winter of 1880 in Hamburg. Florence May provided a more critical account of Brahms's playing of the concerto in a rehearsal in Berlin on the day preceding the performance. See ibid., p. 125. For discussion and documents of Brahms as a pianist, see ibid., pp. 121–36.

8. Quoted in ibid., p. 125. German quoted in Mahlert, *Johannes Brahms*, p. 125.

9. These markings have been transcribed and discussed in Robert Pascall and Philip Weller, "Flexible Tempo and Nuancing in Orchestral Music: Understanding Brahms's View of Interpretation in His Second Piano Concerto and Fourth Symphony," in *Performing Brahms: Early Evidence of Performance Style*, ed. Michael Musgrave and Bernard Sherman (Cambridge: Cambridge University Press, 2003), pp. 220–43. The autograph of the B♭ Concerto is now in the Hamburg Universitäts-and Staatsbibliothek.

10. Johannes Brahms, *Briefwechsel*, vol. 6 (Berlin: Deutsche Brahms-Gesellschaft, 1912; repr., Tutzing: Schneider, 1974), p. 220. Translation quoted from Pascall and Weller, "Flexible Tempo," p. 224. A different translation is in Musgrave, *Brahms Reader*, p. 146.

11. George Henschel, *Personal Recollections of Johannes Brahms* (Boston: Badger, 1907), p. 78. For a comprehensive and insightful study of Brahms's metronome markings, see Bernard Sherman, "Metronome Marks, Timings, and Other Period Evidence Regarding Tempo in Brahms," in *Performing Brahms* (see note 9).

12. Brahms to Clara Schumann, 25 April 1861, in *Johannes Brahms: Life and Letters*, sel. and ann. Styra Avins, trans. Josef Eisinger and Styra Avins (Oxford: Oxford University Press, 1997), p. 232. Original in *Clara Schumann–Johannes Brahms Briefe aus den Jahren 1853–1896*, ed. B. Litzmann, 2 vols. (Leipzig: Breitkopf & Härtel, 1927), 1:359–60.

13. Robert Pascall, "Playing Brahms: A Study in 19th-Century Performance Practice," Papers in Musicology No. 1 (University of Nottingham, Department of Music, 1991), p. 15.

14. The timings of some recordings of the B♭ Concerto—and the slowing trend they represent—have been discussed by José Bowen in "Tempo, Duration and Flexibility: Techniques in the Analysis of Performance," *Journal of Musicological Research* 16 (1996): 116.

15. See Bernard Sherman, "Metronome Marks, Timings, and Other Period Evidence Regarding Tempo in Brahms," in *Performing Brahms* (see note 4), pp. 115–17; Walter Frisch, *Brahms: The Four Symphonies* (New Haven, Conn.: Yale University Press, 2003), pp. 169–73.

16. This performance has been rereleased on Sony SK 60675 with Bernstein's preliminary comments and an interview with Gould.

17. The Horowitz-Toscanini performance is on Appian ARP 6001; the Fleisher-Szell is on Sony MH2K 63225.

18. The Gilels-Jochum is on DGG 447 446–2; the Zimerman-Bernstein is on DGG 413 472–2.

19. See Bowen, "Tempo, Duration and Flexibility."

20. In calculating my ideal timing for the Andante, I have used a metronome setting of ♩ = 63 for the Più Adagio sections at measures 59–70 and 94–99 (see Example 5.1c). This speed is exactly 25 percent below the Andante marking of 84. I selected this proportion because it is almost identical to the one Brahms himself indicated in his metronome markings for *Nänie*, a work composed in the same year as the B♭ Concerto. There, an Andante in ⁶₄ time, marked by Brahms at ♩ = 100, changes at measure 85 to a Più sostenuto marked at ♩ = 76. Taking più sostenuto as roughly analogous to più adagio, I have calculated a similar reduction in speed for the Andante of the concerto.

21. Fanny Davies, "Some Personal Recollections of Brahms as Pianist and Interpreter" (1905), in *Cobbett's Cyclopedic Survey of Chamber Music*, comp. and ed. Walter Wilson Cobbett, 2nd ed., 3 vols. (London: Oxford University Press, 1963), 1:184.

22. Margaret Notley, "Late-Nineteenth-Century Chamber Music and the Cult of the Classical Adagio," *19th-Century Music* 23 (1999): 33–61. See also Lawrence Kramer's chapter on the Adagio in this volume.

23. Quoted in Mahlert, *Johannes Brahms*, p. 107. This does not mean, as Mahlert erroneously asserts (p. 24), that the third movement of the concerto

was originally marked "Adagio" and later changed by Brahms. Other references to the Andante of op. 83 as an "Adagio" include Hermann Kretschmar, in an essay of 1884, cited in Mahlert, *Johannes Brahms*, p. 123; and a review of Brahms's performance of the concerto with the Vienna Philharmonic in *Musikalisches Wochenblatt* 13 (1882): 39. These examples bear out Notley's point about musicians often failing to distinguish between an adagio and andante (Notley, "Late-Nineteenth-Century Chamber Music," p. 44).

24. A helpful table of all Brahms's slow movement designations is given in Notley, "Late-Nineteenth-Century Chamber Music," p. 46.

25. *Encyclopädie der gesammten musikalischen Wissenschaften*, ed. Gustav Schillings (Stuttgart: Köhler, 1835), pp. 192–93.

26. Pascall, "Playing Brahms," p. 15; Michael Musgrave, *Brahms: A German Requiem* (Cambridge: Cambridge University Press, 1996), p. 75.

27. Quoted in Mahlert, *Johannes Brahms*, p. 117.

28. See Billroth to Wilhelm Lübke, October 29, 1881, in Mahlert, *Johannes Brahms*, p. 112.

29. Quoted in Richard Heuberger, *Erinnerungen an Johannes Brahms* (Tutzing: Hans Schneider, 1971), p. 88.

6. THE CIVILIZING PROCESS: MUSIC AND THE AESTHETICS OF TIME-SPACE RELATIONS IN *THE GIRL OF THE GOLDEN WEST*
Richard Leppert

I am grateful for the comments, corrections, and suggestions offered by Helen M. Greenwald, David M. Lubin, and Gary Thomas.

1. A good deal has been written about this opera in recent years; the work of Allan W. Atlas, Helen M. Greenwald, and Annie J. Randall and Rosalind Gray Davis (all cited in these notes) is especially noteworthy. My remarks are indebted to their research, though nonetheless move in a somewhat different direction.

2. Norbert Elias, *The Civilizing Process*, vol. 1, *The History of Manners*, trans. Edmund Jephcott (New York: Pantheon, 1978).

3. On the complex history of the words *civilization*, *culture*, and *nature*, see the separate entries in Raymond Williams, *Keywords: A Vocabulary of Culture and Society*, rev. ed. (New York: Oxford University Press, 1983). *Nature*, Williams suggests, "is perhaps the most complex word in the language" (p. 219); and *culture* "is one of the two or three most complicated words in the English language" (p. 87).

4. Max Horkheimer and Theodor W. Adorno, *Dialectic of Enlightenment: Philosophical Fragments*, ed. Gunzelin Schmid Noerr, trans. Edmund Jephcott (Stanford, Calif.: Stanford University Press, 2002), p. 2.

5. Adorno is thus bluntly positioning himself against Hegel, whose disregard for nature is well known. On this point, see Theodor W. Adorno, *Aes-*

thetic Theory, ed. Gretel Adorno and Rolf Tiedemann, trans. Robert Hullot-Kentor (Minneapolis: University of Minnesota Press, 1997), pp. 63, 75–77; and Richard Wolin, "Utopia, Mimesis, and Reconciliation: A Redemptive Critique of Adorno's *Aesthetic Theory*," *Representations* 32 (Fall 1990): 42.

6. Adorno, *Aesthetic Theory*, pp. 61–62; see also Heinz Paetzold, "Adorno's Notion of Natural Beauty: A Reconsideration," in *The Semblance of Subjectivity: Essays in Adorno's Aesthetic Theory*, ed. Tom Huhn and Lambert Zuidervaart (Cambridge, Mass.: MIT Press, 1997), pp. 213–35.

7. Adorno, *Aesthetic Theory*, pp. 62, 65–66. "Under its optic, art is not the imitation of nature, but the imitation of natural beauty" (ibid., p. 71). See also Roger Behrens, "On Music in Nature and Nature in Music," *Issues in Contemporary Culture and Aesthetics* 5 (1997): 17–26. Cf. composer-philosopher David Dunn, "Nature, Sound Art, and the Sacred," in *The Book of Music and Nature*, ed. David Rothenberg and Marta Ulvaeus (Middletown, Conn.: Wesleyan University Press, 2001), p. 95. Alluding to a lengthy passage in James Agee's *Let Us Now Praise Famous Men* describing the meanings and intelligence audible in late-night calls of two foxes, Dunn comments, "We hear in the world talking to itself a sense of otherness that simultaneously mirrors our deepest sense of belonging"; and "Perhaps music is a conservation strategy for keeping something alive that we now need to make more conscious, a way of making sense of the world from which we might refashion our relationships to nonhuman living systems" (p. 97).

8. Adorno, *Aesthetic Theory*, p. 65. Cf. "Times in which nature confronts man overpoweringly allow no room for natural beauty" (ibid.).

9. Nowhere is this phenomenon more apparent than in the United States, where, as Lee Clark Mitchell has shown, nostalgia for the disappearance (better, disappearedness) of the Native (or, in this context, "Natural") American was at once acknowledged and, from a safe distance, lamented already by the 1830s, a half century in advance of the final slaughter at Wounded Knee in 1890. Lee Clark Mitchell, *Witnesses to a Vanishing America: The Nineteenth-Century Response* (Princeton, N.J.: Princeton University Press, 1981).

10. Michel de Certeau, *The Practice of Everyday Life*, trans. Steven Rendall (Berkeley: University of California Press, 1984), p. 115; he continues: "Every story is a travel story—a spatial practice"; and "Narrated adventures, simultaneously producing geographies of actions and drifting into the commonplaces of an order, do no merely constitute a 'supplement' to pedestrian enunciations and rhetorics. They are not satisfied with displacing the latter and transposing them into the field of language. In reality, they organize walks. They make the journey, before or during the time the feet perform it" (ibid., pp. 115–16).

11. Ibid., p. 117: "Space occurs as the effect produced by the operations that orient it, situate it, temporalize it, and make it function in a polyvalent

unity of conflictual programs or contractual proximities. . . . In contradistinction to the place, [space] has thus none of the univocality or stability of a 'proper.' In short, *space is a practiced place*"; and p. 118: "Stories thus carry out a labor that constantly transforms places into spaces or spaces into places. They also organize the play of changing relationships between places and spaces." Henri Lefebvre, in *The Production of Space*, trans. Donald Nicholson-Smith (Oxford, U.K.: Blackwell, 1991), pp. 26, 71, points out that space is not natural but cultural: it is socially produced—though not as a thing; as such, space responds to both the forces and relation of production. Accordingly, space "serves as a tool of thought and action; that in addition to being a means of production it is also a means of control."

12. See further Gary F. Kurutz, "Yosemite on Glass," in *Yosemite: Art of an American Icon*, ed. Amy Scott (Berkeley: University of California Press, 2007), pp. 54–87.

13. William Deverell, " 'Niagara Magnified': Finding Emerson, Muir, and Adams in Yosemite," in *Yosemite: Art of an American Icon* (see note 12), pp. 11–12; and Kate Nearpass Ogden, "California as Kingdom Come," in ibid., p. 23: "To a nation that was both insecure about the brevity of its history and struggling to rebuild following a brutal civil war, Yosemite was worth its weight in artistic metaphors."

14. John Muir, *Nature Writings* (New York: Library of America, 1997).

15. Frederick Jackson Turner, "The Significance of the Frontier in American History," paper presented to the American Historical Association, 1893, Chicago, available online at http://xroads.virginia.edu/~Hyper/TURNER/chapter1.html. Turner ends his paper thus: "The stubborn American environment is there with its imperious summons to accept its conditions; the inherited ways of doing things are also there; and yet, in spite of environment, and in spite of custom, each frontier did indeed furnish a new field of opportunity, a gate of escape from the bondage of the past; and freshness, and confidence, and scorn of older society, impatience of its restraints and its ideas, and indifference to its lessons, have accompanied the frontier. What the Mediterranean Sea was to the Greeks, breaking the bond of custom, offering new experiences, calling out new institutions and activities, that, and more, the ever retreating frontier has been to the United States directly, and to the nations of Europe more remotely. And now, four centuries from the discovery of America, at the end of a hundred years of life under the Constitution, the frontier has gone, and with its going has closed the first period of American history."

16. See Lee Clark Mitchell, *Westerns: Making the Man in Fiction and Film* (Chicago: University of Chicago Press, 1996), pp. 59–70.

17. Ogden, "California as Kingdom Come," p. 24.

18. Mitchell, *Westerns*, p. 89.

19. The West was also in part the product of popular literature, and the dime novel especially, a genre noted for its sensationalist narrative, and published in staggering quantities during the last four decades of the nineteenth century. The Beadle Dime Novel series, produced by the firm Beadle and Co., later Beadle and Adams, between 1860 and 1885, for example, reached number 631, with Western subjects among the most popular in the aftermath the Civil War. Few of the Beadle narratives achieved the popularity of the stories about Buffalo Bill, a man large in fiction and perhaps even larger in life. Buffalo Bill (William Cody, 1846–1917), Pony Express rider, army scout in the Civil War, and both a scout and fighter in the Indian wars in the West, gained mythic status from Ned Buntline's dime novel *Buffalo Bill, King of the Border Men*, serialized in the *New York Weekly* in 1869 when Buffalo Bill was only twenty-three years old. All told, he was the subject of more than 550 conventionally exaggerated written accounts. See William H. Goetzmann and William N. Goetzmann, *The West of the Imagination* (New York: Norton, 1986), p. 288. See also Henry Nash Smith, *Virgin Land: The American West as Symbol and Myth* (Cambridge, Mass.: Harvard University Press, 1970), pp. 90–111, on the dime novel in general and the Buffalo Bill stories in particular.

In 1872, art (however loosely described) imitating life, Buffalo Bill acted on a Chicago stage with Buntline (Edward Zane Carroll Judson) in a Buntline melodrama, *The Scouts of the Prairie*, supposedly written in four hours. Firing his six-guns at the critical moment, he saved a young couple from certain death at the hands of hostile Indians. The play was a sensation, in large part because the hero was playing himself, as the saying goes, live and in person. The play had a long run, much of it on tour. See further Goetzmann and Goetzmann, *West of the Imagination*, pp. 288–91. In the early 1880s Cody cashed in on his ever increasing fame by mounting what became his fabled "Buffalo Bill's Wild West," a multipart melodrama of "historical" scenes, ranging from episodes from pioneer life to a kind of cowboys-and-Indians extravaganza, involving as many as twelve hundred participants in reenactments of pitched battles of whites against invariably-to-be-vanquished Native Americans. (The exception was Custer's Last Stand, with Cody playing Custer, though Buffalo Bill symbolically triumphed by reenacting his long-held claim to have taken the first scalp in revenge following the Custer massacre.) Cody took the show to Europe beginning in 1887. Puccini saw it at Milan in 1890 and reported enjoying himself. See Emanuele Senici, *Landscape and Gender in Italian Opera: The Alpine Virgin from Bellini to Puccini* (Cambridge: Cambridge University Press, 2005), p. 248.

Puccini's acquaintance with the American West was otherwise formed from his reading of Bret Harte's melodramatic short stories in Italian translation, many of which were set in California gold-mining camps (for example, "The

Luck of Roaring Camp" and "The Outcasts of Poker Flat"). See Senici, *Landscape and Gender in Italian Opera*, pp. 248–49. On Harte's creation of recurring characters and tropes in Western-themes fiction, see Mitchell, *Westerns*, pp. 77–78. See also Ray Allen Billington, *Land of Savagery, Land of Promise: The European Image of the American Frontier in the Nineteenth Century* (New York: Norton, 1981). Billington points out that Europeans were more interested in the Western plains and deserts than in the mountains.

20. Mary Douglas, *Purity and Danger: An Analysis of Concepts of Pollution and Taboo* (Harmondsworth, U.K.: Penguin, 1970), pp. 137, 145.

21. Elias suggests that the noun *civilization* acknowledges Western self-consciousness: "by this term Western society seeks to describe what constitutes its special character and what it is proud of: the level of *its* technology, the nature of *its* manners, the development of *its* scientific knowledge or view of the world, and much more" (*Civilizing Process*, pp. 3–4). However, as Elias points out, German usage is different. *Zivilization* references a value of second rank, one "comprising only the outer appearance of human beings, the surface of human existence." By contrast, *Kultur* expresses a uniquely German sense of national achievement and essence. *Kultur* in German "refers essentially to intellectual, artistic, and religious facts, and has a tendency to draw a sharp dividing line between facts of this sort, on the one side, and political, economic, and social facts, on the other." In French and English, Elias suggests, the concept of civilization, while acknowledging accomplishment, refers as much to attitudes of behavior of people, whereas *Kultur* in German places little value on behavior in the absence of accomplishment. Herbert Marcuse, in "Remarks on a Redefinition of Culture," in *Science and Culture: A Study of Cohesive and Disjunctive Forces*, ed. Gerald Holton (Boston: Houghton Mifflin, 1965), pp. 218–35, elaborates the distinction between *Zivilization* and *Kultur* by describing the former as a realm of necessity and the latter as a realm of higher fulfillment, though one located in class privilege; the former as fact and means, the latter as value and ends. If *Zivilization* marks what is, for Marcuse *Kultur* marks what ought to be: utopia. I am not keen to parse the problematic and indeed politically suspect binary that Marcuse advances; rather, I reference it as a means of delineating the progressive aspects of both Belasco's play and Puccini's opera, and this despite a panoply of profoundly regressive problematics immanent to both.

22. Norbert Elias, *Time: An Essay*, trans. Edmund Jephcott (Oxford, U.K.: Blackwell, 1992), p. 13.

23. Ibid., p. 21.

24. Stuart Hall, "Ethnicity: Identity and Difference," *Radical America* 23 (October-December 1989): 12.

25. Regarding Puccini's deep-seated love of nature, and his dislike of urban life and the trappings of "civilization" (the material benefits of which he

unambiguously enjoyed), see Mary Jane Phillips-Matz, "Puccini's America," in *The Puccini Companion*, ed. William Weaver and Simonetta Puccini (New York: Norton, 2000), p. 215; e.g., "I long for the woods with its many perfumes. . . . I long for the wind that blows my way from the sea, free and smelling of salt water. . . . I hate pavements! I hate palaces! I hate ornate pillars! I hate styles! I love the beautiful shape of the poplar and the pine tree." See also Mosco Carner, *Puccini: A Critical Biography*, 3rd ed. (London: Duckworth, 1992).

26. David Belasco, *The Girl of the Golden West: Novelized from the Play* (New York: Grosset & Dunlap, 1911).

27. Lisa-Lone Marker, *David Belasco: Naturalism in the American Theatre* (Princeton, N.J.: Princeton University Press, 1975), pp. 43, 48: Belasco had collaborated on both playwriting and directing with Cecil's father, Henry, in the late 1880s. Cecil B. DeMille, *The Autobiography of Cecil B. DeMille*, ed. Donald Hayne (Englewood Cliffs, N.J.: Prentice-Hall, 1959), pp. 113–14, says almost nothing about the film. What he principally reports is a close call involving a near car accident in the "extremely crude mountain roads of San Diego County" where the location shooting of mountain scenes took place (near the present site of Mount Palomar).

Larry Langman, *A Guide to Silent Westerns* (New York: Greenwood, 1992), p. ix: The first Western, Edison's brief *Cripple Creek Barroom* from 1898, within five years was superseded by narrative films, such as Edison's *Brush between Cowboys and Indians* (1904), films that quickly grew to feature length. Between 1898 and 1930, fifty-four hundred silent Western films were produced, including documentaries, shorts, and serials, as well as features. The earliest were made on the East Coast and with painted scenery, but by the second decade of the century, Westerns were made in the West, and often partly on location.

28. "She's a gal who would fight for a Buddy / Just a pal who could weather a text / She's a devilish sort / But an angel at heart / She's the girl of the olden west." The song was recorded in 1923 for the Victor label by the popular Canadian ballad singer Henry Burr: 10 in. 78 rpm, Victor #19104-A. Burr (born McClaskey, 1885, d. 1941) began recording in 1902. In all, he recorded a staggering twelve thousand titles, according to the online *Canadian Encyclopedia Historica*. "The Girl of the Olden West," lyrics by Haven Gillespie, music by Charles L. Cooke and Egbert van Alstyne, was published in 1923 by Jerome H. Hemick & Co., New York and Detroit.

29. The musical numbers include a jarringly incorporated "Ave Maria" (Gounod version) and Liszt's "Liebestraum," both sung by the Girl, the latter song accompanied on the saloon piano by the town drunk. Of these four films, only the first, by DeMille, and the 1938 musical are known to have survived.

30. For example, there was the song "The Little Girl of the Golden West," lyrics by Lester M. Stroube, music by Walter A. Stroube, published by Stroube and May Music Publishing Co, Hammond, Indiana, 1920.

31. For details of Belasco's life and work, see Marker, *David Belasco*; and William Winter, *The Life of David Belasco*, 2 vols. (New York: Moffat, Yard, 1918).

32. Marker, *David Belasco*, p. 30.

33. Ibid., p. 63.

34. David Belasco, *The Girl of the Golden West: A Play in Four Acts* (1915; rpt. New York: Samuel French, 1933), pp. 134–58. The production script also includes scene and light plot design sketches for each act, as well as placement instructions for the special effects machinery. Only this edition of the play provides this information. See also the account by Marker, *David Belasco*, pp. 139–60; and Winter, *Life of David Belasco*, 2:205–7.

35. David Belasco, *The Theatre through Its Stage Door*, ed. Louis V. Defoe (New York: Harper and Brothers, 1919), p. 61.

36. The other songs used in the show were "I'll Build Me a Little Home," "Bonnie Eloise," "Sweet Annie of the Vale," "Jim along Josie," "Wait for the Wagon," and "The Old Armchair." The complete set of costume instructions and song cues for the quartet of singers is in Belasco, *Girl of the Golden West: A Play in Four Acts*, pp. 159–62; the song list appears on p. 163. The play text, however, lists additional songs. Belasco, *Theatre through Its Stage Door*, p. 61: "I always aim to avoid fitting old or familiar music to a new play." *The Girl of the Golden West* obviously does not adhere to this claim. At the end of *The Theatre through Its Stage Door*, Belasco indicates a change in his thinking that occurred within the few years preceding the book's publication in 1919: "I became convinced that the use of orchestras and entr'acte music in the theatre was often destructive to the illusion of what was taking place on stage and calculated to interfere with the imaginative quality of what I was attempting to put into my productions. In other words, I came to believe that an orchestra, however delightful its music, produced a discordant note in the theatre. Therefore I resolved to do away with my orchestra altogether. I dismissed my musicians and concealed my orchestra pit beneath a canopy of flowers" (p. 245).

37. The New York Public Library's Theater Division at Lincoln Center holds several more or less complete copies of the music for the play. Furst's work is hand copied, rather than set, as one would expect; the popular tunes sung solo are in the form of published sheet music with piano accompaniment, again several copies of each. The conductor's score (marked "Leader") is simply the first violin part. There is no full orchestral score. One set has a great deal of the music crossed out (most of the prelude and about half the

entr'acte music, for example), indicating changes made somewhere along the
way, perhaps for the on-tour production. There are also copies of published
piano-vocal sheet music used as source material for orchestral entr'acte medleys by Furst, including a few tunes not listed in the printed script for the play.
The music cues for orchestra in *The Girl of the Golden West* are most heavily
concentrated in act 1 (fourteen cues); throughout the play, the cues are mostly
short, usually sixteen bars or fewer. (In the New York Public Library's extensive Belasco holdings, seventy-five reels of microfilm are given to incidental
music for his plays.) For additional information on Furst and the New York
Public Library holdings of music for the play, see Allan W. Atlas, "Belasco
and Puccini: 'Old Dog Tray' and the Zuni Indians," *Musical Quarterly* 75, no.
3 (Fall 1991): 394–95nn. 19–20. In 1905 Furst also published a sheet-music
arrangement of the play's first-act waltz music: "The Girl of the Golden West
Waltz," in seven pages; the cover reproduces a photograph of Blanche Bates.

38. Belasco's representation of the play's Native Americans, Wowkle and
Billy Jackrabbit, by contrast, is both clichéd and fundamentally racist. The
character description for Billy registers him as "shifty, beady-eyed, lazy and
lying; toes in" (Belasco, *Girl of the Golden West: A Play in Four Acts*, p. 7).
Wowkle and Billy speak largely in monosyllables, in a combination of broken
English and gutturals ("Ugh" and "Huh" being the favorites). Regarding anti-
racist aspects of the play, see Roxana Stuart, "Uncle Giacomo's Cabin: David
Belasco's Direction of *La fanciulla del West*," in *Opera and the Golden West: The
Past, Present, and Future of Opera in the U.S.A.*, ed. John L. DiGaetani and Josef
P. Sirefman (Rutherford, N.J.: Fairleigh Dickinson University Press, 1994),
p. 145.

39. Belasco's voluminous papers were left to the New York Public Library
following his death, forming the initial core of the library's extensive theater
history collections. Belasco meticulously clipped reviews and saved programs,
which he mounted in large scrapbooks. The scrapbooks were eventually
microfilmed by the library, and unfortunately, the originals were then
destroyed. Belasco's plays were well documented in production photographs
as well; the NYPL retains these scrapbooks. The clippings record for *The Girl
of the Golden West* are extensive. Reviews for the play were mixed. While
acknowledging Belasco's lavish production qualities and the solid cast, Bates
especially, some critics were notably weary of the predictable nature of the
playwright's melodramas, which to some seemed very old hat.

40. Belasco, *Girl of the Golden West: A Play in Four Acts*, pp. 11–12.

41. Louis Hartmann served as Belasco's lighting designer beginning in
1901 and continued in that capacity until Belasco's death nearly thirty years
later. For an account of his work, see Louis Hartmann, *Theatre Lighting: A
Manual of the Stage Switchboard* (New York: D. Appleton, 1930); regarding

Belasco's lighting rehearsals, see pp. 14, 19, 21. For extensive discussion of Belasco's interest in lighting and the effort spent on the lighting of his plays, see Belasco, *Theatre through Its Stage Door*, esp. pp. 50–57 and 162–83.

42. Donald R. Anderson, "The West of Frederick Jackson Turner in Three American Plays," *Journal of American Culture* 23, no. 3 (Fall 2000): 89–97, briefly discusses Belasco's play.

43. Belasco's novel of *Girl of the Golden West* provides the initial view of the Sierra Nevada (pp. 78–80); the description is based on the First Picture panorama.

44. Ibid., epigraph.

45. The effect of Belasco's lighted sunburst curtain seems to have been magical. Here is the report of an enthused critic: "As you seat yourself in your orchestra chair you are confronted with a drop-curtain of dazzling beauty. It is made of embossed leather, and shows in shadowy outline a dark green and red valley, a chain of inky black mountains surmounted by a blazing sunset scene. A skillfully concealed spot-light kept always focused upon this sun makes it seem a living ball of fire." And here is the main point: "Under the spell of this curtain you gradually drift far, far away from Forty-second street on your long journey across the continent. In less than two minutes you have arrived." Review of *The Girl of the Golden West*, *Red Book* (January 1906): 404.

Another critic, writing in the *New York Sun*, reacted in kind, repeating the metaphor of time and space travel. Referring to "the decorative beauty, the apt symbolism" of the act curtain, he noted, "Words cannot describe such beauty. . . . The disc of the sun and its flaring streamers were laid on in opaque gold. Their light was reflected from a spotlight in the gallery. How were the beams kept from striking also beneath the summits? The sides of the mountains were of rich, nappy cloth, which drank in every straying beam. . . . Only Belasco could be the father of such striking and perfect scenic art. . . . The curtain had transported us to the golden West, and the panorama view . . . showed us the spot in which *The Girl* lived . . . in which the story of her fate was to be enacted." Review of *The Girl of the Golden West*: "Belasco and His Three Aces," *New York Sun*, December 1905 (the precise date and page number are indecipherable on the microfilm). Belasco's novel of *Girl of the Golden West* provides a variety of nature tropes including that of a pastoral paradise (pp. 94–95), stormy violence (p. 218), and anthropomorphized friend (p. 200), which replicates Minnie's text in act 2 of the play. David Belasco, *Six Plays* (Boston: Little, Brown, 1929), p. 357: "Oh, my mountains! My beautiful peaks! My Sierras! God's in the air here, for sure. You can see Him layin' peaceful hands on the mountain tops. He seems so near, you want to let your soul go right on up."

46. As is typical, Belasco's stage directions for the play precisely describe the stage set, the gist of which is as follows: "The scene is a great stretch of

prairie. In the far background are foothills in with here and there a suggestion
of a winding trail leading to the West. The foliage is the pale green of sage
brush,—the hills the deeper green of pine and hemlock" (Belasco, *Six Plays*,
p. 402).

47. The act 4 lighting design is reproduced in Belasco, *Girl of the Golden
West: A Play in Four Acts*, last page (unpaginated).

48. Belasco, *Six Plays*, p. 403.

49. Here the music reprises the G-major waltz tune first heard at the end
of act 1 when the new lovers have first declared themselves to each other.
Belasco worked three months on the sunrise for act 4, spending, he says, the
considerable sum of five thousand dollars to replicate correctly the magic of
the California sunrise, though in the end he was displeased with the result,
thereafter selling it to another manager for a different production. "It was a
very beautiful sunset [*sic*] that we contrived, but it was not even remotely Californian" (quoted in Belasco, *Theatre through Its Stage Door*, p. 173). Belasco
also discusses the "sunset" (Belasco obviously had forgotten that the effect was
for a sunrise) in ibid., pp. 56–57. For more on Belasco's lighting, see Helen
M. Greenwald, "Realism on the Opera Stage: Belasco, Puccini, and the California Sunset," in *Opera in Context: Essays on Historical Staging from the Late
Renaissance to the Time of Puccini*, ed. Mark A. Radice (Portland, Ore.: Amadeus, 1998), pp. 292–93; and Marker, *David Belasco*, pp. 78–98.

50. Belasco, *Girl of the Golden West: Novelized from the Play*, pp. 340–41.

51. Ibid., p. 343.

52. Ibid., p. 345.

53. I have previously written about this subject, explored here in greater
detail, in "Paradise, Nature, and Reconciliation, or, a Tentative Conversation
with Wagner, Puccini, Adorno, and The Ronettes," *Echo* (online journal) 4,
no. 1 (Fall 2002).

54. For a full accounting of the opera's advance publicity, see Annie J.
Randall and Rosalind Gray Davis, *Puccini and the Girl: History and Reception of
The Girl of the Golden West* (Chicago: University of Chicago Press, 2005), pp.
96–98, 107–13.

55. See Belasco, *Theatre through Its Stage Door*, pp. 101–8. The critics were
divided, not about the production but about the music and, for some, on the
very question of a wild-west Western as the subject for an opera, especially
one written by an Italian who—so obviously, some surmised—knew so little
about the country. The reviews were lengthy, many requiring a half page and
more, and often with pictures of the principals, as well as of Puccini and
Belasco, and the stage sets. For a sampling of the reviews, see Randall and
Davis, *Puccini and the Girl*, pp. 113–15; for reviews of early productions in
Europe, see ibid., pp. 118–24. For the history of Metropolitan Opera produc-

tions to the present, see ibid., pp. 208–25. Anton Webern saw *La fanciulla del West* in 1918 and confided his impressions to Schoenberg in a letter (27 March 1918): "I am a little surprised that it is a score that sounds original in every way. Splendid. Every measure astonishing. Very special sounds. Not a shade of kitsch! And mine is a first-hand impression. I have to say I really liked it." Quoted in Michele Girardi, *Puccini: His International Art*, trans. Laura Basini (Chicago: University of Chicago Press, 2000), pp. 283–84.

56. Theodor W. Adorno, "On Some Relationships between Music and Painting," trans. Susan H. Gillespie, *Musical Quarterly* 79, no. 1 (Spring 1995): 66; Theodor W. Adorno, "On the Contemporary Relationship of Philosophy and Music," in *Theodor W. Adorno: Essays on Music*, ed. Richard Leppert, trans. Susan H. Gillespie (Berkeley: University of California Press, 2002), p. 144: "The time that is immanent in every music, its inner historicity, *is* real historical time, reflected as appearance."

57. *The Girl of the Golden West* (New York: F. Rullman, 1910), edition for the Chicago Grand Opera Company, p. 5. Concerning the redemption trope—far more important to Puccini's opera than to Belasco's play—see the detailed and insightful discussion, including its history in the creative process and advancement in the publicity efforts of both Puccini himself and the Metropolitan Opera, in Randall and Davis, *Puccini and the Girl*, pp. 148–56.

58. Randall and Davis, *Puccini and the Girl*, pp. 45n. 17, 57. On 27 August 1907, Puccini wrote to his librettist Zangarini, "Increasingly the California-disease takes hold of me. I have copied several photographs of the most beautiful part of the forest where the highest and largest trees are, all for the scene in the third act. I am *determined* that it must be in the open air in a large clearing of a forest with colossal trees and with ten or more horses and sixty men" (ibid., p. 59).

59. Giacomo Puccini, *La fanciulla del West* (full score) (Mineola, N.Y.: Dover, 1997).

60. William Ashbrook is reminded by the second motif of "the swaying branches of huge trees" (*The Operas of Puccini* [New York: Oxford University Press, 1968], p. 146).

61. There are good discussions of the prelude in Randall and Davis, *Puccini and the Girl*, pp. 12–15; and Girardi, *Puccini*, pp. 286–89, though the points made in each are somewhat different from mine.

62. Concerning Puccini's unusual orchestrations, see Ashbrook, *Operas of Puccini*, pp. 146–47.

63. Carner, *Puccini*, p. 460. Richard Specht, *Giacomo Puccini: The Man, His Life, His Work*, trans. Catherine Alison Phillips (London: J. M. Dent and Sons, 1933), p. 198: "It is significant to note how often the expression-mark *ruvido* (harsh) occurs in the score," and he adds, "the rough, jagged, untamed quality

of the [opera's] natural surroundings imparts itself to the melodies too" (p. 201).

64. For a list of recordings of individual arias and duets, see *La Fille du Far West* (Paris: Editions Premières Loges, 1995), pp. 128–29. The opera's lack of conventional arias had negative financial consequences for Puccini, who realized considerable income from sheet-music royalties; see Ashbrook, *Operas of Puccini*, p. 146.

65. Lawrence Kramer, *Opera and Modern Culture: Wagner and Strauss* (Berkeley: University of California Press, 2007), pp. 128–66.

66. Walter Benjamin, "Theses on the Philosophy of History," in *Illuminations*, ed. Hannah Arendt, trans. Harry Zohn (New York: Schocken, 1969), p. 261.

67. Allan W. Atlas, in "Belasco and Puccini: 'Old Dog Tray' and the Zuni Indians," has carefully traced the sources for the tune that Jake Wallace sings in both Belasco's play and Puccini's opera. In the play the tune is "Old Dog Tray," also known as "Echoes of Home," for which more than one version exists, though today the best known is by Stephen Foster. Foster's setting was sung by minstrels in the California mining camps. Contrary to oft-repeated claims by scholars prior to Atlas, Puccini's source, identified by Atlas, is entirely unrelated to what Belasco employed, though the imagery and sentimentality of the lyrics are similar.

68. Belasco describes Wallace in Winter, *Life of David Belasco*, 1:74–75.

69. Belasco, *Six Plays*, pp. 321–22; and Belasco, *Girl of the Golden West: Novelized from the Play*, pp. 43–48.

70. Allan W. Atlas has also written about this song in a second essay, one that lays out what he perceives as the opera's three interrelated tropes: distance, return, and redemption: "*Lontano-Tornare-Redenzione*: Verbal Leitmotifs and Their Musical Resonance in Puccini's *La fanciulla del West*," *Studi Musaicali* 21, no. 2 (1992): 359–97. Atlas points out that by the time Jake Wallace first sings the word *lontano*, the word has already appeared ten times in the stage directions as well as one other time in the opera's "Preliminary Note" (ibid., pp. 364–65). Atlas also points out that the word *lontano* appears a total of twenty-four times in the opera's dialogue and seventeen times in the stage directions and the score's prefatory note, that *tornare* appears twenty-one times in dialogue and four times in the stage directions; and finally that Puccini uses *redenzione* four times, whereas its English equivalent never appears in Belasco's play (ibid., p. 361n. 7). See also Senici, *Landscape and Gender in Italian Opera*, p. 252.

71. Belasco, *Six Plays*, pp. 356–57; cf. Belasco, *Girl of the Golden West: Novelized from the Play*, pp. 199–200, repeating the play's dialogue. Puccini, *La fanciulla del West*, act 2, rehearsal no. 19, m. 1, to rehearsal no. 21, m. 2.

72. Belasco, *Six Plays*, pp. 337–38; and Belasco, *Girl of the Golden West: Novelized from the Play*, pp. 129–30.

73. Belasco, *Six Plays*, p. 334. This unlikely utterance does not appear in the novel.

74. Catherine Clément, judging *La fanciulla* a "masterpiece," refers to Minnie as "the rising sun; contrasted to her nocturnal sisters, she is the day that does not close on an act of mourning. Opera lovers do not love this antiheroine. She is made for tomorrow. Tomorrow she will set out, lit by the brilliance of her victory." Catherine Clément, *Opera, or, The Undoing of Women*, trans. Betsy Wing (Minneapolis: University of Minnesota Press, 1988), p. 95.

75. Yet whatever the opera's invocation of nature and the redemption trope it supports, the premiere was governed by other principles, duly registered in reviews and in wholly separate articles, often printed alongside the reviews. "Such was the beauty of the women [in the audience], and the magnificence of the toilettes, that the filmy attire, the revealed physical charms, and the jewels, which seemed a sort of mediaeval armor, conspired to make a background that was simply overwhelming" (from Metropolitan Opera Archives, microfilm [1910], review: "'The Girl' Proves Puccini Triumph," 11 December 1910 [source unidentified]). And: "Many of the socially elect sat in the orchestra, where jeweled coronets and necklaces worth several kings' ransoms vied with the electrics overhead. Silks, satins, and rare old laces were still trailing in from the corridor when Toscanini, looking thinner than ever after long rehearsals, hurried out to the conductor's desk amid a general salvo of applause" (Metropolitan Opera Archives, microfilm [1910]; the newspaper source cannot be identified, but the date is almost certainly 11 December). Such lead-ins are typically followed by long lists describing the costumes of individual society women, of the following sort: "Mrs James W. Gerard wore white satin, with a tunic of tangerine chiffon and embroidery with pearl ornaments" (from Metropolitan Opera Archives, microfilm [1910]: Cholly Knickerbocker, "First Night Any City in the World Might Envy: Society Flock to Greatest Opera Opening City Ever Saw," *New York American*, 11 December 1910). The Metropolitan Opera Archive has microfilmed its numerous scrapbooks of clippings. Those from the early twentieth century were already in poor condition when photographed, and the quality of the photography is very uneven. Many clippings are incomplete due to deterioration, and the source data, as a result, is often impossible to discern. My thanks to John Pennino, Metropolitan Opera Archivist, for his kind assistance during my research at the opera house.

76. The primeval Western setting of the final act attracted some critics' attention: "And so, the opera ends, amid one of the loveliest of stage settings

[the review includes a reproduction of the set], a forest of huge redwoods, through which one sees the snow clad Sierras lit with the pink light of dawn, a regular Maxfield Parrish study with the two [lovers] turning their faces toward the East[,] the sunlight, and with an adieu, the familiar Italian 'addio' to their beloved California, the snowy Sierras and the Golden West" (Metropolitan Opera Archives, microfilm [1910]: "'The Girl' Proves Puccini Triumph," 11 December 1910 [source unidentified]).

77. Indeed, at the opera's end, as Atlas has shown ("*Lontano-Tornare-Redenzione*," p. 377), Puccini quotes the tune one final time (see act 3, rehearsal no. 42, mm. 12–14), giving it to Minnie as she successfully pleads for Johnson's life. Senici suggests that in *La fanciulla* Puccini has created "a particularly powerful ear, a giant one, capable of hearing the action beyond the fixed field of visibility—an ear capable of 'seeing' the action that the eye cannot see" (*Landscape and Gender in Italian Opera*, p. 255). Senici further suggests that "the capabilities of the giant ear that the opera offers its audience go beyond anything of which any human ear is capable: they allow us to hear beyond reality" (ibid., p. 259).

78. Quoted in Girardi, *Puccini*, pp. 260–61. See also Puccini to Sybil Seligman, 41 July 1907, in Vincent Seligman, *Puccini among Friends* (New York: Macmillan, 1938): "But the scene must take place outside the *Polka* in a big wood, and in the background . . . there are paths leading to the mountains—the lovers go off and are lost from sight, then they are seen again in the distance embracing each other, and finally disappear—how does that strike you?" See also Randall and Davis, *Puccini and the Girl*, p. 171n. 3, regarding the stage directions that describe the act 3 setting. See Specht, *Giacomo Puccini*, p. 195, regarding the elaborate act 3 scenery used for the Boston production, used again in 1911 in Rome; the trees were modeled in plaster and the foliage cut from leather.

79. Greenwald points out that Puccini began seven of his twelve operas at sunset ("Realism on the Opera Stage," pp. 284–85).

80. Byron Nelson, in "The Isolated Heroine and the Loss of Community in Puccini's Belasco Operas," *Yearbook of Interdisciplinary Studies in the Fine Arts* 2 (1990): 404–5, makes a similar point and also compares the opera's conclusion to the final act of *Aida*. Concerning Puccini's unusual orchestral scoring of the closing measures, see Girardi, *Puccini*, p. 324.

81. The stage manual probably used for the 1910 production calls for the mountains to be visible even in the first and second acts, both of which are interior settings, through a door and windows. See the insightful commentary in Senici, *Landscape and Gender in Italian Opera*, pp. 229, 250–51, and 318nn. 4–5. A copy of the rare stage manual by Jules Speck, *La fille du West: Opera en tois actes* . . . (Paris: G. Ricordi, c. 1911–12), is in the Cornell University Music

Library. Speck at the time of the Puccini premiere was the stage manager at the Metropolitan Opera.

82. Horkheimer and Adorno, *Dialectic of Enlightenment*, pp. 42–43.

7. A FAREWELL, A FEMME FATALE, AND A FILM: THREE AWKWARD MOMENTS IN TWENTIETH-CENTURY MUSIC
Peter Franklin

1. See Lawrence Kramer, *Opera and Modern Culture: Wagner and Strauss* (Berkeley: University of California Press, 2004), pp. 7–8.

2. Ibid., p. 8.

3. Ibid., pp. 6–7.

4. Julian Johnson, *Who Needs Classical Music? Cultural Choice and Musical Value* (New York: Oxford University Press, 2002), p. 100.

5. Susan McClary, "Terminal Prestige: The Case of Avant-Garde Musical Composition," in *Keeping Score: Music, Disciplinarity, Culture*, ed. David Schwarz, Anahid Kassabian, and Lawrence Siegel (Charlottesville: University of Virginia Press, 1997), p. 69. The essay, first published in 1989, opens with the text of Laurie Anderson's "Difficult Listening Hour."

6. Friedrich Nietzsche, *The Case of Wagner*, in *The Birth of Tragedy and The Case of Wagner*, trans. Walter Kaufmann (New York: Vintage Books 1967), p. 166.

7. Arnold Schoenberg, *Style and Idea* (London: Williams and Norgate, 1951), pp. 7–36. My own comments on the subject may be found in Peter Franklin, *The Idea of Music: Schoenberg and Others* (London: Macmillan, 1985), pp. 77–90.

8. Schoenberg, *Style and Idea*, p. 34.

9. Ibid.

10. See Elias Canetti, *The Play of the Eyes* [*Das Augenspiel*, 1985] (London: Picador/ Pan Books, 1991), p. 51.

11. The annotations are omitted in all the recent versions of Basil Creighton's translation; see Alma Mahler, *Gustav Mahler: Memories and Letters*, ed. Donald Mitchell and Knud Martner, 4th ed. (London: Sphere Books, 1990)—the only reference to the omitted material is a footnote on p. 332, which fails to mention the annotations in the Tenth that were transcribed, and their location described, in Alma Mahler, *Gustav Mahler: Erinnerungen und Briefe* (Amsterdam: Allert de Lange, 1949), p. 479.

12. Gustav Mahler, *A Performing Version of the Draft for the Tenth Symphony*, prepared by Deryck Cooke (New York and London: Associated Music Publishers and Faber Music Ltd., 1976).

13. *Gustav Mahler: Zehnte Symphonie; Faksimile-Ausgabe* (Berlin: Paul Zsolnay, 1924).

14. I allude here to the "letter" that Schoenberg recorded in 1947 to the National Institute of Arts and Letters after becoming an elected member, in which he describes his development by saying, "I had the feeling as if I had fallen into an ocean of boiling water." See Arnold Schoenberg, *Letters*, ed. Erwin Stein, trans. Eithne Wilkins and Ernst Kaiser (London: Faber, 1964), p. 245.

15. See Thomas Mann, *Dr. Faustus*, trans. H. T. Lowe-Porter (Harmondsworth, U.K.: Penguin Books, 1968), p. 176.

16. Ibid., chap. 15, pp. 130–31.

17. See Juliane Brand, Christopher Hailey, and Donald Harris, eds., *The Berg-Schoenberg Correspondence: Selected Letters* (London: Macmillan, 1987), p. 168.

18. See Christopher Hailey, *Franz Schreker, 1878–1934: A Cultural Biography* (Cambridge: Cambridge University Press, 1993), pp. 74–75.

19. Karol Szymanowski, *Szymanowski on Music: Selected Writings of Karol Szymanowski*, ed. and trans. Alistair Wightman (London: Toccata, 1999), p. 218n. 6.

20. H. Schreker-Bures, H. H. Stuckenschmidt, and W. Oehlmann, *Franz Schreker* (Vienna: Elisabeth Lafite, Österreichischer Bundesverlag, 1970), p. 20.

21. "Doch alle Lust will Ewigkeit— / —will tiefe, tiefe Ewigkeit!" Franz Schreker, *Das Spielwerk und die Prinzessin: Ein dramatisches Märchen in einem Vorspiel und zwei Aufzügen* (Vienna: Universal-Edition, 1913), p. 1.

22. As *Das Spielwerk: Mysterium in einem Aufzug.*

23. The one surviving extract, a significant portion of the final scene of the opera, is included in the complete set of Schreker's recordings issued by Symposium Records in conjunction with the Franz Schreker Foundation, 2005 (CDs 1271, 1272, 1273).

24. "Heiah, wir ziehn in / selige Weiten! / Heiah, wir wandern / ins Abendrot! / Doch kommt des Morgens / eisig Erwachen— / ach, da sind wir /schon lange tod."

25. "Zittert dahin des Spielwerks Klang: / Der Sang, urewig von Tod und Gebären,— / ein mild Verklären schmerzwilder Triebe,— / das Lied der Liebe."

26. Mary Ann Doane, *The Desire to Desire: The Woman's Film of the 1940s* (London: Macmillan, 1988); chap. 4, "Love Story," deals initially at some length with *Humoresque.*

27. Lawrence Kramer, *After the Lovedeath: Sexual Violence and the Making of Culture* (Berkeley and Los Angeles: University of California Press, 1997), p. 12.

28. For the most articulate spokesman of the Second Viennese School, see Theodor W. Adorno's essay "Franz Schreker" in his *Quasi una Fantasia*, trans. Rodney Livingstone (London: Verso, 1992), pp. 142–43.

29. See Doane, *Desire to Desire*, pp. 99–100.

30. Ibid., p. 97.

31. All dialogue transcriptions are my own.

32. See Susan McClary, *Feminine Endings: Music, Gender, and Sexuality* (Minnesota: University of Minnesota Press, 1991), pp. 57–58.

33. Friedrich Nietzsche, *The Birth of Tragedy*, in *The Birth of Tragedy and The Case of Wagner* (see note 6), p. 126.

34. Ibid., pp. 126–27.

35. Carolyn Abbate, *Unsung Voices: Opera and Musical Narrative in the Nineteenth Century* (Princeton, N.J.: Princeton University Press, 1991), p. 16.

36. Translation adapted by the author from Richard Wagner, *Tristan and Isolde*, trans. Stewart Robb (New York: Dutton, 1965), p. 149.

37. *Richard Wagner to Mathilde Wesendonck*, trans. William Ashton Ellis (London: H. Grevel and Co., 1905), includes the so-called Venice Diary (1858–59), in which Wagner communicated passionately with Mathilde, whom he had left with the husband (Otto Wesendonck) who had acted as his patron and whom he clearly wished to replace in her affections. The printed diary (p. 31) begins with an imagined scene in which Wagner dies in Mathilde's arms, as if encouraging her to read the connection with the third act of *Tristan*, the text of which she knew.

8. "POUR OUT . . . FORGIVENESS LIKE A WINE": CAN MUSIC "SAY AN EXISTENCE IS WRONG"?
Walter Bernhart

1. Stefan Kunze, "Bösewichter, Außenseiter und Gescheiterte in der Oper," in *Gesungene Welten*, ed. Udo Bermbach and Wulf Konold (Berlin: Dietrich Reimer, 1992), pp. 209–22. The idea that negative characters are manifestations of great passion even applies to the powerful scenes of invocation in seventeenth-century French opera as, for example, Armide's invocation of Hate in Lully's *Armide* of 1686 (act 3, scenes 3 and 4).

2. Kunze, "Bösewichter, Außenseiter und Gescheiterte in der Oper," pp. 211–18.

3. Ibid., p. 216.

4. Cf. ibid.

5. "durch Dissoziation des musikalischen Zusammenhangs" (ibid., p. 221).

6. W. H. Auden, *Secondary Worlds* (London: Faber and Faber, 1968), pp. 83, 90; Walter Bernhart, "Prekäre angewandte Opernästhetik: Audens 'sekundäre Welt' und Hans Werner Henzes *Elegie für junge Liebende*," in *Die Semantik der musiko-literarischen Gattungen. Methode und Analyse: Eine Festgabe für Ulrich Weisstein zum 65. Geburtstag* (Tübingen: G. Narr, 1994), pp. 236–37.

7. Hans Werner Henze, "Der Künstler als bürgerlicher Held: Eine Einführung in die Oper: *Elegie für junge Liebende*" (1975), in *Musik und Politik:*

Schriften und Gespräche 1955–1984, ed. Jens Brockmeier, exp. ed. (Munich: Deutscher Taschenbuch Verlag, 1984), p. 236.

8. Cf. Hans Werner Henze, "Meine Musik auf dem Theater," *Österreichische Musikzeitschrift* 21 (1966): 371.

9. Rolf Urs Ringger, "Gregor Mittenhofer oder: Schnittpunkt der Wahne," in *Neue Zürcher Zeitung* 2/3 (June 2001): 371; Edward Callan, "Exorcising Mittenhofer," *London Magazine* 14 (1974): 73–85.

10. W. H. Auden and Chester Kallman, "Elegy for Young Lovers: A Singspiel," in *Libretti and Other Dramatic Writings by W. H. Auden: 1939–1973*, ed. Edward Mendelson (Princeton, N.J.: Princeton University Press, 1993), pp. 653–61.

11. "admirable character": Monroe K. Spears, *The Poetry of W. H. Auden: The Disenchanted Island* (New York: Oxford University Press, 1963), p. 287; "keine gehässige Desavouierung": Günther Lohse, "Röntgenstunde gegen ein Genie," in program booklet *Elegie für junge Liebende* (Klagenfurt: Stadttheater Klagenfurt, 1985–86); "Die Autoren erklären, daß sie dem Mythos vom ungebundenen 'Künstlergenie' zur Auferstehung verhelfen wollen": Claus-Henning Bachmann, "Henze: *Elegie für junge Liebende*. Uraufführung bei den Schwetzinger Festspielen," *Österreichische Musikzeitschrift* 16 (1961): 384.

12. "das Offenlassen der Schuldfrage": Hans Werner Henze, "Komponist und Regisseur: *Gespräch mit Horst Goerges*" (1960), in *Musik und Politik* (see note 7), p. 89. "Am Ende steht dann, wortlos, die Musik allein, die einzige Kunst, die, wie Auden sagt, nicht in der Lage ist, zu verurteilen oder zu richten, und die daher Vergebung über die Menschen auszuschütten vermag wie reinen Wein" (In the end, after all, music stands alone, wordless, the only art, as Auden says, which is unable to condemn or to judge, and which can therefore pour out forgiveness over people like pure wine). Hans Werner Henze, "Über *Elegie für junge Liebende*" (1962), in *Musik und Politik* (see note 7), p. 86.

13. W. H. Auden, "The Composer," in *Collected Poems*, ed. Edward Mendelson (London: Faber and Faber, 1974), p. 148.

14. Bernhart, "Prekäre angewandte Opernästhetik," (see note 6), pp. 234–35.

15. Hanspeter Krellmann, "Moderne Oper—zeitgenössische Oper—zeitgerechte Oper?" *Musica* 31 (1971): 121; Auden and Kallman, "Genesis of a Libretto" (1961), in *Libretti and Other Dramatic Writings* (see note 10), p. 245.

16. "den angeklagten Dichter," "Der Meister, der gewaltige, Dracula": Henze, "Künstler als bürgerlicher Held," (see note 7), pp. 236, 242.

17. "Die Brandmarkung des 'Künstlers als Held' gefällt mir sehr": Hans Werner Henze, "Musica impura—Musik als Sprache: *Aus einem Gespräch mit Hans-Klaus Jungheinrich*" (1962), in *Musik und Politik* (see note 7), p. 195.

18. Edward Mendelson, *Early Auden* (London: Faber, 1981), p. 361.

19. "das jugendstilhafte Weben und Flüstern der entfremdeten Natur": Henze, "Künstler als bürgerlicher Held," pp. 237–38.

20. "dumpfe Tamtamschläge," "Klavier- und Harfenarpeggien," and "ein wimmerndes Flexaton . . . , das . . . eine Atmosphäre von Gruselfilm schafft": ibid., p. 243.

21. "Da der Dichter sein Verbrechen, halb bewußt, halb unbewußt, plant—die Musik überführt ihn schon": ibid.

22. "wenn das Verbrechen de facto ausgeübt wird": ibid.

23. "das metallische Klappern eines schweren Gegenstandes": Henze, "Über *Elegie für junge Liebende*," p. 85.

24. Hans Werne Henze, *Elegy for Young Lovers* (opera in three acts), libretto by W. H. Auden and Chester Kallman, vocal score (Mainz: B. Schott's Söhne, 1961), p. 361.

25. Cf. Henze, "Künstler als bürgerlicher Held," p. 241.

26. "realistische Klänge," "wenn etwas in Unordnung gerät": Henze, "Über *Elegie für junge Liebende*," (see note 12), p. 85.

27. Auden, *Secondary Worlds*, (see note 6), p. 94.

28. "Die Schlußszene der Oper bringt uns das Grauenhafte solcher Konzeptionen vor Augen": Henze, "Künstler als bürgerlicher Held," (see note 7), p. 237.

29. "von der in Anführungszeichen gesetzten kristallenen Klanglichkeit": ibid., pp. 239–40.

30. Cf. Walter Bernhart, "Cardillac, the Criminal Artist: A Challenge to Opera as a Musico-Literary Form," in *Interart Poetics: Essays on the Interrelations of the Arts and Media*, ed. Ulla-Britta Lagerroth, Hans Lund, and Erik Hedling (Amsterdam: Rodopi, 1997), pp. 137–43.

31. A significant analogous situation can be found in Francis Poulenc's *Dialogues of the Carmelites* (1957), in which the murderous death by guillotine of the nuns is similarly marked by musical silence, that is, a long fermata pause in the eighth bar before the end of the opera, at which "La foule commence à se disperser." Francis Poulenc, *Dialogues of the Carmelites* (opera in twelve acts and three scenes), text of the drama by Georges Bernanos, adapted to a lyric opera with the authorization of Emmet Lavery, vocal score (Milan: Ricordi, 1987), p. 255.

32. The opera's revised version of 1952 shows an identical musical arrangement of the scene. Only the stage direction is considerably shorter.

33. Cf. Walter Bernhart, "Ambivalenz der Unschuld: Benjamin Britten auf der Suche nach dem kindlichen Sein," *Kunstpunkt* 18 (1999): 22–23; Bernhart, "*The Turn of the Screw*: Ein Glanzstück der Literaturoper," in Programmheft *Benjamin Britten: "The Turn of the Screw"* (Graz: Theater Graz, 2002), pp. 6–11.

34. Benjamin Britten, *The Turn of the Screw*, op. 54 (opera in a prologue and two acts), libretto after the story by Henry James by Myfanwy Piper, vocal score by Imogen Holst (London: Boosey & Hawkes, 1955), p. 82.

35. Ibid., pp. 144, 145.

36. Lawrence Kramer, *Musical Meaning: Toward a Critical History* (Berkeley: University of California Press, 2002), pp. 52, 61, and 51–67 generally.

37. Ibid., pp. 54, 53; emphasis added.

38. Henry James, *The Turn of the Screw: An Authoritative Text, Backgrounds and Sources, Essays in Criticism*, ed. Robert Kimbrough (New York: Norton, 1966), pp. 123, 118, 122; emphasis in the original.

39. Kramer, *Musical Meaning*, p. 62.

WALTER BERNHART is Professor of English Literature at the University of Graz, Austria, Director of the university's Center for Intermediality Studies in Graz, and founding and current president of the International Association for Word and Music Studies. His most recent publications include "Functions of Description in Poetry" (2007), and "From Novel to Song via Myth: *Wuthering Heights* as a Case of Popular Intermedial Adaptation" (2008). He is Executive Editor of *Word and Music Studies* and *Studies in Intermediality*, and has edited or co-edited ten individual volumes.

MARSHALL BROWN is Professor of Comparative Literature at the University of Washington and editor of *Modern Language Quarterly*. His books include *The Shape of German Romanticism* (1979), *Preromanticism* (1991), *Turning Points: Essays in the History of Cultural Expressions* (1997), *The Gothic Text* (2002), and *"The Tooth That Nibbles at the Soul": Essays on Music and Poetry*, forthcoming from the University of Washington Press.

KEITH CHAPIN is Lecturer in Music at the New Zealand School of Music (Wellington). He is co-editor of *Eighteenth-Century Music* and an associate editor of *Nineteenth-Century Music*. His research focuses on the aesthetics of counterpoint, especially in the eighteenth century, and on the interrelationships between music and literature. His most recent essays include "Scheibe's Mistake: Sublime Simplicity and the Criteria of Classicism" (2008) and "Classicist Terms of Sublimity: Christian Friedrich Michaelis, Fugue, and Fantasy" (2006).

PETER FRANKLIN is Professor of Music at the University of Oxford and a Fellow of St Catherine's College. His research areas are Gustav Mahler and the post-romantic symphony, early twentieth-century Austrian and German opera, and Hollywood film music (with a focus on European émigré composers in the 1930s and '40s). Publications include the books *Mahler: Symphony No. 3* and *The Life of Mahler*. His writing on film music includes essays in *Film Music: Critical Approaches* (2001) and *Beyond the Soundtrack: Representing Music in Cinema* (2007).

WALTER FRISCH is H. Harold Gumm and Harry and Albert von Tilzer Professor of Music at Columbia University, where he has taught since 1982. He has published widely on the music of the Austro-German tradition, especially Schubert, Brahms, and Schoenberg. His most recent book is *German Modernism: Music and the Arts* (2005). He is currently serving as general editor for a new series of period music histories from Norton for which he is writing the volume on the nineteenth-century.

RICHARD LEPPERT is Regents Professor and Morse Alumni Distinguished Teaching Professor in the Department of Cultural Studies and Comparative Literature at the University of Minnesota. The most recent of his books include an edition of selected *Essays on Music* by Theodor W. Adorno; *Beyond the Soundtrack: Representing Music in Cinema* (co-edited with Lawrence Kramer and Daniel Goldmark); and *Sound Judgment*, a volume of collected essays for the Ashgate Press series Contemporary Thinkers on Critical Musicology.

SUSAN MCCLARY is Professor of Musicology at the University of California at Los Angeles and specializes in the cultural criticism of music, both the European canon and contemporary popular genres. Best known for her book *Feminine Endings: Music, Gender, and Sexuality* (1991), she is also author of *Georges Bizet: Carmen* (1992), *Conventional Wisdom: The Content of Musical Form* (2000), and *Modal Subjectivities: Renaissance Self-Fashioning in the Italian Madrigal* (2004). McClary received a MacArthur Foundation Fellowship in 1995.

*   *   *

LAWRENCE KRAMER is Professor of English and Music at Fordham University. His work—nine books to date and scores of articles—was the inspiration for both this volume and the conference that gave rise to it.